DATE DUE

AP 17 '97			
AG 8 '97			
TE 8 '01			

DEMCO 38-296

Justice Oliver Wendell Holmes

Justice Oliver Wendell Holmes

Free Speech and the Living Constitution

H. L. Pohlman

New York University Press

NEW YORK AND LONDON

Library of Congress Cataloging-in-Publication Data
Pohlman, H. L., 1952–
Justice Oliver Wendell Holmes : free speech and the living
Constitution / H. L. Pohlman.
p. cm.
Includes bibliographical references and index.
ISBN 0-8147-6614-5 (cloth)
  1. Freedom of speech—United States.   2. Holmes, Oliver Wendell,
1841–1935.   3. United States. Supreme Court.   4. Judicial process—
United States.   I. Title.
KF4770.P64   1991
342.73'0853—dc20
[347.302853]   90-44269
                         CIP

New York University Press books are printed on acid-free paper,
and their binding materials are chosen for strength and durability.

Book design by Ken Venezio

To Patricia

Contents

Acknowledgments

I WOULD LIKE TO thank Dickinson College and Dickinson School of Law, especially James Fox and his staff at the library, for all their support and assistance. Also, the National Endowment for the Humanities generously provided me with a summer stipend in 1986, and the American Philosophical Society awarded me the Henry M. Phillips Research Grant in Jurisprudence in 1989. I am also grateful to my colleagues in Dickinson's Political Science Department, who have endured my idiosyncracies with patience and humor. The conversations that I had with Eugene Hickok concerning American constitutionalism were especially helpful in clarifying my ideas. My students, especially those who ventured into my Free Speech Seminar during the last few years, deserve my heartfelt thanks. Scholars who have read the manuscript or earlier versions of it and given me their advice include Robert Amdur, Vincent Blasi, G. Edward White, Jesse Goodale, and Paul Kens. I owe each a great deal. Gary and Sue Mescher are friends whose help was indirect but immeasurable. They made the job of writing this book easier if not possible. And a very special person whose praises cannot be left unsung is Victoria Kuhn. Her energy is matched only by her conscientiousness and the warmness of her heart.

Justice Oliver Wendell Holmes

1. Introduction

JUSTICE OLIVER WENDELL HOLMES occupies an anomalous position in American jurisprudence. Many admire his rhetoric and most find him insightful, but there is the widespread suspicion that his basic approach is fundamentally impoverished and that his legal/constitutional philosophy lacks any overarching structure or internal coherence. Though there are different explanations of why he went wrong, the most prevalent one focuses on his positivism. Holmes may have been brilliant and eloquent, but his positivism, it is argued, conflicted with central features of American constitutionalism: the ideal of legally limited government and the judiciary's role of protecting individual rights. It inclined him to a narrow understanding of the judicial function, one that encouraged a passive and acquiescent judiciary. Such an outlook made Holmes a popular figure in the early twentieth century, when much popular socio-economic legislation was declared unconstitutional over his dissents. But what he failed to see was that the essential function of the judiciary was the protection of individual rights.[1] Positivism blinded him to this feature of American constitutionalism, and this is why there is an almost "un-American" quality to his legal thought. Therefore all agree that Holmes deserves a place in the pantheon of American jurisprudence, but there are some who insist that he should wear a black hat.

Defenders of Holmes cry foul.[2] They agree that he generally deferred to legislatures, but in their opinion it is too much to say that he failed to see the judiciary's special role of protecting individual rights. After all, Holmes was in the forefront of those who tried to protect the right of free speech during the hysteria of World War I and its aftermath. Though there are a few other cases in which Holmes appears as a guardian of individual rights,[3] certain of his free-speech decisions are central to the controversy over his theory of constitutional adjudication. They puzzle his critics and supporters alike. Critics claim that his free-speech decisions, and the other examples of Holmes's opposition to majority will, are exceptions. They only show that he was inconsistent and that his legal philosophy was so out of tune with American constitutionalism that as a judge even he could not consistently adhere to it. Defenders also have a difficult time reconciling Holmes's positivism with his protection of free speech. In contrast to the critics, however, they discount its importance, arguing that a few ill-chosen rhetorical asides should not mar his reputation as a civil libertarian. The end result is that Holmes is a rather puzzling figure in American legal thought. Why would a man apparently wearing a black hat occasionally help the good guys?

This book attempts to provide an alternative account. It recognizes that there is a tension between Holmes's positivism and his defense of the individual right of free speech. This tension, however, is resolved in Holmes's understanding of the special role that judges play in the American constitutional order. Judges are not "mouthpieces" of a written constitution, nor are they entitled to "rewrite" the Constitution as they like. They are special representatives of the sovereign American people. In this capacity, they do not mirror the people's beliefs and wishes in a direct fashion because their job is to take the long-range point of view. They must tie the constitutional values of the past to those of the present and the future. Precedent and the intent of the framers are therefore relevent, but they are not the whole story. Judges must slowly adapt the powers of government and the corresponding rights of individuals to the evolving values and beliefs of the American people. In the case of free speech, Holmes used his theory of legal liability to adjust the right of free speech to the character of early twentieth-century American society. The wishes of the popular sovereign and the dictates of Holmes's theory of legal liability converged in his theory of free speech.

This brief summary of my conclusion is meant only to suggest the direction my book takes. Holmes's theory of free speech will serve ultimately as a window into the wider context of his thought. But there are many obstacles that first must be overcome. There is an enormous controversy concerning Holmes's theory of free speech. What was his theory? Was it coherent? Did he adhere to it consistently? How protective was it? Was it more protective than the theories of his peers? Answers to these questions require a detailed exposition of his theory of legal liability, his free-speech opinions, and the contrasting ideas of his peers. Much of what follows is concerned with these issues. The conclusion is that Holmes was a moderate defender of free speech who had a coherent, well-structured theory that he consistently adhered to throughout his judicial career. This interpretation, which cuts against the grain of much of the recent commentary on this topic[4] and which must stand or fall on its own, is then used to probe the meaning of Holmes's constitutionalism. I think Holmes's theory of free speech can fulfill this role, but it, of course, is an important topic in its own right.

The issue of how Holmes's theory of free speech fits into his positivism and constitutionalism is considered in the last chapter, but a couple of questions call for attention here. Why does his commitment to positivism make his defense of individual rights difficult to understand and how was it related to his theory of legal liability, which defined (I argue) his sense of the limits of free speech? The meaning of the term *positivism* is unfortunately very vague. It is possible to disentangle at least three different senses of the term found in the various charges of positivism that have been levelled against Holmes.[5] First, there is his belief that law was "not a brooding omnipresence in the sky, but the articulate voice of some sovereign or quasi-sovereign."[6] By this statement, he meant that all law had an identifiable human source. This is the least controversial tenet of his positivism, but believers in natural law have claimed that it was the source of a totalitarian strain in his thought.[7]

In 1918, Holmes explained why he thought that those who grounded legal rights in an objective moral world were "in that naive state of mind that accepts what has been familiar and accepted by them and their neighbors as something that must be accepted by all men everywhere."[8] Of course, all of our familiar social institutions could not be abandoned. Just as humans have to eat and drink to live, so also "if they live in society, so far as we can see, there are further conditions. Reason working on experience does tell us, no doubt, that if our wish to live continues, we can do it only on those terms."[9] But that is the end of the matter. There was no *a priori* duty to live or to live in society, but only

a statement of what I must do if I wish to remain alive. If I do live with others they tell me that I must do and abstain from doing various things or they will put the screws on to me. I believe that they will, and being of the same mind as to their conduct I not only accept the rules but come in time to accept them with sympathy and emotional affirmation and begin to talk about duties and rights.[10]

Law consists of rules necessary for a form of social life. It was not objective in the sense that the believer in natural law has demanded.

Holmes's critical attitude toward natural law was a part of his intellectual makeup from the early 1870s. Indeed, it is arguable that during this early period his efforts to keep the common law insulated from Kantian-inspired reforms were motivated by his contempt for the idea of natural rights. In an early article entitled "Possession," Holmes argued that it was sensible for the common law to give legal remedies to possessors who did not intend to appropriate the object. German jurists had disagreed with this practice, and Holmes explained how Kantian philosophy had misguided them:

Apart from the direct working of the Roman theory, Kant was much influenced in this part of his work by the speculations of Rousseau. He believed in the Rights of Man, and approached the law from that point. Possession was for him an extension of the ego, a setting of the will into somewhat external to it, and thus an appropriation of that somewhat, or, as Hegel would have said, possession is an objective realization of free will; and the realized free will of the individual can only be restrained when in opposition to the freedom of all, to the universal will expressed by the State.[11]

Holmes disagreed. General utility was sufficient to restrict liberty and to decide if a possessor should be given remedies. In the same vein, over forty years later, he noted that it "is fashionable nowadays to emphasize the criterion of social welfare as against the individualistic eighteenth century bills of rights." He then cited his book *The Common Law* "to show that it is no novelty."[12] Here again the community is conceived as the source of all law.

Truth itself was perceived in an analogous way. Repeatedly, Holmes insisted that humankind does not have cosmic truth. Even though "there is in all men a demand for the superlative,"[13] they must humbly recognize that they are born in the universe, not it in them. Accordingly, human categories will never completely capture the world. Even if we "fancy" that we hear "a clang from behind the phenomena,"[14] we can only really know how the world appears to us. Hence a person's beliefs are a "system of intellectual limitations."[15] To think about the world in a certain way is not to think about it in various other ways. Any objectivity found in truth only comes from the fact that others share one's intellectual limitations:

what gives it objectivity is the fact that I find my fellow man to a greater or less extent (never wholly) subject to the same *Can't helps*. If I think that I am sitting at a table I find that the other persons present agree with me; so if I say that the sum of the angles of a triangle is equal to two right angles. If I am in a minority of one they send for a doctor or lock me up; and I am so far able to transcend the to me convincing testimony of my senses or my reason as to recognize that if I am alone probably something is wrong with my works.[16]

Therefore, law, morality, and truth have a common source. They are all rooted in one's social interaction with the external world.

A more controversial aspect of Holmes's positivism was his denial of any necessary relationship between law and morality.[17] This idea was central to his view of legal education. "When I emphasize the difference between law and morals I do so with a single end, that of learning and understanding the law. . . . But I do say that distinction is of the first importance for the object which we are here to consider—a right study and mastery of the law as a business with well understood limits, a body of dogma enclosed within definite lines."[18] He did not mean that morality could be ignored because it never effected the law. Though a few commentators have made this suggestion,[19] it is extremely unlikely that anyone, much less Holmes, would be so out of touch with reality to come to that conclusion. The law "is the witness and external deposit of our moral life. Its history," he argued, "is the history of the moral development of the race."[20] Therefore a student should separate the law as it now is from what it ought to be, no matter the degree to which it has been influenced in the past by morality.

For the objective of the improvement of legal education, Holmes advised the student to look on the law as a "bad man, who cares only for the material consequences which such knowledge enables him to predict."[21] If he followed this recommendation, the student would not be inadvertently studying something outside of the law. The danger of this was especially acute since ordinary terms of morality—for example, *malice, intent,* and *duty*—were in use throughout the law. The student had to resist the temptation to give to these terms the meaning that they would have in a moral context. The best option would be to get rid of all such terms. Holmes himself dreamed of writing a book that would do exactly that.[22] The student could then more readily attend to the types of sanctions that courts would apply to different factual settings. For the lawyer, in Holmes's opinion, this was what the law was all about.

By separating law from morality for the sake of legal education, Holmes did not mean that judges should never take morality into account in their decisions. It was, after all, Holmes himself who reminded judges of "their duty of weighing considerations of social advantage."[23] Utility was a moral standard and in this way morality shaped legal development. And to the degree to which judges were making policy in this manner, even lawyers had to take morality into account. Just as a "bad man" wants to know how the moral commitments of those around him will affect their actions, so also the lawyer will want to know how morality is shaping the law. Only then can he give prudent advice and litigate successfully. If and when it helps him predict how a court will apply sanctions, his job would entail taking it into account. And Holmes's famous definition of law as "the prophecies of what courts will do in fact"[24] coincided with his "bad-man" conception of legal education. Thus, his positivism was not only expressed in his rejection of natural rights, but also in his basic understanding of the nature of law. Both morality and law may be human creations, but they were not equivalent. Law consisted of the sanctions applied by courts.

The last aspect of Holmes's positivism concerns his understanding of who determined the content of law, who determined when courts would apply what sanctions. His clear and simple answer was that political power was the source of law. "Now it is admitted by everyone that who is the sovereign is a question of fact equivalent to the question who has the sum of the political powers of a state in his hands. That is to say, sovereignty is a form of power, and the will of the sovereign is law, because he has power to compel obedience or punish disobedience, and for no other reason."[25] All law could be ultimately traced back to human beings who had the power and the will to enforce compliance.

Holmes understood morality in a very similar way. It seemed to him "clear that the *ultima ratio,* not only *regum,* but of private persons, is force, and that at the bottom of all private relations, however tempered by sympathy and all the social feelings, is a justifiable self-preference."[26] Since Holmes believed that "force (mitigated by politeness)" ruled the world, he said that if he "were asked certain *whys* by a woman [he] should reply, 'Because Ma'am I am the bull.' " Sympathy, social feelings, and politeness could soften the effects of power, but it was, in Holmes's opinion, what made the world go around.

In the wider social context, an individual's power was unimportant. One person could not accomplish anything politically. Individuals had to join together to make the kind of world they wanted. The morality of a society would correspondingly depend on the power of various social groups. In a letter, Holmes tried to explain how morality, rights, and power were related to legal development.

As to the *right* of citizens to support and education I don't see it. It may be a desirable ideal to aim at, but I see no right in my neighbor to share my bread. I mean moral right of course—there is no pretense of any other, except so far as he in combination has power to take it. I always have said that the rights of a given crowd are what they will fight for. I once heard the older Agassiz say of some place in Germany that there would be a revolution if you raised the price of a glass of beer. If that was true and believed they had a right to beer at that price.[27]

Moral rights are equivalent, not to natural rights, but to what a group will fight for. They are not legal rights unless courts will apply sanctions against those who violate them. But social groups are invariably trying to realize their ideals into law. Of course, whether a group can accomplish this, whether it can transform a moral into a legal right, also depends on its power.

Holmes's early comment on the Gas-Stokers' strike in England contains a clear statement of his understanding of the relationship between law and power.[28] He first reminded his readers that the Darwinian struggle of life takes place not only between different animal species and nations, but also within a state between different groups. Each group is struggling to make the world that it wants. Since man is an "idealizing animal,"[29] each group "dresses up" its actions in the language of morality, but this is epiphenomenal. The real action is the underlying struggle of power. The struggle may be "mitigated by sympathy, prudence, and all the social and moral qualities,"[30] but it is nonetheless a struggle of power. The law can do little to change the nature of the contest. "All that can be expected from modern improvements is that legislation should easily and quickly, yet not too quickly, modify itself in accordance with the will of the *de facto* supreme power in the community, and the spread of an educated sympathy should reduce the sacrifice of minorities to a minimum."[31] To show that Holmes never changed his mind, one need only refer to the short introduction that he wrote in 1900 for a new edition of Montesquieu's *Esprit des lois*. In answer to the question of what constitutes the first requirement of good government, Holmes responded that it was "the correspondence to the actual equilibrium of force in the community—that is, conformity to the wishes of the dominant power." He went on to admit that the dominant powers might be stupid and their laws may end in "destruction," but added that "the test of good government is that the dominant power has its way."[32]

Though law rested on power, it was not unlimited. All legal authorities were limited since "no human power is unlimited."[33] Legally, it is true, the ultimate political power of a community was absolute, because "there can be no legal right as against the authority that makes the law on which the right depends."[34] But when legal theory was put aside, sovereignty was "a question of strength and may vary in degree."[35] But the limit was always a *"de facto* limit in the common consciousness that various imaginable enactments would provoke a general uprising, . . . an extra-legal fact of uncertain boundaries."[36] It is not at all clear, for example, what price will provoke beer drinkers to fight for their rights.

Holmes's legally absolute sovereign was therefore not a de facto tyrant. As noted earlier, the sovereign could treat less-powerful social groups with toleration, sympathy, and social feeling. And even if the dominant power of a society preferred a certain alternative, the determined opposition of a less-powerful group might well be successful. A dominant power could prefer a certain option but not think it worth a fight. In this way, the dominant authority's power was not only limited by its own sympathy and social feeling, but also by the "moral rights" of inferior groups—the things a given crowd will fight for.

The judicial role, however, was understood by Holmes to be completely passive in its relationship to ultimate political power. A court could not resist the power that established and maintained it.

What I mean by law in this connection is that which is or should be enforced by the Courts and I can't understand how anyone should think that an instrumentality established by the United States to carry out its will . . . should undertake to enforce something that *ex hypothesi* is against its will. It seems to me like shaking one's fist at the sky, when the sky furnishes the energy that enables one to raise the fist. There is a tendency to think of judges as if they were independent mouthpieces of the infinite, and not simply directors of a force that comes from the source that gives them their authority.[37]

Courts only had power if they conformed to the desires of the dominant group. A measure of the depth of Holmes's commitment to this notion of the judicial function can be taken from his proposed epitaph: "Here lies the supple tool of power."[38] It indicates his commitment to an *ultimately* passive conception of the judicial role.

Of the three aspects of Holmes's positivism, only the last can legitimately raise significant doubts about his view of the judicial role in the American constitutional setting. Obviously, Holmes's belief that law and morality are human creations in no way prevents him from protecting individual rights. Many contemporary judges have a similar understanding of law and morality and have no trouble fulfilling their constitutional responsibilities. The problem with Holmes's constitutionalism, if there is a problem, does not arise here. The same can be said for his insistence that there is no necessary relationship between law and morality. If individual rights are a matter of law, this aspect of his positivism would not prevent a judge from performing his duty.

Can we say the same thing about the third aspect of Holmes's positivism? Can a judge believe that law is ultimately reducible to power and still perform his responsibilities in the American constitutional order? More specifically, in Holmes's historical context, how could he have written his famous free-speech dissents if at the time the overwhelming majority of Americans, the dominant power in the constitutional order, favored punishing such seditious speech? How did he reconcile his proposed epitaph with his defense of free speech? Is his explanation plausible or defensible? These are the types of questions that this book hopes to answer. Besides a better comprehension of Holmes's theory of free speech, the goal is a fuller appreciation of his constitutionalism, especially his sense of the judicial role.

Before explaining the relationship between Holmes's positivism and his theory of legal liability, it is first necessary to emphasize that my topic is generally confined to the limits of free speech. The important issue of why he favored free speech will only be touched on in passing. It is, after all, common knowledge that he was a skeptic and that he supported free speech, to the degree that he did, because of his skeptical outlook. In the following famous passage from his dissent in *Abrams v. United States*, he revealed the role that skepticism played in his point of view.

But when men have realized that time has upset many fighting faiths, they may come to believe even more than they believe the very foundations of their own conduct that the ultimate good desired is better reached by free trade in ideas,— that the best test of truth is the power of the thought to get itself accepted in the competition of the market; and that truth is the only ground upon which their wishes safely can be carried out. That, at any rate, is the theory of our Constitution. It is an experiment, as all life is an experiment. Every year, if not every day, we have to wager our salvation upon some prophecy based upon imperfect knowledge.[39]

The eloquence of this language should not hide the influence of John Stuart Mill. Holmes was deeply shaped by the philosophy of British empiricism and it is therefore hardly surprising that he adopted Mill's rationale for free speech.[40]

It might seem counterintuitive that Holmes's definition of the limits of free speech can be understood without paying a lot of attention to his underlying rationale. How could he decide whether a particular type of speech was protected without evaluating its positive value in the marketplace of ideas. The more value an utterance had, the more protection; the less value, the less protection. Such an approach integrates the justification of free speech with the definition of its limits. It produces a nicely interwoven theory.

Though this more integrated approach to free speech may be more preferable, Holmes's method was different. Of course, he could not define the limits of free speech without probing the value of different forms of speech. However, he was able to assess the value of speech from a perspective other than his metaphor of a marketplace of ideas. It was, I claim, Holmes's general theory of legal liability that helped him conceptualize the limits of free speech. His basic orientation was therefore not to protect speech that was valuable, but to deny protection to speech that satisfied the criteria of his theory of legal liability. He defined free speech negatively, not positively, by excluding speech that failed the test. What constituted free speech was what was left over. It was the residue. How big a residue is the crucial issue.

My claim that Holmes used his theory of legal liability to define a constitutional right may seem implausible. How could he have defined a constitutional right, a right that purportedly gives a form of activity special protection, by applying a theory that was applicable to all types of action? Indeed, if my interpretation is true, Holmes gave speech no special protection whatsoever. He applied the same standard whether speech was involved or not. Constitutional protection was only granted to speech that was not punishable in any case. What kind of value does free speech have if it is defined in this way? Is it possible that Holmes's theory of free speech, and perhaps his entire approach to individual constitutional rights, is tainted from the very beginning, from the fact that he approached these types of issues by way of his theory of legal liability?[41]

This question is not an easy one, but it is also true that the practice of defining free speech negatively—ascertaining what it is by excluding what it is not—has a long tradition in this country. Soon after many of the new state constitutions were in place at the end of the eighteenth century, judges had to decide whether free-speech or free-press clauses had altered traditional common-law categories of liability: libel, slander, obscenity, blasphemy. And much of the history of free speech involves the slow narrowing of these categories. If so, it is hard to avoid the conclusion that questions of common-law liability and freedom of speech have been intertwined for a long time. In the same vein, many modern books on free speech discuss the different rationales of free speech, but the substantive chapters refer to obscenity, libel, incitement. Holmes's approach, therefore, may not be so unusual. The orthodox way to define the limits of free speech may very well be to define what it is not.

It is also not clear that a negative approach will *necessarily* lead to a restrictive sense of the limits of free speech. To argue that a person does not really believe in free speech unless he gives speech more protection than other acts is a sophistical argument. Even if speech was given additional protection, how much of it would in fact be protected would depend on the severity of the underlying theory of legal liability. If the general theory is harsh, with liability easily incurred, then the fact that free speech is given somewhat more protection is hardly comforting. Above the baseline established by the theory of legal liability, any particular form of speech would bear the burden of proving its value.

Conversely, there is something comforting about Holmes's alternative approach. Speech is not punishable unless it fits into traditional categories of liability, unless it is as pernicious or as harmful as other types of acts. But whether a theory of legal liability functions as a baseline from which to measure the value of speech or as the decisive standard on which to decide whether speech is liable or not, the important issue is the substance of the general theory. How that question is answered will have a large impact on how much speech is really free from liability— which is the most important issue. Consequently, Holmes's reliance on his theory of liability does not preclude the possibility that he had a moderate sense of the limits of free speech. It does, however, mean that his reputation as a defender of free speech will depend, to a great extent, on the content of his theory of legal liability.

Whether the negative approach to free speech is the best way to proceed or not, there is a general feature of Holmes's legal philosophy that substantiates my position that he approached it in this way. I am referring to his substantial doubts about the intellectual viability of the concept of "a right." He denigrated all talk of primary rights and duties as "apt to get the cart before the horse, and to consider the right or the duty as something existing apart from and independent of the consequences of its breach, to which certain sanctions are added afterward."[42] The law did not attach sanctions to preexisting rights, but created rights and duties by attaching sanctions to different types of acts. Nonetheless, Holmes preferred the concept of "a duty" to that of "a right." Though at times he suggests that it would be better if both terms were thrown out of the law, *duty* was in his mind less troublesome.

His basic problem with the term *duty* was that it normally meant "something more than a tax on a course of conduct."[43] It suggested to a lawyer or a layperson that if someone violated their duty, a court would do something more than impose a tax. The problem was that often a violation of a so-called duty would not mean that a court would do anything more than tax the activity in question. In such a case, Holmes responded, a "legal duty cannot be said to exist if the law intends to allow the person supposed to be subject to it an option at a certain price. The test of a legal duty is the absolute nature of the command."[44] The conclusion was that there were few legal duties, strictly speaking, at civil law. The agent could do what he or she wanted—for example, the agent could violate his or her contract—as long as the agent paid the tax. But Holmes still believed that there were some legal obligations, especially in criminal law or in a case where a judge enjoined someone from acting. In these areas there were absolute commands, shown by the fact that the law did not recognize any contract to do the forbidden act.[45] Hence the term *duty* had a meaningful, though somewhat circumscribed, role to play in the law.

But Holmes could not consistently use the term *duty* in this restricted fashion. In an early attempt to formulate a universal classification of the law, after he argued "that it should be based on *duties* and not on *rights*," he expressed his suspicion that the opposing "custom" was "at the bottom of some difficulties which have been felt. Duties precede rights logically and chronologically."[46] He then divided the law into duties of sovereigns to each other, duties of citizens to the sovereign, duties of all the world to all the world, and duties of all the world to persons in particular positions or relations.[47] In later articles, he shifted the categories, but he still used the concept of duties rather than rights.[48] Since Holmes knew that his classificatory sense of the term was less restrictive than his own definition, he confessed that he used the word to avoid "circumlocutions."[49] But that does not affect the basic point. Holmes was never fond of the term *duty* but he did think that it was preferable to *right*.

The reason why Holmes in general preferred duty to right illuminates why he saw the right of free speech from the perspective of his theory of liability and how that theory was linked to his positivism. The basic insight was that the law worked only through coercion. A person can have a right only if a duty, a sanction, is imposed on others.

Even those laws which in form create a right directly, in fact, either tacitly impose a duty on the rest of the world, as, in the case of patents, to abstain from selling the patented article, or confer an immunity from a duty previously or generally imposed, like taxation. The logical priority of the duty in such instances is clear when we consider that in its absence any man might make and sell what he pleased and abstain from paying for ever, without assistance from law. Another illustration is, that, while there are in some cases legal duties without corresponding rights, we never see a legal right without either a corresponding duty or a compulsion stronger than duty.[50]

Law creates rights by creating duties, by threatening agents with coercion if they disobey.

Law therefore does not give freedom to humankind. Only if there was no law would a person be perfectly free to do whatever he or she had the power to do. As Holmes said in regard to the rights of ownership, "The so-called right of use in the owner is not derived from the law. Any man, unless restrained, may use anything he can lay his hands on, in any way he can devise."[51] Law's goal is therefore to limit freedom, whether one describes the limitations as taxes or as duties. "To put it more broadly," he argued, "and avoid the word duty, which is open to objection, the direct operation of the law is *to limit freedom of action or choice on the part of a greater or less number of persons in certain specified ways*." Accordingly, "the law does not enable me to use or abuse this book which lies before me. *That is a physical power which I have without the aid of the law*. What the law does is simply to prevent other men to a greater or less extent from interfering with my use or abuse" (emphasis mine).[52] Law does not give freedom; it takes it away. Law operates by imposing duties. The so-called rights that are thereby created are the natural powers that we had all along.[53] The only difference is that the law will punish those who try to interfere with the exercise of the natural power.

Holmes understood the right of free speech as a natural power. The law did not give me the freedom to talk and write. That ability, like the ability to use the above book, is a physical power that I have as the creature that I am. All that the law can do is impose duties, whether against me or others. The law could punish or tax me for what I have said or written or my neighbors for what they have said or written. It could also punish or tax me if I violated a duty not to interfere with my neighbor's speech activity or my neighbors if they have violated their duty by interfering with my right to talk and write. But the question will always be one of an individual violating his or her duty, whether the duty is owed to the state or to some other individual.

The link between free speech and Holmes's theory of legal liability can therefore be discerned. The theory specified the conditions under which a court should apply sanctions. It established the criteria by which a judge imposed duties and thereby created rights. Moreover, in Holmes's opinion, the substance of his theory reflected the general drift of the law in the age of the modern, secular nation-state. Its key concept was harm, because the purpose of law today is utility. In earlier historical periods, revenge had been the primary purpose of law, and, in a corresponding way, liability had been confined to "sinful," "intentional" acts. But this more religious approach to the law fell out of favor as the modern scientific outlook developed.[54] Though unwanted "survivals" and even obsolete rules remained, the general substance of law adapted to its new role. Communities wanted to punish harmful action, not sin, and they wanted to punish it whether the actor was a sinner or not.

Since Holmes's theory of liability was meant to capture this general trend of the law, it can be understood as an indirect reflection of political power. It specified the conditions under which the modern American sovereign wished to apply legal sanctions. There was therefore a connection between Holmes's positivism and his theory of legal liability. The link's abstract character does not undermine its significance. Holmes's theory of legal liability was a statement of the existing sovereign's desire to impose sanctions. Thus, Holmes's theory of liability and his positivism converged in his understanding of the individual right of free speech. The right was a residue. It was the natural power I had to talk and write that the sovereign did not punish or tax, but in fact protected by applying sanctions against those who tried to interfere with it.

Notes

1. The important critics of Holmes's positivism are Lon Fuller, *The Law in Quest of Itself* (Boston: Beacon Press, 1966); Henry M. Hart, Jr., "Holmes's Positivism—An Addendum," *Harvard Law Review* 64 (1951): 929–37; Samuel J. Konefsky, *The Legacy of Holmes and Brandeis* (New York: Macmillan, 1956), chap. 12; and Yosal Rogat, "Mr. Justice Holmes: A Dissenting Opinion," *Stanford Law Review* 15 (December 1962; March 1963): 3–44; 254–308; idem, "The Judge as Spectator," *The University of Chicago Law Review* 31 (1964): 213–56. More recent articles that bear on this theme include Robert Gordon, "Holmes' *Common Law* as Legal and Social Science," *Hofstra Law Review* 10 (1982): 719–46; G. Edward White, "The Integrity of Holmes' Jurisprudence," *Hofstra Law Review* 10 (1982): 633–71; idem, "Looking at Holmes in the Mirror," *Law and History Review* 4 (Fall 1986): 439–65; P. S. Atiyah, "The Legacy of Holmes through English Eyes," *Boston University Law Review* 63 (1983): 341–82; Jan Vetter, "The Evolution of Holmes, Holmes and Evolution," *California Law Review* 72 (1984): 343–68; Mary L. Dudziak, "Oliver Wendell Holmes as a Eugenic Reformer: Rhetoric in the Writing of Constitutional Law," *Iowa Law Review* 71 (1986): 833–67.
2. Holmes's greatest defender was Mark DeWolfe Howe. He specifically addressed Holmes's positivism in "The Positivism of Mr. Justice Holmes," *Harvard Law Review* 64 (1951): 529–46, and in "Holmes' Positivism—A Brief Rejoinder," *Harvard Law Review* 64 (1951): 937–39.
3. For Holmes's defense of rights other than the right of free speech, see his opinions or dissents in *Pennsylvania Coal Co. v. Mahon*, 260 U.S. 393 (1922); *Nixon v. Herndon*, 273 U.S. 536 (1927); *Olmstead v. United States*, 277 U.S. 438 (1928); *Frank v. Mangum*, 237 U.S. 309 (1915); *Moore v. Dempsey*, 261 U.S. 86 (1923).
4. See Konefsky, *The Legacy of Holmes and Brandeis*, especially chaps. 9–10; Rogat, "The Judge as Spectator," 214–17; Fred D. Ragan, "Justice Oliver Wendell Holmes, Jr., Zechariah Chafee, Jr., and the Clear and Present Danger Test for Free Speech: The First Year, 1919," *Journal of American History* 58 (1971–72): 24–45; Gerald Gunther, "Learned Hand and the Origins of Modern First Amendment Doctrine: Some Fragments of History," *Stanford Law Review* 27 (1975): 719–55; David S. Bogen, "The Free Speech Metamorphosis of Mr. Justice Holmes," *Hofstra Law Review* 11

(1982): 97–188; David M. Rabban, "The First Amendment in Its Forgotten Years," *Yale Law Journal* 90 (1981): 514–95; "The Emergence of Modern First Amendment Doctrine," *University of Chicago Law Review* 50 (1983): 1205–1355; Yosal Rogat and James M. O'Fallon, "Mr. Justice Holmes: A Dissenting Opinion—The Free Speech Cases," *Stanford Law Review* (1984): 1349–1406; Richard Pollenberg, *Fighting Faiths: The Abrams Case, the Supreme Court, and Free Speech* (New York: Viking Penguin, 1987), 207–28; Edward J. Bloustein, "Holmes: His First Amendment Theory and His Pragmatist Bent," *Rutgers Law Review* 40 (Winter 1988): 283–302.

5. H. L. A. Hart, *The Concept of the Law* (Oxford: Clarendon Press, 1961), 253, described five senses of the term *positivism:* "(1) that laws are commands of human beings; (2) that there is no necessary connection between law and morals, or law as it is and law as it ought to be; (3) that the analysis or study of meanings of legal concepts is an important study to be distinguished from (though in no way hostile to) historical inquiries, sociological inquiries, and the critical appraisal of law in terms of morals, social aims, functions, &c; (4) that a legal system is a 'closed logical system' in which correct decisions can be deduced from predetermined legal rules by logical means alone; (5) that moral judgments cannot be established, as statements of fact can, by rational argument, evidence or proof ('non cognitivism in ethics')." As the text makes clear, I think another sense, one that reduces law to power, is needed. It is the most important sense in which Holmes was a positivist.

6. *Southern Pacific Co. v. Jensen,* 244 U.S. 205, 222 (1917).

7. See Ben Palmer, "Hobbes, Holmes, and Hitler," *American Bar Association Journal* 31 (1945): 569–73; idem, "Defense against Leviathan," *American Bar Association Journal* 32 (1946): 328–32, 360; idem, "The Totalitarianism of Mr. Justice Holmes: Another Chapter in the Controversy," *American Bar Association Journal* 37 (1951): 809–11; Francis E. Lucey, "Natural Law and American Legal Reform: Their Respective Contributions to a Theory of Law in a Democratic Society," *Georgetown Law Journal* 30 (1942): 493–533; idem, "Holmes-Liberal-Humanitarian-Believer in Democracy?" *Georgetown Law Journal* 39 (1951): 523–62; Harold R. McKinnon, "The Secret of Mr. Justice Holmes," *American Bar Association Journal* 36 (1950): 261–64, 342–46.

8. Oliver Wendell Holmes, Jr., "Natural Law," *Harvard Law Review* 32 (1918), in Oliver Wendell Holmes, Jr., *Collected Legal Papers* (New York: Peter Smith, 1952), 312. All references to works by Oliver Wendell Holmes, Jr., are hereafter cited as "Holmes."

9. Ibid., 313.

10. Ibid.

11. "Possession," *American Law Review* 12 (July 1878), in *The Formative Essays of Justice Holmes,* ed. Frederic Rogers Kellogg (Westport, Conn.: Greenwood Press, 1984), 180 (hereinafter cited as *The Formative Essays*). See also Holmes, *The Common Law* (Cambridge: Belknap Press, 1963),

37–41, where he criticized Kant's retributive theory of punishment and defended a utilitarian one.

12. Holmes, "Ideals and Doubts," *Illinois Law Review* 10 (1915), in *Collected Legal Papers,* 307.

13. Ibid., 310.

14. "Natural Law," in *Collected Legal Papers,* 315.

15. See "Ideals and Doubts," in *Collected Legal Papers,* 304–5.

16. Holmes, "Natural Law," in *Collected Legal Papers,* 310–11.

17. See Fuller, *The Law in Quest of Itself;* Hart, Jr., "Holmes' Positivism—An Addendum."

18. Holmes, "The Path of the Law," *Harvard Law Review* 10 (1897), in *Collected Legal Papers,* 170–71.

19. See references cited in n. 17 above.

20. Holmes, "The Path of the Law," in *Collected Legal Papers,* 170. See also Holmes, *The Common Law,* 38: "rules of law are or should be based upon a morality which is generally accepted."

21. Holmes, "The Path of the Law," in *Collected Legal Papers,* 171.

22. See *Holmes-Pollock Letters,* ed. Mark D. Howe, 2 vols. (Cambridge: Harvard University Press, 1941), 2:212–13.

23. Holmes, "The Path of the Law," in *Collected Legal Papers,* 184. Also see idem, *The Common Law,* 31–32: The very considerations which judges most rarely mention, and always with an apology, are the secret root from which the law draws all the juices of life. I mean, of course, considerations of what is expedient for the community concerned. Every important principle which is developed by litigation is in fact and at bottom the result of more or less definitely understood views of public policy."

24. Holmes, "The Path of the Law," in *Collected Legal Papers,* 173.

25. Holmes, review of "Law and Command," by Frederick Pollock, *American Law Review* 6 (1872), in *The Formative Essays,* 91.

26. Holmes, *The Common Law,* 38.

27. *Holmes-Laski Letters,* ed. Mark P. Howe, 2 vols. (Cambridge: Harvard University Press, 1953), 1:762. Also see ibid. 1:8, 2:948.

28. See Holmes, "The Gas-Stokers' Strike," *American Law Review* 7 (1873), in *Harvard Law Review* 44 (1931): 795–96.

29. *Holmes-Laski Letters* 2:1183.

30. Holmes, "The Gas-Stokers' Strike," 795.

31. Ibid., 796.

32. See Holmes, *Collected Legal Papers,* 258. See also, idem, *The Common Law,* 36: "The first requirement of a sound body of law is, that it should correspond with the actual feelings and demands of the community, whether right or wrong."

33. *The Western Maid,* 257 U.S. 419, 432 (1922).

34. *Kawananakoa v. Polyblank,* 205 U.S. 349, 353 (1907).

35. *Carino v. Insular Government of the Philippine Islands,* 212 U.S. 449, 458 (1909).

36. *Holmes-Laski Letters* 1:115.

37. *Holmes-Laski Letters* 2:822.

38. See Merlo Pusey, *Charles Evans Hughes,* 2 vols. (New York: Macmillan, 1951), 1:287.

39. *Abrams v. United States* 250 U.S. 616, 630 (1919).

40. For Holmes's relationship to British empiricism, see H. L. Pohlman, *Justice Oliver Wendell Holmes and Utilitarian Jurisprudence* (Cambridge: Harvard University Press, 1984), especially chap. 5.

41. For a discussion of the problem described in this paragraph, see Frederick Schauer, *Free Speech: A Philosophical Inquiry* (Cambridge: Cambridge University Press, 1982), chap. 1.

42. Holmes, "The Path of the Law," in *Collected Legal Papers,* 168–69.

43. Holmes, review of "Law and Command," by Frederick Pollock, in *The Formative Essays,* 92.

44. Ibid.

45. Ibid. When Holmes wrote "The Path of the Law," he said that the term *duty* could be fruitfully used only if the law attached some further "disadvantage" or "consequence" over and above the "tax" of a civil sanction. He then referred to two doctrines that were relevant to some civil actions. "One is, that a contract to do a prohibited act is unlawful, and the other, that, if one of two or more joint wrongdoers has to pay all the damages, he cannot recover contribution from his fellows" (*Collected Legal Papers,* 174). But on the same page, Holmes described these doctrines as "insignificant" and said that they could be abolished "without disturbance." It is arguable that Holmes was saying that the term legal duty had no role to play in the law. But the better position is that these two doctrines no longer, in his view, indicated the existence of an "absolute command." He still believed that if a state did not merely "tax" a course of action, but was understood to prohibit it absolutely, a legal duty existed. Even when he wrote "The Path of the Law," he still believed that there were duties in criminal law, and that there was a duty to obey an injunction. See *Collected Legal Papers,* 173, 175–76.

46. Holmes, "Codes and the Arrangement of the Law," *American Law Review* 5 (1870), in *The Formative Essays,* 79.

47. Ibid., 81–82.

48. Holmes, "The Arrangement of the Law: Privity," *American Law Review* 7 (1872), in *The Formative Essays,* 97, and idem, "The Theory of Torts," *American Law Review* 7 (1873), in ibid., 128.

49. Holmes, "Theory of Torts," in *The Formative Essays,* 125 n. 1.

50. Holmes, "Codes and the Arrangement of the Law," in *The Formative Essays,* 79–80.

51. Ibid., 83.

52. Holmes, "Possession," *American Law Review* 12 (1878), in *The Formative Essays,* 181.

53. Holmes, *The Common Law,* 169: "A legal right is nothing but a permission to exercise certain natural powers."
54. See Patrick J. Kelley's fine discussion of the relationship between Holmes's theory of liability and the rising scientific and positivistic outlook in "Oliver Wendell Holmes, Utilitarian Jurisprudence, and the Positivism of John Stuart Mill," *American Journal of Jurisprudence* 30 (1985): 189–219.

2. Holmes's Theory of Legal Liability

HOLMES'S THEORY OF free speech will not be understood until its relationship to his theory of legal liability is completely uncovered. This approach is not entirely novel. Several commentators have linked Holmes's theory of free speech to his doctrine of criminal attempt.[1] But the problem with this interpretation is that it is too narrow. Holmes's doctrine of attempts is relevant, but it is not the whole story. To understand his theory of free speech, his entire theory of legal liability must be examined.[2] This chapter explores the relevant aspects of his general theory, and the two following chapters show how it is related to Holmes's free-speech decisions.

Harmful Acts

Holmes built his theory of legal liability on the premises of British utilitarian jurisprudence.[3] First, like the utilitarians, he favored comprehensive principles that defined both civil and criminal liability.[4] Second, by denying that either a "bad" motive or a personal moral fault was a necessary condition for punishment or civil liability, he endorsed "general" and "external" standards. Even if a person's motive for acting illegally was "good" in some sense, or even if that person had a shortcoming that made compliance personally impossible, Holmes thought it proper of the law to impose liability to prevent harms.[5] One reason for these rather harsh requirements is that a court cannot "see men as God sees them" and so the "law takes no account of the infinite varieties of temperament, intellect, and education which make the internal character of a given act so different in different men."[6] However, a "more satisfactory account" of why the law ignored the agent's motive and personal capacities was that "when men live in society, a certain average of conduct, a sacrifice of individual peculiarities, going beyond a certain point, is necessary to the general welfare." No doubt an "awkward" or "hasty" person will be excused in heaven, but because "his slips are no less troublesome to his neighbors than if they sprang from guilty neglect,"[7] they were to be discouraged by law, whether by civil or criminal liability.

Holmes's explanation of his commitment to external and objective standards has been criticized and ignored. The contemporary academic mind rebels at the simplicity and coldness of his reasoning. H. L. A. Hart has argued that the argument is a non sequitur, and that the theory itself violates elementary notions of justice by punishing those who lack the capacity to comply with the law.[8] But since all utilitarian arguments require a calculation of benefits over costs, they invariably contain questionable assessments of empirical fact. In this sense, any utilitarian justification of a practice is a non sequitur, and it is therefore difficult to appreciate the force of this particular criticism.[9] The fairness of Holmes's theory is also a controversial matter. In contrast to Hart's criticism, Sheldon Novick[10] argues that the theory was meant to reflect the common law's gradual evolution toward "modern ideas of fairness."[11] It is, however, not clear what Novick means by *fairness* or how much significance he attaches to this alleged characteristic of Holmes's criteria of liability. At one point, he says that he uses "the term *fairness* as a shorthand for Holmes's somewhat artificial definition of 'culpability,' "[12] but at others he claims that Holmes understood a lawsuit as "a plea for fairness"[13] and believed that a judge could find in the common law "fundamental principles of fairness" even in cases involving constitutional adjudication.[14] In regard to the first usage of the term, Novick seems to be saying that Holmes's theory was fair because it refused "to impose liability for accidents, and that the unforeseeable consequences of a person's acts were simply accidents."[15] But Hart's claim that the theory is unfair rests on the possibility that it would permit the imposition of liability on the basis of consequences that were personally unforeseeable on the part of the agent, even if the average person of the community could have foreseen them.[16] It therefore seems misleading to use the term *fair* as a "shorthand" for Holmes's notion of culpability. The harsh truth is that Holmes's theory did treat individuals of meager ability unfairly, but he thought it was justified for the sake of "the general welfare."

The real problem, however, lies with the stronger senses of fairness that are present in Novick's work. The idea that there are "fundamental principles of fairness" seems at odds with Holmes's well-known rejection of natural law and any other conception of law as "an omnipresence in the sky." Law consisted of the will of those who had the power to compel obedience. Of course, the power of different groups waxed and waned, resulting in changes in the law, including the common law. For this reason, it was not wise to repress the Gas-Stokers' strike, not because the law had to reflect some kind of fundamental fairness between all groups, but because there was legitimate doubt whether the English ruling group had the power and will to stop the rising labor movement. In the same spirit, Holmes's theory of liability expressed the political will of the dominant socioeconomic groups of the modern age. The theory, in short, was flexible enough to adapt to evolving political realities. Utility was the basis of the theory, but every effective political group had its own interpretation of the good society.

Novick, however, thinks it is a fundamental mistake to place Holmes and his theory of liability in the utilitarian tradition because it was a-historical and antievolutionary.[17] But this conclusion is too extreme. Even if Jeremy Bentham was completely ahistorical, it is doubtful whether John Austin was that insensitive to the value of history, and it is clearly wrong to believe that John Stuart Mill was.[18] Moreover, even if the utilitarian tradition in the nineteenth century was antievolutionary, Holmes could have rejected this feature of their thought but remained heavily indebted to the tradition in other aspects of his legal philosophy. Novick himself, for example, recognizes the role that policy played in both Holmes's theory of judicial decision making and in his theory of liability itself, at least in the case of privileges.[19] Such an admission does much to undermine his exclusion of Holmes from the utilitarian tradition. At a minimum, Holmes thought utilitarian considerations should guide legal development. And since utility is such a flexible standard, allowing different groups to have different estimates of it, an interpretation of Holmes's theory of liability that relies on utility seems to be more compatible with the generally accepted view that he was an evolutionist than an interpretation based on "fundamental principles of fairness."

Patrick S. Atiyah has also offered a few explanations of Holmes's commitment to external standards other than the utilitarian one he himself gave. First, since Holmes believed that a person was not punishable for wicked intentions if that person complied with the law, he may have concluded that the law had to exclude intent in cases of noncompliance. Second, he believed that through history the law necessarily adopted external standards, and therefore he endorsed them because they were inevitable. Third, since he separated law from morality, he did not want to make the legal liability of a person depend on that person's moral culpability.[20]

Atiyah's purpose in suggesting these various explanations of Holmes's commitment to his theory of liability seems to be critical. Since none of these explanations justify his theory, the implication is that he had no rationale for his *general* and *external* standards.[21] They were therefore indefensible. But since Holmes never used any of these arguments to justify his theory, I think Atiyah's approach is oblique. Ascribing arguments and positions to a theorist that the theorist did not use or defend seems a questionable practice, especially if the arguments and positions are then subjected to criticism. The danger of attacking a straw adversary is very great.

Elsewhere I have commented on the third argument,[22] which Yosal Rogat also used to criticize Holmes's theory.[23] The simple truth is that there are many legal positivists in the world who do not accept Holmes's theory of liability, and therefore it is difficult to see how his separation of law from morality explains his attachment to external standards of liability. The first argument—the idea that an agent's intentions are irrelevant because bad intentions do not suffice for liability—is so weak that I think nothing is gained by ascribing it to Holmes. Very few, if any, jurists believe that bad intentions suffice for legal liability, yet there is no widespread support for an external theory. How then can his support for the idea that bad intentions do not suffice for legal liability be used to explain his position that a person can be liable despite good intentions? Clearly, the answer to the question of why Holmes favored an external theory of legal liability must be found elsewhere.

The second argument, however, may have a point. I think Holmes did believe that external standards were inevitable (in some sense) because of the growth of political power in the age of nation-states and because of the development of science and the secular point of view. The "modern state has the power to draw the line of liability where it wills," and "the modern secular and scientific attitude [has] encouraged the state to draw the line where it served utility, that is, it [has] encouraged external general standards."[24] The assumption is that the powerful modern state has no other basis on which to decide the question than experience. In this sense, external standards are worth more to society, in Holmes's opinion, than their cost, and the modern state has acted accordingly.

Modern criminal law, however, as Atiyah notes, seems to have moved in a direction opposite to the one suggested by Holmes.

By the time that the issue was finally presented to the House of Lords for decision, Holmes's view had been abandoned or rejected by all serious criminal lawyers and academics, as well as judges actually engaged in the trial of criminal cases. Objective standards of liability in the criminal law are seen as illiberal and unacceptable for three interrelated reasons: first, they result in the conviction of someone who did not *choose* to violate society's prohibitions; second, the deterrent effect of law is of much more doubtful efficacy when the accused does not choose to act; and third, objective standards of culpability penalize the thoughtless and careless in a way which many today find offensive given that such conduct may be the result of temperament and character rather than of choice.[25]

This is surely an interesting development. Holmes had thought that the modern state would punish in accordance with an objective standard because it had the power to do so and because it would benefit the community. Was he wrong? Is it in fact more useful not to punish those who did not intend or foresee the harm they caused? Has contemporary society lost its respect for the scientific and secular outlook? Has a nonutilitarian outlook become more popular in the post–World War II academic world? Or has this revulsion against punishing those who are incapable of complying with the law occurred only in our imagination? Does the law continue to punish the incapable with the happy thought that the agent intended, foresaw, or could have foreseen the harm? Holmes would probably have found the latter questions worth pursuing. He was always fond of pointing out how human beings rarely have the stomach to face the facts. But this speculative question is not worth pursuing in detail. The important point is that Holmes's justification for the external standard of liability was utility.

The most important personal capacity that Holmes's theory of legal liability ignored was the agent's ability to foresee the harmful consequences of his or her actions. If the agent should have foreseen the harm according to community standards, he or she was liable regardless of his or her personal incapacity. For this reason, words like *malice, intention,* and *negligence* had special meanings. Whether an act was malicious,

intentional, or negligent depended on the likelihood of harmful consequences, not on the agent's actual motive or foresight. "If the manifest
probability of harm is very great, and the harm follows, we say that it is
done maliciously or intentionally; if not so great, but still considerable,
we say that the harm is done negligently; if there is no apparent danger,
we call it mischance."[26] The differences between malicious, intentional,
and negligent homicide were therefore ones of degree, depending on the
likelihood that death would result from the agent's act. If the likelihood
of death was "very great," then the agent was liable for malicious or
intentional homicide, even though the agent did not actually intend or
foresee the death. And the agent could be liable for negligence even if he
or she lacked the capacities necessary to foresee the harm. Holmes's
criterion for separating negligence from accident was the foresight of the
reasonably prudent person. If an average person of the community
would have foreseen a "considerable" likelihood that death would result, the agent was guilty of manslaughter; if the average person would
not have foreseen the likelihood, the death was an accident and the agent
went free.

Although Holmes imposed liability regardless of the motive, the intentions, and the foresight of the agent, it is incorrect to say that he
excluded from consideration all aspects of the agent's consciousness.[27]
His theory was not external or general in this sense. The standard of a
rational and prudent person did not operate in a vacuum. Whether an
average person would have estimated the danger of the act as great,
considerable, or unlikely is a question that could not be answered without some notion of the person's knowledge of the circumstances of the
act. "Does he know the gun is loaded? Does he know that people
frequently walk behind the fence upon which his target hangs? Does he
know the fence to have weak spots or holes?"[28] The rational and
prudent person cannot estimate the degree of danger of the act—pulling
the trigger of the gun—unless that person has some conception of the
relevant circumstances of the act.

It was Holmes's general position that what the rational and prudent
person could foresee should be determined by what the actual agent
knew of the circumstances of an act. "An act cannot be wrong, even
when done under circumstances in which it will be hurtful, unless those
circumstances are or ought to be known." This is so because insofar "as
the threats and punishments of the law are intended to deter men from

bringing about various harmful results, they must be confined to cases where circumstances making the conduct dangerous were known."[29] Consequently, though the agent's motive, intent, and foresight were not necessary conditions for his or her liability, the agent's actual knowledge was always a relevant consideration. It showed what harmful consequences the agent ought to have foreseen or what other circumstances of his or her act ought to have been known. If the agent knew facts that would have warned a rational and prudent person of the dangerousness of a contemplated act, or, in the more complicated case, if the agent knew facts from which a rational and prudent person would have inferred the existence of other facts that would have in turn warned the prudent person of danger, then the agent was liable regardless of what he or she in fact intended or foresaw.[30] In either case, the agent's knowledge of the circumstances of the act was the basis for liability according to Holmes. It was the "key to the whole subject" and "the essential element."[31] Therefore, though his theory of liability was external in one sense, the crucial criterion of liability was an internal feature of the agent's actual state of knowledge. It was what the prosecution or the plaintiff had to prove.

Holmes, however, did grant the prosecution and the plaintiff some leeway in how to establish the crucial issue of the defendant's knowledge of the circumstances of his or her act. First, since he always required for liability a voluntary act—a willed muscular contraction—on the part of the agent, inferences could be made from the nature of the agent's activity.[32] Though next to nothing could be inferred as to the defendant's state of knowledge from a *simple* act, the more likely situation would be that the agent was engaged in a coordinated series of acts, which would be a sufficient basis to infer either the agent's intent or state of knowledge. "But the coordination of a series of acts shows a further intent than is necessarily manifested by any single act, and sometimes proves with almost equal certainty the knowledge of one or more concomitant circumstances. And there are cases where conduct with only the intent and knowledge thus necessarily implied is sufficient to throw the risk of it on the actor."[33] Examples include liability for trespass and for keeping dangerous animals. When "a man does the series of acts called walking, it is assumed for all purposes of responsibility that he knows the earth is under his feet." If he goes through the motions of walking "on the surface of the earth, it cannot be doubted that he knows that the earth is there. With that knowledge, he acts at his peril in certain respects. If he crosses his neighbor's boundary, he is a trespasser."[34] In the same way, an owner of a tiger is liable for any damage the pet may cause because the "fact that tigers and bears are dangerous is so generally known, that a man who keeps them is presumed to know their peculiarities. In other words, he does actually know that he has an animal with teeth, claws, and so forth, and he must find out the rest of what an average member of the community would know, at his peril."[35] The court therefore can infer from the defendant's activity of walking or keeping a wild animal that he or she knew of the earth or of teeth and claws, and this would be enough to warn a prudent person of the dangerous character of the activity. The agent's conduct itself established that he or she knew circumstances that either made the act dangerous or from which an average person would have inferred the existence of other circumstances that in turn would have indicated the danger.

An agent's activity could also establish intent. Though Holmes denied that an agent's actual intent had to be harmful to incur liability, he never doubted that an agent's intent, whether illegal or not, could in certain circumstances be more easily established than the agent's knowledge of the circumstances of the act. In such cases, "if intent to cause a certain harm is shown, there is no need to prove knowledge of facts which made it likely that harm would follow."[36] After all, the person could not very well have intended the harm without knowing what made the act dangerous. Even if the agent's intent was lawful, it could reveal the agent's awareness of relevant facts. A command to an employee to "break a horse" in a public street indicates not only the employer's intention but also his or her knowledge. The employer knew that the horse was wild. Thus, if a passerby is injured, the employer is liable because he or she knew enough to be forewarned of the danger.[37]

Holmes, therefore, had no objection if the agent's awareness of the circumstances of the act was inferred from the nature of the agent's activity. At times, Holmes characterized an agent's knowledge to be of a certain kind because his or her activity was of a certain character. But this does not justify any distortion of Holmes's fundamental criterion of liability: the agent's actual knowledge of what would have warned a rational and prudent person of danger.[38] The evidence used to prove a proposition should not be confused with the proposition itself.

Holmes thought a court could infer the agent's knowledge from conduct only in relatively simple cases. For example, after discussing strict liability for trespass and for keeping dangerous animals, Holmes said, "I now pass to cases one degree more complex than those thus far considered. In these there *must be another concomitant circumstance known to the party* in addition to those of which the knowledge is necessarily or practically proved by his conduct" (emphasis mine).[39] Consequently, the prosecution or the plaintiff must prove that the agent knew this "concomitant circumstance" in a way different from inferring the knowledge from the agent's conduct. Though malice, intention, or foresight did not have to be established to impose liability, in the usual case the state or the plaintiff had to show that the agent knew whatever would have warned an average person of the dangerous character of the activity.

Although Holmes based liability on certain factors of the agent's internal life, it should be emphasized that his criterion of liability was still factual in nature. "The question what a prudent man would do under given circumstances is then equivalent to the question what are the teachings of experience as to the dangerous character of this or that conduct under these or those circumstances; and as the teachings of experience are matters of fact, it is easy to see why the jury should be consulted with regard to them."[40] When called on to perform this legislative role, the jury's job was "to determine the circumstances necessary to be known in any given case in order to make a man liable for the consequences of his act."[41] Once the jury determined what facts, if known, would have warned a rational and prudent person of danger, then the jury had only to make up its mind about what the agent knew. Did the agent know the facts that would have warned an average person. Only if the agent knew such facts was he or she liable.

Holmes realized that the jury's finding as to which known facts indicated danger was a decision "with a special and peculiar function." Its "only bearing is on the question, what ought to have been done or omitted under the circumstances of the case, not on what was done. Their function is to suggest a rule of conduct."[42] Juries made law as they decided what knowledge threw the risk of the action on the agent. But once a number of juries had made similar findings as to what, if known, made the agent liable, a judge could then simply apply the rule. From that point on, the jury's function would be restricted to determining if the agent knew the crucial facts. It would no longer play a legislative role. Holmes considered an example of this kind of development. The "co-ordinated acts necessary to point a gun and pull a trigger, and the intent and knowledge shown by the co-ordination of those acts, are all consistent with entire blamelessness. They threaten harm to no one without further facts. But the one additional circumstance of a man in the line and within range of the piece makes the conduct manifestly dangerous to any one who knows the fact." Consequently, "there is no longer any need to refer," by way of the jury, "to the prudent man, or general experience. The facts have taught their lesson, and have generated a concrete and external rule of liability. He who snaps a cap upon a gun pointed in the direction of another person, known by him to be present, is answerable for the consequences."[43]

These concrete external rules of law were the culmination of legal development.[44] Holmes opposed the general doctrine of strict liability, according to which an agent was responsible for all of the consequences of his or her actions,[45] but favored the practice of holding individuals strictly liable to rules that specified what consequences an agent must foresee if he or she knew certain facts. But the agent actually had to know them. The above gunman was liable only if he knew that some other person was within the line of fire. Even in a case of strict liability, the agent's knowledge of circumstances was the key to liability. Holmes's endorsement of strict liability at the level of particular rules and his assessment that such rules constituted the culmination of legal standards in no way conflicts with his fundamental criterion of liability: the agent's actual knowledge of the particular circumstances of his or her act.

Holmes's general theory of legal liability required a voluntary muscular contraction—an act—and the agent's awareness of circumstances that would have warned a rational and prudent person of danger, but nothing further was needed. He denied that the agent's act had also to violate someone's legal rights and described the opposing view as a "familiar" but "wrong" doctrine.[46] It was wrong because judge-made law had to evolve to fit new historical circumstances. Judges had to create new duties by imposing legal sanctions on acts that had never been sanctioned before. In such instances of judicial legislation, there was an *ex post facto* creation of the duty. The agent was liable even though no one's rights had been violated. Since the theory of legal liability had to be consistent with the practice of judicial legislation, all that was needed, besides the act, was a community judgment that the agent knew enough of the circumstances to have been warned of the dangerous character of his or her conduct.

This theory of legal liability was designed to capture the general trend of the law,[47] but Holmes recognized its limited scope. First, the law could for special reasons make the standard of liability more severe. This is exactly what it did when it applied the felony-murder rule. The rule required the agent to foresee the death even though the rational and prudent person would have failed to foresee it. It is murder "if a man does an act with intent to commit a felony, and thereby accidentally kills another; for instance, if he fires at chickens, intending to steal them, and accidentally kills the owner, whom he does not see."[48] Second, the law could require "a man to find out present facts, as well as to foresee future harm, at his peril, although they are not such as would necessarily be inferred from the facts known."[49] Holmes cited the English law that prohibited the abduction of girls "under sixteen from the possession of the person having lawful charge of her."[50] The English courts had ruled that if an agent abducts a girl he must find out her age at his peril even though he had every reason to think that she was over the age limit. In both of these examples, the lawmaker had lowered the standards of liability. An agent was liable even though unaware of facts that would have warned a prudent person of danger or that would have indicated the existence of other facts that would in turn have warned the prudent person. Even though common experience did not warrant the assessment of danger, the legislature had apprehended it and that was sufficient to throw the risk on the agent.[51] Holmes generally had no real objections to these legislative extensions of liability, though he doubted whether the law would go too far in this direction. Extensive punishment of conduct that was not blameworthy in the average member of the community would "shock the moral sense of any civilized community" and "would be too severe for that community to bear."[52] Community sentiment ordinarily limited liability to cases of harmful acts.

Privileged Acts

Requiring an agent to foresee harmful consequences (the accidental death of someone during a felony) or to know present facts (the age of an abducted girl) were, it is arguable, consistent extensions of Holmes's basic theory. The acts were *harmful* as defined by what a rational, prudent person would foresee or know, whether the assessment was made by a legislature or a jury, as long as they did not extend liability too far. Liability, however, was not reducible to harmful acts. In certain cases, the agent not only had to know facts that would warn a prudent person of danger, but the agent also had to act with actual *malicious* intent or purpose. This condition meant "not only that a wish for the harmful effect is the motive, but also that the harm is wished for its own sake, or, as Austin would say with more accuracy, for the sake of the pleasurable feeling which knowledge of the suffering caused by the act would excite."[53] Holmes squared this requirement with his general theory by arguing that certain "prohibited conduct may not be hurtful unless it is accompanied by a particular state of feeling." For instance, "everyone knows that sometimes secret harm is done by neighbor to neighbor out of pure malice and spite. The damage can be paid for, but the malignity calls for revenge."[54] Thus, in a case of malicious destruction of property, the agent's purpose had to be actually malicious before the agent could incur liability. Holmes's external standard of liability did not apply.

Further, not only was "actual malice" required for certain crimes, but the law could grant privileges to certain harmful forms of action. In the case of privileged action, the defendant harmed another and knew facts that warned of the danger, but the defendant was free of liability because he or she acted with "just cause."[55] Of course, for Holmes the question whether a certain harmful act should be privileged was strictly a policy one, even if it was presented in the language of just cause.[56] Once "the question of policy is faced," he continued, "it will be seen to be one which cannot be answered by generalities, but must be determined by the particular character of the case." In his judgment, "plainly the worth of the result, or the gain from allowing the act to be done, has to be compared with the loss which it inflicts."[57] His favorite example was that of a wealthy businessman opening up a store in a small town knowing that he will drive his only competitor—a deserving widow—

out of business. Such action, though harmful in the short-term, was privileged by the law because of the long-term advantages of a free market.[58] Another privilege involved the "right [of a person] to give honest answers to inquiries about a servant, although he intends thereby to prevent his getting a place."[59] Here again it was thought that society benefits, in the long-term, if employers were given access to information concerning prospective employees, even if the employees were occasionally harmed.[60] Thus Holmes endorsed the view that policy justified withdrawing liability from certain acts that were ordinarily subject to liability on general principles, acts that were indisputably harmful according to the standard of the rational and prudent person.

The important point, however, concerns the limits of these privileges. Though the law had often granted to an agent the right to harm another, it usually did so with qualifications, and one of the more important qualifications concerned the agent's purpose. The law could and often would withdraw the privilege if the agent's actual purpose was malevolent. For example, if a person in authority advised another not to employ a certain doctor, that person would lose the privilege if the motive was malicious, if the purpose was not to help the patient but to harm the doctor.[61] Holmes, true to his general approach, argued that the question of the limit of a certain privilege—like the question of its existence— was a matter of policy, and that in such cases "the advantages to the community, on the one side and the other, are the only matters really entitled to be weighed."[62] Some harmful acts were privileged even if malice was present, but only because policy substantiated the absolute character of the privilege. "Apart from statutory exceptions, the right to make changes upon or in a man's land is not affected by the motive with which the changes are made." This was so because "were it otherwise, and were the doctrine carried out to its logical conclusion, an expensive warehouse might be pulled down on the finding of a jury that it was maintained maliciously [to block a neighbor's light], and thus a large amount of labor might be wasted and lost."[63]

Nonetheless, policy often justified the withdrawal of the privilege if the agent's purpose was malicious. The reason was simple. "The gratification of ill-will, being a pleasure, may be called a gain, but the pain on the other side is a loss more important." There was "no general policy in favor of allowing a man to do harm to his neighbor for the sole pleasure of doing harm."[64] In many cases of privilege, the actual purpose or intent of the agent was a crucial factor. According to Holmes, the agent was liable if the purpose was malicious and was free if it was not.

Attempts

Though Holmes's general theory imposed liability if the agent acted while knowing a fact that should have warned of danger, his discussion of the role of malicious intent in cases of privileged harmful actions reveals the limited scope of his general theory. While usually the defendant's knowledge of circumstances was enough to decide the question of liability independent of the agent's intent, in cases of privilege the agent's intent was always relevant and often crucial to liability. But since privileged actions were short-term harmful acts that the law insulated from liability because of their long-term advantages, liability for abuses of privilege was not inconsistent with the general theory. Privileged acts were, in a sense, subject to liability because they were harms even though the state declined to impose it. It made no difference that the intent of the agent was the reason why the state withdrew the privilege.

But the law, according to Holmes, was not satisfied with merely imposing liability on harmful acts, whether the harmful acts had to be conjoined to an unlawful purpose or not. Innocent harmless acts, of all things, were also at times punishable. For example, the harm that the crime of larceny was meant to prevent was a permanent loss of an owner's property, which of course did not occur if the thief was caught. "If then the law punishes the mere act of taking, it punishes an act which will not of itself produce the evil effect sought to be prevented, and it punishes it before that effect has in anyway come to pass."[65] But of course Holmes knew that the "law cannot wait until the property has been used up or destroyed in other hands than the owner's, or until the owner has died, in order to make sure that the harm which it seeks to prevent has been done."[66] If the state was to act at all, it had to act on probabilities rather than on the accomplished facts of harmful consequences, unreasonably dangerous action, or maliciously motivated privileged acts. The probability referred to is the likelihood that but for the state's interference, the agent's innocent act would have been followed by other acts that would have in time resulted in the permanent deprivation of the owner's property. The actual intent of the agent became relevant for this reason. It was "an index to the external event which probably would have happened."[67] Accordingly, unreasonably dangerous activity as defined by Holmes's rational and prudent person was not a necessary condition for liability in every instance. An innocent act could establish liability if the agent's intention indicated that harm was likely to follow unless the state interfered.

But Holmes insisted that there were limits to this kind of liability, if the purpose of law was to remain the prevention of harm and not the punishment of sinners. Unlawful intent alone was not enough. "If a man starts from Boston to Cambridge for the purpose of committing a murder when he gets there, but is stopped by the draw and goes home, he is no more punishable than if he had sat in his chair and resolved to shoot somebody, but on second thoughts had given up the notion."[68] But how was the line to be drawn between this case, in which unlawful intent was not enough for liability, and larceny, in which liability was imposed, even though the owner had not been permanently deprived of property. Holmes, once again, responded that it was ultimately a policy question, the relevant factors being "the nearness of the danger, the greatness of the harm, and the degree of apprehension felt."[69] The larcenist had come near enough to a harm great enough to justify punishment from a policy-making point of view; the Bostonian had not.

Since the issue was one of policy, differences of opinion were to be expected as to where to draw the line. In the case of purchasing a die for coining, liability could be placed further back because the object could not be used legally. Even if ownership of such a die was a completely nonharmful act, it could still be punished because the owner could only have intended at some point in the future to counterfeit coins—a substantial harm that would raise the apprehension of the community.[70]

One type of attempt also involved imposing liability on an innocent act on the ground that unlawful intent was present. Criminal attempts were of two kinds: harmful acts and innocent acts done with an intent to cause harm. The first kind of attempt included acts—pulling the trigger of a gun pointed in the direction of another person—that were dangerous (assuming that the agent knew facts that should have warned of the danger) even if the harmful result did not come to pass. Such an attempt was consequently punished on ordinary principles of liability without any consideration of the actual foresight, intent, or motive of the agent. As Holmes put it, such "an act is punishable as an attempt, if, supposing it to have produced its natural and probable [not intended] effect, it would have amounted to a substantive crime."[71]

In contrast to this type of attempt, Holmes continued, there was "another class of [attempts] in which actual intent is clearly necessary, and the existence of this class as well as the name (attempt) no doubt tends to affect the whole doctrine."[72] This class of attempts consisted of acts "which could not have effected the crime unless followed by other acts on the part of the wrongdoer. For instance, lighting a match with intent to set fire to a haystack has been held to amount to a criminal attempt to burn it, although the defendant blew out the match on seeing that he was watched."[73] Here again the state steps in and punishes, though no dangerous activity took place, on the theory that it is probable that the agent's innocent act (the agent may only be lighting a cigarette) "will be followed by other acts in connection with which its effect will be harmful, although not so otherwise."[74]

But how can the state know that the dangerous acts would probably have occurred? Holmes responded that the state must show that the agent would have chosen to do the dangerous acts, "and the only way generally available to show that he would have chosen to do them is by showing that he intended to do them when he did what he did."[75] Therefore, as in the cases of larceny and the purchase of a die for coining, harmful action was in certain cases unnecessary for liability. An innocent act conjoined to an actual intent to cause some future harm was enough.

The nearness and greatness of danger, along with the apprehension felt by the community, determined when a nonharmful act could be punished on the ground that it constituted an attempt. The line of illegality was therefore very fuzzy. "It has been thought that to shoot at a block of wood thinking it to be a man is not an attempt to murder, and that to put a hand into an empty pocket, intending to pick it, is not an attempt to commit larceny, although on the latter question there is a difference of opinion."[76] It seems that Holmes in the end favored not imposing liability in these cases, but he added that "it might be said that even such things as those should be punished, in order to make discouragement broad enough and easy to understand."[77] In any case, unlawful intent was a sufficient basis for liability only if it was conjoined to an act that was close enough to a serious harm to justify punishment. If the law's purpose was to prevent harm, and not punish sinners, only then was the punishment of a nonharmful act justified.

A consideration of Holmes's decisions helps to buttress my interpretation of his doctrine of attempts. In *Hyde v. United States*, Holmes reaffirmed the twofold nature of attempts. An "attempt, in the strictest sense, is an act expected to bring about a substantive wrong by the forces of nature."[78] Here he was referring to the first category of harmful acts: the category in which the external standard of the rational and prudent person was used to ascertain if the agent, from what was known, should have foreseen the danger. But along with this type of attempt "is classed the kindred offense where the act and the natural conditions present or supposed to be present are not enough to do the harm without a further act, but where it is so near to the result that if coupled with an intent to produce that result, the danger is very great."[79] He then cited *Swift v. United States*[80] as an example of a case in which the defendants had done nothing harmful per se, but had done various things sufficiently proximate to a harm that their intent to monopolize the meat industry was a sufficient basis for finding a probability of harm and for the state to enjoin the defendants.[81]

Two early Massachusetts decisions also deserve some consideration. The first was an arson case.[82] A Mr. Peaslee arranged materials in a room for the purpose of having another person set them afire; he then solicited that person to set fire to them; and he drove in a carriage toward the scene of the proposed crime with the intent to set the building aflame himself, but changed his mind within a quarter of a mile of the site. Was there anything here that could in Holmes's opinion be the basis for an attempted arson conviction?

In the end, he said yes, but it seems clear that in his opinion neither the first nor the last act sufficed.[83] In regard to the first act, Peaslee had placed in the room a piece of wood in a pan of turpentine and had laid a candle on a shelf six feet away.[84] But this in itself was a nonharmful act. Punishment of it would push the law too far, according to Holmes, in the direction of retribution for moral wrongs when its true purpose was the prevention of harmful acts. This act constituted an attempt only if the agent intended harm, which he certainly did, and only if the actual harm was serious enough and sufficiently proximate to the act to justify punishment. The issue was debatable, but Holmes and the Massachusetts Supreme Court decided that punishment on this theory was inappropriate.

A mere collection and preparation of materials in a room for the purpose of setting fire to them, unaccompanied by any present intent to set the fire, would be too remote. If the accused intended to rely upon his own hands to the end, he must be shown to have had a present intent to accomplish the crime without much delay, and to have had this intent at a time and place where he was able to carry it out.[85]

Since he had not intended to light the fire himself, since he intended further acts—the solicitation of another to light the turpentine—the innocent act was not close enough to a harm itself serious enough to justify punishment from a policy-making point of view. The act was a preparation to commit a crime, but it was not an attempt.

The same can be said for the last act—driving toward a building with an intent to set it afire. If the law's main purpose was to prevent harmful acts, this last act was too far away from the harm to impose liability. It was analogous to the case of the Bostonian on his way to Cambridge to murder someone. Peaslee could have changed his mind just as the hypothetical Bostonian had done. Moreover, in the arson case mentioned earlier, while Holmes agreed with the decision that a person who lights a match by a haystack with the intent to set it afire is guilty of attempted arson, he also approvingly cited the same court's understanding that "if the defendant had gone no further than to buy a box of matches for the purpose, he would not have been liable."[86] The point is that Holmes's conception of the purpose of the law—to prevent harm—made him suspicious of punishing innocent acts conjoined to evil intentions unless there was some real proximity to harm.[87]

If policy justified liability, however, Holmes had no qualms about imposing it, even if no harm commensurate with the punishment took place. The relevant considerations—proximity of actual harm, greatness of danger, and the degree of apprehension felt by the community—were discussed by Holmes in another early Massachusetts case.[88] Here a Mr. Kennedy had placed a teaspoonful of rat poison in a pint of tea and caused another teaspoonful to adhere to the underside of the crossbar of Mr. Leoroyd's mustache cup. Kennedy was convicted of attempted murder even though his expectation that Learoyd would die from the poison "may have been unfounded and unreasonable."[89]

In this case, liability for attempted murder was imposed by Holmes even though, from the facts that Mr. Kennedy knew, a rational and prudent person would not have foreseen the likelihood of death. The defendant was therefore not guilty of the first type of an attempt: an unreasonable harmful action likely to cause death. A small amount of rat poison was not likely to cause death. Kennedy was, however, guilty of the second type of attempt. His actual intent to commit murder was what turned the scales of liability, even if it was conjoined to an act unlikely in itself to cause death. Holmes thought that the gravity of the threatened harm (death), the seriousness of the actual resulting harm (arsenic poisoning), and the apprehension felt by the community were enough to convict Kennedy of attempted murder.[90] This was so even if the likelihood of death was small. Again, the question of whether an unlawful intent was conjoined to an act close enough to a harm itself serious enough to justify imposing liability was one of policy. Each case had to be decided on its own terms.[91]

As noted earlier, Holmes favored liability in *Peaslee* on the ground that the defendant had solicited another to commit arson. His general position was that inducements of illegal acts constituted attempts even if the harmful result did not come to pass. With unlawful intent Peaslee had done something that was, from a policy-making point of view, sufficiently proximate to the harm to justify liability for an attempt. Holmes was a little troubled that liability for illegal solicitation violated the principle "pretty well established, in this country at least, that everyone has a right to rely upon his fellow-men acting lawfully, and, therefore, is not answerable for himself acting upon the assumption that they will do so, however improbable it may be."[92] For example, a gun dealer who foresees that a buyer will use a purchase illegally is not punished. Despite the dealer's foresight of a particular harm and the fact that the dealer's act was a necessary condition for the harm, the dealer goes free on the principle that one can assume that others will act lawfully.[93] Was there any justification for treating the gun dealer differently from someone like Peaslee who induces another person to commit a crime?

Holmes thought that the significant difference was between foresight and intent. The assumption that everyone has a right "to rely upon his fellow-men acting lawfully" was to be withdrawn if the agent's intent was unlawful. The question was one of privilege. In general, Holmes believed that inducements made to others were a potential basis for liability, even though the free flow of information and conversation justified a general privilege. The agent kept a privilege if the harm was foreseen but not if it was intended. If the agent "not only has expected unlawful conduct, but has acted with the intent to bring about consequences which could not happen without the help of such unlawful acts on the part of others,"[94] then the agent was liable for an attempt even if the contemplated harm did not occur. Therefore the privilege of relying on one's fellows to act lawfully was overridden in *Peaslee* because the defendant's actual intent was unlawful. He naturally lost the privilege of assuming that the addressee would obey the law.

Inducements of lawful action could also be the basis of liability, at least of civil liability, though the privilege was stronger than in the case of an inducement of unlawful action.[95] Holmes's example was that of an agent who advised friends not to use the services of a certain doctor. Now clearly the agent's friends had the legal right not to use the services of that particular doctor, and therefore the agent was inducing lawful action. The advice was accordingly privileged; the agent was free of liability even if the resulting harm to the doctor was foreseen. But he was not free of liability if he did not believe that his advice was in the best interest of his friends, if his purpose was rather to hurt the doctor's practice.[96] Holmes applied the same criteria in *Tasker v. Stanley*,[97] which concerned the liability of a person who persuaded a woman to abandon her husband. He argued that the person's advice was privileged, but hinted that the case would have come down differently if the advice was not honestly given or if the agent's purpose was malicious in regard to the husband. Therefore, according to Holmes's theory, even in the case of inducements of lawful action, the actual purpose of the agent had a direct bearing on liability for damages.

Conspiracies

One privilege that deserves special attention is the right of association. Holmes's point of view in this regard was shaped by the early trade union movement. He was willing to concede that the acts of such associations were likely to be harmful. Nonetheless he privileged union activity unless it was part of a conspiracy. The law of conspiracy qualified the privilege or the right of association.

In *Hyde v. United States*,[98] Holmes carefully distinguished conspiracies from attempts. In his view, danger or its proximity was a necessary condition for both kinds of attempts discussed above: harmful acts that failed to produce a harmful result and innocent acts that were proximate to a harm and conjoined to an unlawful intent. Moreover, an attempt necessitated an overt act; it was the "essence of the offense."[99] Conspiracy was different. In Holmes's words, "the essence of the conspiracy is being combined for an unlawful purpose—and if an overt act is required, it does not matter how remote they may be from accomplishing the purpose, if done to effect it; that is, I suppose, in furtherance of it in any degree."[100] It is true that Holmes did not equate a conspiracy with the unlawful agreement. A conspiracy "is the result of the agreement, rather than the agreement itself, just as the partnership, although constituted by a contract, is not the contract, but is a result of it."[101] But even so, conspiracy could be established without proof of an overt act (other than the act of conspiracy itself)[102] or any proximity to harm.

It is my belief that Holmes understood conspiracy as an abuse of privilege. Certainly he believed that the right of association was to the long-term advantage of society. At every opportunity, he applauded man's tendency to combine. In his theoretical writings, his correspondence, and in his judicial opinions, he repeatedly characterized modern society as based on the individual's right to form groups by way of the right to contract. Capitalists had the right to form ever-larger corporations and laborers the analogous right to form corresponding unions. As he claimed in *Vegelahn v. Guntner*,[103] "free competition means combination, and . . . the organization of the world, now going so fast, means an ever increasing might and scope of combination." Holmes added that it seemed to him "futile to set our faces against this tendency. Whether beneficial on the whole, as I think it, or detrimental, it is inevitable, unless the fundamental axioms of society, and even the fundamental conditions of life, are to be changed."[104]

Of course, what was true of all privileges was true of the right of association and contract: it had its limits. *Vegelahn v. Guntner* concerned workmen who were charged with conspiring to prevent their employer from hiring additional laborers. Holmes argued, in dissent, that the union's activity was protected as long as they did not advocate unlawful action, threaten bodily harm, spread lies about their employer, *or act from malicious motives.*[105] Accordingly, even if a union refrained from unlawful advocacy and libel, it lost its privilege and became a conspiracy if its purpose was to harm the employer rather than to help its members in the "struggle for life." But according to Holmes, the union's purpose was not to harm the employer; it was only trying to help its membership. Even though the union foresaw the harms that its actions inflicted on the employer, it did not intend them. The distinction between foresight and intent, according to Holmes, explained why the state could not justifiably withdraw the union's privilege.[106]

Several years after *Vegelahn v. Guntner,* Holmes, now on the Supreme Court, returned to this theme of the privileged nature of man's associational activity. In his famous dissent in *Northern Securities Company v. United States,*[107] he argued that the majority's interpretation, if strictly applied, "would make eternal the *bellum omnium contra omnes* and disintegrate society so far as it could into individual atoms." His conclusion was that if the statute's purpose was to prohibit man's inclination to combine, then it was not a law to regulate commerce but "an attempt to reconstruct society."[108] Hence Holmes understood man's inclination to form larger social, economic, and political groups to be an inevitable and beneficial characteristic of modern society. The law privileged it for this reason.

Holmes's assessment of the human tendency to combine did not prevent him from realizing the harmful effects that such combinations had in particular cases. If two of three competitors form a partnership, then the third is harmed, perhaps even ruined. As long as the purpose of the partnership was not malicious in character, the law gave the third no remedy. This was true even if the competitors foresaw the harm that their combination would cause. The "policy of allowing free competition justifies the intentional inflicting of temporal damage . . . when the damage is done not for its own sake, but as an instrumentality in reaching the end of victory in the battle of trade."[109] Consequently, all acts of combination were privileged, even if they caused damage, unless the purpose of the agents was to harm other persons or the public. In contrast, if the purpose of the agents who combined was malicious, they were then outside of the privilege, subject to liability under the law of conspiracy. Holmes's doctrine of conspiracy functioned as a qualification to the general right (privilege) of association.

Holmes's opinion in *Aikens v. Wisconsin*[110] shows how he used his doctrine of conspiracy in constitutional adjudication. In this case, the Court examined the constitutionality of a statute that punished "combining for the purpose of wilfully or maliciously injuring another in his business." [111] Several newspapers had agreed that if any person paid the higher rate of advertising charged by a competitor, then they would also charge that person the higher rate; but if that person refused to buy space from the competitor entirely, then they would continue to charge the traditional lower rate. Holmes's judgment was that the law was constitutionally applied in this case because the purpose of the agreement was malicious. His basic position was that a combination whose purpose was malicious was outside of the Constitution and punishable.

By *malicious* Holmes meant "doing harm malevolently, for the sake of the harm as an end in itself, and not merely as a means to some further and legitimately desired." [112] Consequently, if the purpose of the newspaper combination had been greater efficiency or self-interest, then the combination would have been privileged, even though the contractors had foreseen their competitor's economic ruin. The Wisconsin law thus caused Holmes some misgivings since it imposed liability if the parties combined for the purpose of either "wilfully or maliciously" injuring another in business. The clause that imposed liability on those who conspired "wilfully" to injure another went too far. The law, if read literally, would

embrace all injuries intended to follow from the parties' acts, although they were intended only as the necessary means to ulterior gain for the parties themselves. Taken in that way the word would hit making a new partnership, if it was intended thereby [in the sense of foreseen] to hurt someone's else business by competition. [113]

Holmes refused to say explicitly whether the law would be unconstitutional if applied to a combination that "wilfully" rather than "maliciously" harmed another's business. But he did say that if the statute was extended to combinations that were done "partly from disinterested malevolence and partly from a hope of gain," then "the statute would be open to all the objections at which we have hinted in dealing with the word 'wilfully'. [114]

It seems clear enough that Holmes would have granted a constitutional privilege to the combination that only "wilfully" harmed another economically. Understood to be "confined to combinations with intent to do wrongful harm . . . , the statute would punish only combinations of a kind for which no justification could be offered and those which *were taken out of the justification by the motive with which they were made*" (emphasis mine). [115] Once again an unlawful purpose was the reason why a state could take away a privilege. Foresight of harm was not enough; the conspirators had to have a malicious purpose to lose the constitutional privilege of association and contract.[116]

The defendants objected that the means by which they had attempted to obtain their objective were legal. The means "to be used by this particular combination were simply the abstinence from making contracts; that a man's right so to abstain cannot be infringed on the ground of motives; and further, that it carries with it the right to communicate that intent to abstain to others, and to abstain in common with them.[117] Holmes responded that "the fallacy of this argument lies in the assumption that the statute stands no better than if directed against the pure nonfeasance of singly omitting to contract." But this case and statute were not of this character. "The statute is directed against a series of acts, and acts of several,—the acts of combining with the intent to do other acts."[118] Even if a single newspaper could legally have refused to contract for any reason and even if the acts of the combination were normally protected by the right of contract, these claims were irrelevant to the case at hand. Newspapers had combined for the purpose of destroying another. Acts of association lost their privilege if the underlying motives of the combination were malicious.

When the acts consist of making a combination calculated to cause temporal damage, the power to punish such acts, *when done maliciously,* cannot be denied because they are to be followed and worked out by conduct which might have been lawful if not preceded by the acts. No conduct has such an absolute privilege as to justify all possible schemes of which it may be a part. The most innocent and constitutionally protected of acts or omissions may be made a step in a criminal plot, and if it is a step in a plot, neither its innocence nor the Constitution is sufficient to prevent the punishment of the plot by law. (Emphasis mine)[119]

Holmes's view was that privileged acts lose their protection if actual malice was present. A combination became a conspiracy if and when its purpose was malicious.

In *Aikens,* Holmes's assessment of the constitutionality of the statute depended on his conception of the limits of liability in common law. If some act, including a combination, was punishable according to the common law, then the Constitution would be no bar. The common law's view was "that, *prima facie,* the intentional infliction of temporal damage is a cause of action which . . . requires justification if the defendant is to escape." Holmes then said that if "this is the correct mode of approach, it is obvious that justifications may vary in extent, according to the principle of policy upon which they are founded, and that while some—for instance, at common law, those affecting the use of land— are absolute, others may depend *upon the end for which the act is done"* (emphasis mine).[120] Holmes used his understanding of the role that policy played in questions of privilege in common law to decide if a particular state statute was within the constitutional right to contract and associate.

> It has been held that even the free use of land by a single owner for purely malevolent purposes may be restrained constitutionally, although the only immediate injury is to a neighboring landowner. Whether this decision was right or not when it comes to the freedom of the individual, malicious mischief is a familiar and proper subject for legislative repression. Still more are combinations for the purpose of inflicting it. It would be impossible to hold that the liberty to combine to inflict such mischief, even upon such intangibles as business or reputation, was among the rights which the 14th amendment was intended to preserve.[121]

Policy justifies withdrawing the privilege from malicious combinations in common law, and therefore such conspiracies are outside of constitutional rights of contract and association. A better example of how Holmes's theory of legal liability shaped his constitutional judgment is hard to imagine, and it should be kept in mind when evaluating whether common law principles had a fundamental impact on his doctrine of free speech.

The importance of Holmes's condition of actual malicious purpose is also evident in his restraint-of-trade decisions. He favored liability in *Swift v. United States* and *Nash v. United States,* but opposed it in *Northern Securities Company v. United States* and *United States v. Winslow* because of his findings of foresight versus malevolent purpose.[122] He denied liability in the latter cases because there was not sufficient evidence that the conspirators had an unlawful purpose. In *Northern Securities,* the question was whether "several men [can] unite to form a corporation for the purpose of buying more than half the stock of each of two competing interstate railroad companies . . . [if] ending competition between the companies"[123] was the goal of the combination? Holmes's affirmative answer relied on his opinion that the purpose of the parties was self-interested, not malicious.

In his dissent, he dismissed the relevance of the provisions of the Sherman Anti-Trust Act that dealt with contracts in restraint of trade because, as defined by common law, they were contracts that restricted how the contractor would ordinarily carry on his or her business.[124] They had nothing to do with this case because the contract or combination at issue in no way restricted the freedom of the contractors; rather, the contract united them into a corporation. The real issue was whether the agreement constituted a conspiracy in restraint of trade if the purpose of the incorporation was to suppress competition. Holmes argued that it did not because conspiracies in common law "were combinations to keep strangers to the agreement out of the business. . . . In other words, they [such combinations] were regarded as contrary to public policy because they monopolized, or attempted to monopolize, some portion of the trade or commerce of the realm."[125] Therefore, an agreement constituted a conspiracy in restraint of trade only if the purpose of the agreement was to harm the public (monopolize trade) by excluding strangers to the contract from the particular trade.

Holmes's crucial finding was that the Northern Securities Company was "not formed for the purpose of excluding others from the field."[126] Regardless of the size of the railroads involved or the fact that "one purpose of the purchase was to suppress competition between the two roads,"[127] there was no conspiracy because there was no purpose to keep others from entering the business. To conclude otherwise, he argued, "rests on a popular instead of an actual and legal conception of what the word 'monopolize' in the statute means."[128] Agreements that were meant to suppress competition were unlawful conspiracies only if their purpose was to exclude others from the business to the detriment of the public. The purpose of the stockholders of the Northern Securities Company was not of this character, and Holmes denied liability accordingly.

He applied the same analysis in *United States v. Winslow*. Three companies who sold machinery used in the manufacture of shoes merged, and the new corporation would only lend equipment to shoe manufacturers that used their equipment exclusively. Was there an unlawful purpose to this agreement to unite? Was the purpose of the agreement to monopolize in the legal sense? Holmes said no. "On the face of it the combination was simply an effort after greater efficiency."[129] His assessment in *Swift v. United States* and *Nash v. United States* was quite different. In these cases, he found a malicious purpose to exclude others from the relevant business and to harm the public and accordingly placed the contractual activity outside of the privilege. In *Swift,* Holmes found that the purpose of the combination was "not merely to restrict competition among the parties, but to aid in an attempt to monopolize commerce among the states."[130] And in *Nash,* against the defendant's objection that the acts that their combination had planned were lawful, Holmes responded that it was "enough to say that some of them conceivably might have been adequate to accomplish the [unlawful] result, and that the intent alleged would convert what on their face might be no more than ordinary acts of competition or the small dishonesties of trade into a conspiracy of wider scope."[131] If the purpose or intent of a combination was malicious or unlawful, then the conspiracy in restraint of trade was established. This was so even if the planned activities were relatively harmless.

Summary

Holmes's theory of legal liability is composed of more than one branch. No doubt the main branch consisted of the external test that he applied to harmful acts. If an agent, knowing facts that would have warned a rational person of danger, acted anyway, that agent was liable no matter what he or she foresaw or intended. The degree of liability would depend on the degree of danger that the rational person perceived and on what the agent knew about his or her circumstances. Certain harmful acts, however, were ordinarily privileged from liability because of their long-term advantages. But even here liability could be imposed if the agent's actual purpose was malicious, harmful in regard to another person or the public in general. Abuses of privilege constituted a subordinate but important branch of Holmes's theory of legal liability, especially the abuse of the right of association as defined by the law of conspiracy. Attempts were a different branch. In the case of an attempt, liability could be imposed on a nonharmful act, but only if the agent actually intended harm and had done something proximate to it. What is crucial to remember is that the two subordinate branches required actual illicit intent.

Notes

1. See Note, *Harvard Law Review* 41 (1927): 525–28; Livingston Hall, "The Substantive Law of Crimes, 1887–1936," *Harvard Law Review* 50 (1937): 616–53; Yosal Rogat, "The Judge as Spectator," *University of Chicago Law Review* 31 (1964): 216–217; Fred D. Ragan, "Justice Oliver Wendell Holmes, Jr., Zechariah Chafee, Jr., and the Clear and Present Danger Test for Free Speech: The First Year, 1919," *Journal of American History* 58 (June-March 1972): 28–31; David S. Bogen, "The Free Speech Metamorphosis of Mr. Justice Holmes," *Hofstra Law Review* 11 (1982): 154–63; David M. Rabban, "The First Amendment in Its Forgotten Years," *Yale Law Journal* 90 (1981): 580; "The Emergence of Modern First Amendment Doctrine," *University of Chicago Law Review* 50 (Fall 1983): 1271–73.

2. I do, however, ignore those elements of Holmes's theory of liability—for example, his understanding of contracts—that have no bearing on the substance and the consistency of his free-speech doctrine.

3. See H. L. Pohlman, *Justice Oliver Wendell Holmes and Utilitarian Jurisprudence* (Cambridge: Harvard University Press, 1984), chap. 2.

4. Ibid., 26–27.

5. Ibid., 27–39.

6. Holmes, *The Common Law* (Cambridge: Harvard University Press, 1963), 86.

7. Ibid. For Holmes's general discussion of the community's right to sacrifice the individual for the common good, see ibid., 37–42.

8. See H. L. A. Hart, *Punishment and Responsibility* (Oxford: Oxford University Press, 1986), 242–44.

9. See Pohlman, *Holmes and Utilitarian Jurisprudence*, 162–63.

10. Sheldon Novick, *Honorable Justice: The Life of Oliver Wendell Holmes* (Boston: Little, Brown, 1989).

11. Ibid., 159.

12. Ibid., 434 n. 67.

13. Ibid.

14. Ibid., 446 n. 67, 456 n. 29.

15. Ibid., 434 n. 67.

16. See Hart, *Punishment and Responsibility*, 243–44.

17. Novick, *Honorable Justice*, 431 n. 23, 434 n. 67.

18. See Pohlman, *Holmes and Utilitarian Jurisprudence*, 94–96. For a recent view that also places Holmes in both the historical and the utilitarian traditions, see Thomas Grey, "Holmes and Legal Pragmatism," *Stanford Law Review* 41 (1989): 805–15.

19. Novick, *Honorable Justice*, 446 n. 50.

20. See Atiyah, "The Legacy of Holmes through English Eyes," *Boston University Law Review* 63 (1983): 344.

21. Hereinafter I use the terms *general* and *external* interchangeably to refer to the *objective* character of Holmes's theory of legal liability.
22. See Pohlman, *Holmes and Utilitarian Jurisprudence*, 161–62.
23. See Rogat, "The Judge as Spectator," 217–26.
24. Pohlman, *Holmes and Utilitarian Jurisprudence*, 148.
25. Atiyah, "The Legacy of Holmes through English Eyes," 347.
26. Holmes, "Privilege, Malice, and Intent," *Harvard Law Review* 8 (1894), in Holmes, *Collected Legal Papers* (New York: Peter Smith, 1952), 117–18. See also *Commonwealth v. Pierce*, 138 Mass. 165, 178 (1884): "But it is familiar law that an act causing death may be murder, manslaughter, or misadventure according to the degree of danger attending it. . . . As implied malice signifies the highest degree of danger, and makes the act murder; so, if the danger is less, but still not so remote that it can be disregarded, the act will be called reckless."
27. Jerome Hall is responsible for popularizing the notion that Holmes's theory of legal liability made the defendant's mental state "irrelevant in modern penal law" (*General Principles of Criminal Law*, 2d ed. [New York: Bobbs-Merrill, 1960], chap. 5). Francis A. Allen makes the same error when he claims that Holmes's "external standard assumes subjective awareness of the circumstances in which conduct occurs" ("Mr. Justice Holmes: The Criminal Law," *University of Chicago Law Review* 31 [1964]: 260. Patrick S. Atiyah is much closer to my view that Holmes's crucial criterion of legal liability was an internal fact: what the agent knew of the circumstances of the act ("The Legacy of Holmes through English Eyes," 343).
28. Pohlman, *Holmes and Utilitarian Jurisprudence*, 43.
29. Holmes, *The Common Law*, 46.
30. For the more complicated case, see ibid., 46–47.
31. Ibid., 116, 117. See also Holmes, "Privilege, Malice, and Intent," *Harvard Law Review* 8 (1894), in *Collected Legal Papers*, 123: "In a proper sense, the state of man's consciousness always is material to his liability."
32. Holmes, *The Common Law*, 45–46.
33. Holmes, *The Common Law*, 121.
34. Ibid., 121.
35. Ibid., 124.
36. Ibid., 126.
37. Holmes, "Agency," *Harvard Law Review* 4 (1891), in *Collected Legal Papers*, 64.
38. In an earlier work, I was guilty of this misinterpretation of Holmes's theory of liability. Since Holmes in certain cases allowed the law to assume the agent's knowledge of circumstances that would render him liable, I too quickly assumed that he required that everyone have the knowledge of an average person of the community. Having made this mistake, I compounded the error by arguing that his criterion of liability was completely external: the objective dangerousness of external acts. I now see that it is impossible to assess, in most cases, the agent's knowledge by using such an abstract

standard as the "knowledge of the average man" and that Holmes never entertained such a delusion. Consequently, his criterion of liability was not external in the sense in which I earlier maintained. According to his general theory, liability depended on a voluntary act and on the agent's knowledge of what would have warned a rational and prudent person of danger. For my earlier discussion, see Pohlman, *Holmes and Utilitarian Jurisprudence*, 137–39.

39. Holmes, *The Common Law*, 125.
40. Ibid., 119.
41. Ibid., 117.
42. Ibid., 120.
43. Ibid., 119.
44. See Holmes, *The Common Law*, 89–92. Also see Pohlman, *Holmes and Utilitarian Jurisprudence*, 137.
45. Holmes, *The Common Law*, 44.
46. See Holmes, "The Path of the Law," *Harvard Law Review* 10 (1897), in Holmes, *Collected Legal Papers*, 191.
47. See Holmes, *The Common Law*, 63.
48. Ibid., 48.
49. Ibid., 48.
50. Ibid.
51. Ibid.
52. Ibid., 42
53. Ibid., 44. Also see 104 and Holmes, "Privilege, Malice, and Intent," *Harvard Law Review* 8 (1894), in *Collected Legal Papers*, 118–19.
54. Holmes, *The Common Law*, 53.
55. See Holmes, "Privilege, Malice, and Intent," *Harvard Law Review* 8 (1894), in *Collected Legal Papers*, 119.
56. Ibid., 120.
57. Ibid.
58. Ibid., 120–21.
59. Ibid., 121.
60. Ibid.
61. Ibid., 124–25.
62. Ibid., 130–31.
63. Ibid., 122.
64. Ibid., 124.
65. Holmes, *The Common Law*, 58.
66. Ibid.
67. Ibid., 59.
68. Ibid., 56.
69. Ibid.
70. See Ibid., 56–57.
71. Ibid., 55.
72. Ibid., 55.

73. Ibid.
74. Ibid.
75. Ibid., 56.
76. Ibid., 57.
77. Ibid.
78. *Hyde v. United States*, 225 U.S. 347, 387 (1911).
79. Id.
80. 196 U.S. 375 (1905).
81. Id. at 396.
82. *Commonwealth v. Peaslee*, 177 Mass. 267 (1901).
83. In fact, Peaslee escaped liability because the act of criminal solicitation was not mentioned in the indictment. But Holmes added that if the solicitation had been alleged, he had no doubt that Peaslee would have been liable. See Id. at 274.
84. Id. at 271.
85. Id. at 273–74.
86. Holmes, *The Common Law*, 56. See also 55.
87. For example, I think it is plausible to say that Holmes doubted the wisdom of punishing for attempted rape a slave who "ran after a white woman, but desisted before he caught her." See *The Common Law*, 56 and 57, where Holmes refers to the "peculiar fears," of a slave-owning society.
88. *Commonwealth v. Kennedy*, 170 Mass. 18 (1897).
89. Id. at 21.
90. Id. at 22.
91. For example, Holmes argued in *Northern Securities Co. v. United States* that even if the stockholders intended to monopolize the railroads, their activity was too remote from the harm to constitute an attempt. See 193 U.S. 197, 409 (1904).
92. Holmes, "Privilege, Malice, and Intent," *Harvard Law Review* 8 (1894), in *Collected Legal Papers*, 132.
93. Ibid., 131.
94. Ibid., 133.
95. See Ibid., 135: "I cannot believe that *bona fide* advice to do an unlawful act to the manifest harm of the plaintiff ought to be any more privileged than such advice, given maliciously, to do a lawful act. Of course, I am speaking of effectual advice. It seems to me hard for the law to recognize a privilege to induce unlawful conduct."
96. See ibid., 124–25.
97. 153 Mass. 148 (1891).
98. 225 U.S. 347, 387–88 (1911).
99. Id. at 388.
100. Id. According to Holmes, a conspiracy was "a partnership in criminal purposes." See *United States v. Kissel*, 218 U.S. 601, 608 (1910).
101. *United States v. Kissel*, 218 U.S. 601, 608 (1910).
102. *Nash v. United States*, 229 U.S. 373, 378 (1912): "the Sherman Act

punishes the conspiracies at which it is aimed on the common law footing
—that is to say, it does not make the doing of any act other than the act
of conspiring a condition of liability."

103. *Vegelahn v. Guntner*, 167 Mass. 92 (1896).
104. Id. at 108.
105. Id. at 104–9.
106. Holmes's reasoning in his dissent in *Plant v. Woods*, 176 Mass. 492, 504–5 (1900), is identical to that described above. In this case, one union of painters threatened employers with harm if they hired any painters from a competing union. Here again Holmes insisted that " the presence or absence of justification may depend upon the object of their conduct, that is, upon the motive with which they acted" (id. at 504). In this case, though the union's purpose "was not directly concerned with wages," its actions were still privileged because its aim was "to strengthen the defendants' society as a preliminary and means to enable it to make a better fight on questions of wages or other matters of clashing interests" (id. at 505). The conclusion was that since the union's purpose was self-serving, not malicious, it was protected. The privilege was maintained by Holmes not because labor in general would secure by these threats of strikes and boycotts a larger share of the annual product. Though more powerful labor organizations may get a larger share for their members, "they get it at the expense of the less organized and less powerful portion of the laboring mass" (id). Policy considerations justified this struggle between competing unions. They did not become conspiracies, even if they foresaw the harm they inflicted on others, unless their purpose was malicious.
107. *Northern Securities Co. v. United States*, 192 U.S. 197, 411 (1903).
108. Id. at 411. See also 407.
109. *Vegelahn v. Guntner*, 167 Mass. 106 (1896).
110. 195 U.S. 194, 202 (1904).
111. Id. at 202.
112. Id. at 203. Holmes of course meant the actual purpose of the agent. He explicitly denied that the external standard had any role in the law of conspiracy. "It is no sufficient answer to this line of thought that motives are not actionable, and that the standards of the law are external. That is true in determining what a man is bound to foresee, but not necessarily in determining the extent to which he can justify harm which he has foreseen" (id. at 204).
113. Id. at 202–3.
114. Id. at 206.
115. Id.
116. Holmes certainly emphasized the fact that malice existed in this case. "The malevolent purpose is alleged, it is admitted by the demurrer, it is not sufficiently denied by the pleas, whatever we may conjecture would have been done if counsel had this decision before them. A purely malevolent act may be done even in trade competition" (id. at 203–4).

117. Id. at 205.
118. Id.
119. Id. at 205–6.
120. Id. at 204.
121. Id. at 205.
122. *Swift v. United States*, 196 U.S. 375 (1904); *Nash v. United States*, 229 U.S. 373 (1912); *Northern Securities Co. v. United States*, 193 U.S. 197 (1903); *United States v. Winslow*, 227 U.S. 202 (1912).
123. *Northern Securities Co. v. United States*, 193 U.S. 197, 401 (1903), Holmes dissenting.
124. Id. at 104.
125. Id.
126. Id. at 408.
127. Id. at 409. Holmes agreed that if it was unlawful to conspire to suppress competition, then the conspiracy provisions of the Sherman Anti-Trust Act would apply to the facts of this case. But he then denied that suppressing competition was an unlawful purpose. Those who combined to suppress competition were subject to liability only if they also had the unlawful purpose of excluding others from the business (id. at 409–10).
128. Id. at 408–9.
129. *United States v. Winslow*, 227 U.S. 202, 217 (1912).
130. *Swift v. United States*, 196 U.S. 398 (1904).
131. *Nash v. United States*, 229 U.S. 378 (1912).

3. The Major Opinions

H OLMES'S MAJOR FREE-SPEECH opinions fit into the categories of his theory of legal liability. Speech was punishable if it was harmful per se or if the speaker intended harm and either one of two conditions was met. Besides actual illegal intent, the speech had to be sufficiently proximate to harm to constitute an attempt, or it had to be part of an unlawful conspiracy. The theory therefore had two main branches. If the speech was harmful in itself, the speaker was liable on the external standard of liability. No matter what the speaker intended or foresaw, he or she was punishable if the agent knew facts that would have warned a reasonable person of the danger. But if the speech was not harmful in itself, the speaker could still be liable if harm was intended and either the speaker said something proximate to the harm or conspired with others to obtain through speech the unlawful objective. This chapter examines Holmes's opinions to see how he applied these different standards of liability to various factual settings.

Harmful Speech

Holmes's libel and slander decisions are important because they show that he thought that speech alone could constitute a harmful act subject to liability on general principles. An agent who libeled another was punishable irrespective of motive or intent. Liability was grounded on the harmful act and that alone. In an early article, Holmes wrote: "So in slander and libel, the distinction between malice in law and malice in fact seems to give the result, that the usual ground of liability in such actions is simply doing certain overt acts; viz., making the false statements complained of, irrespective of intent."[1] In *The Common Law*, he returned to the same theme, arguing that "the rule that it [libel] is presumed upon proof of speaking certain words is equivalent to saying that the overt conduct of speaking those words may be actionable whether the consequence of damage to the plaintiff was intended or not." This conclusion "falls in with the general theory," he added, "because the manifest tendency of slanderous words is to harm the person of whom they are spoken."[2] Libel was a harmful speech act to which the external standard of liability was applied. A publisher knew facts that would have warned a rational and prudent person of danger and was therefore liable if his or her actions harmed another. No internal facts of intent or motive had to be proved of the defendant.

Holmes's later judicial opinions followed the same reasoning. In 1891, he held that even though a newspaper acted in good faith and had reasonable grounds to believe that what it had published in a particular story was true, it was yet liable for the false statements it made about a customs official.[3] Good faith was not exculpatory because the publisher knew facts that should have warned of the dangerous character of his or her business. The danger was so obvious that the law had developed a concrete external rule: "A person publishes libellous matter at his peril."[4] Holmes had no inclination to treat libel differently because freedom of speech was involved; his theory of legal liability qualified the import of constitutional guarantees. He concluded that, apart from any statutory reforms, liability for libel or slander was no more or less than "the usual liability in tort for the natural consequences of a manifestly injurious act."[5]

Hanson v. Globe Newspaper Co.[6] is an even better example of Holmes's general presumption that libel was subject to the external principle of liability. Though the majority of the Massachusetts Supreme Court decided for the newspaper, Holmes dissented. In its description of a prisoner, the newspaper had referred to him as H. P. Hanson when his real name was H. P. H. Hanson. This simple innocent mistake took on more serious overtones when the real H. P. Hanson stood up and sued. The majority rejected the suit since the newspaper had not libeled the actual person that the article was meant to describe, but Holmes insisted that general principles made the newspaper's actual intention or purpose irrelevant. "The publication is so manifestly detrimental that the defendant publishes it at the peril of being able to justify it in the sense in which the public will understand it."[7] To grant an excuse in this case "would be very like firing a gun into a street, and, when a man falls, setting up that no one was known to be there."[8]

Firing a gun in a crowded street was, in Holmes's mind, much like publishing a newspaper in a crowed city. While in the former case, there was considerable likelihood that someone's body would be harmed, in the latter there was as much likelihood that someone's reputation would be hurt. The gunman knew facts that should have warned of the risk and was liable if harm occurred regardless of actual foresight, intent, or purpose. The publisher was in the same position. Both had engaged in conduct manifestly dangerous according to the standard of the rational and prudent person.

Holmes's libel decisions are also important because they reveal his doctrine of privilege at work. Again, whether a certain privilege against libel should be recognized and, if it should, whether the privilege held if the agent libeled another maliciously were policy questions. Early in his judicial career, Holmes read any privilege against libel narrowly. In 1884 he refused to widen the privilege attached to fair reports of judicial proceedings.[9] Though the *Boston Herald* had published a fair and correct report of the contents of a petition for the removal of an attorney from the bar, Holmes restricted the privilege to fair reports of what goes on in open court. A newspaper that published a report of a petition filed in the office of the clerk of court took the risk that the contents of the petition were false. If there were any false statements of fact, it was libel.

In 1891 Holmes upheld a privilege of fair criticism on matters of public interest,[10] but excluded from the privilege statements of fact. What is privileged "is criticism, not statement, and however it might be if a person merely quoted or referred to a statement as made by others, and gave it no new sanction, if he takes upon himself in his own person to allege facts otherwise libellous, he will not be privileged if those facts are not true."[11] The privilege was confined to comment and criticism. A publisher was still strictly liable for factual claims.

Holmes may have later widened this narrow conception of the privilege of fair criticism on matters of public interest. In 1911, as a Justice on the Supreme Court, he rejected a libel suit against a Puerto Rican newspaper that had charged a public official with immoral conduct. As reported by the newspaper, a United States attorney had worked as a private counsel for persons suing the government of Puerto Rico.[12] Holmes reasoned that a charge of libel failed for a number of reasons: (1) the facts as presented were true; (2) the conduct attributed to the attorney was lawful and therefore could not constitute a libel; (3) the plaintiff "was a public officer in whose course of action connected with his office the citizens of Puerto Rico had a serious interest, and *anything bearing on such action was a legitimate subject of statement* and debate." (emphasis mine).[13] This language seemed to privilege statements of fact, not just criticism and comment on the facts. But in any case, Holmes held that the privilege was made out unless the defendants acted maliciously. In "the absence of express malice or excess the defendant was not liable at all."[14] Accordingly, the actual purpose of the agent became crucial in the law of libel only to override a privilege.

Holmes's libel decisions therefore show that in his judgment speech alone could constitute a harmful act subject to liability on ordinary principles. He also thought that harmful speech was privileged if it was a report of official court proceedings, if it contained only comment and criticism, or if it concerned the activities of a public officer.[15] But there was more than a hint that if the publisher acted with a malicious purpose, the privilege was withdrawn.

Contempts, like libels, were subject to liability because they were harmful acts. But unlike libels, contempts were never privileged and the agent's intent was therefore always irrelevant. Two types of contempt were delineated: interference with the administration of justice and disobedience of a court order. *Patterson v. Colorado,*[16] which is often used to denigrate Holmes's commitment to free speech, concerned the first type of contempt. An ex-senator had published an editorial and articles that were extremely critical of the Colorado Supreme Court. The court had, in his opinion, unjustifiably thrown out the results of a recent election held in Denver. But most important, since it concerned the integrity of the court, he hinted that utility corporations were scheming "to buy" a couple of seats on the court to free themselves from restrictions on their franchises. The state brought a charge of contempt of court since the cases that Patterson excoriated were technically still before the court or were ones that might come before the court in the near future. In his defense, Patterson said he was able and willing to prove the truth of what he had written. His position was that Colorado's constitution and the Ninth Amendment protected all truthful statements from subsequent punishment.[17]

Holmes rejected those aspects of Patterson's argument that relied upon the federal Constitution. Neither the Ninth Amendment or the Fourteenth Amendment protected truth in every instance. Even if a statement was true, it was subject to liability on the external standard if it was harmful per se.

A publication likely to reach the eyes of the jury, declaring a witness in a pending cause a perjurer, would be none the less a contempt that it was true. It would tend to obstruct the administration of justice, because even a correct conclusion is not to be reached or helped in that way, if our system of trials is to be maintained. The theory of our system is that the conclusions to be reached in a case will be induced only by evidence and argument in open court, and not by any outside influence, whether of private talk or public print.[18]

Private talk or public print that "obstructed" or "interfered" with the courts constituted a contempt because it harmed the system of judicial administration. That what was said was true made no difference. The agent knew facts that should have revealed the danger that his or her speech activity posed to the administration of justice. He or she was liable on general principles.

The agent's foresight, intent, and motive were irrelevant in such a case. Holmes was willing to concede that Patterson was acting with the best of motives and intentions, that he only wanted to perform "a public duty" by telling the public the truth about Republican electoral fraud.[19] Nonetheless, he was guilty of a contempt because a rational and prudent person would have foreseen, from facts that Patterson knew, that his publications were very likely to harm the administration of justice, and that was all that was necessary for liability.

A Massachusetts case that Holmes cited in *Patterson* confirms the view that he understood contempt as a manifestly harmful act, even though Judge Field wrote the earlier opinion. The question was whether a newspaper company could be guilty of contempt if it had published the following: "The town offered Loring $80 at the time of the taking, but he demanded $250, and, not getting it, went to law."[20] At the time of publication, Silas H. Loring was suing for damages that he suffered when the town took his land to remove a grade crossing. Judge Field said that the newspaper could be held in contempt though there was no finding "that there was an intent to influence the trial of the cause referred to on the part of anybody."[21] Field and Holmes therefore agreed. Contempt did "not depend upon the intention of the party, but upon the act he has done."[22] This meant that the act had actually to obstruct the administration of justice. Holmes made this clear in a case involving a newspaper that criticized a judge who was, at the time, considering enjoining the enforcement of a popular ordinance: one that limited the railroad fare to three cents.[23] The newspaper depicted the judge as being biased in favor of the railroad. After he gave the railroad the injunction it wanted, the judge directed an indictment against the newspaper and later found it to be in contempt of court.

Holmes was critical for two reasons. First, the summary proceedings by which the judge found the newspaper to be in contempt were completely inappropriate.[24] But, second, the "words of the [contempt] statute . . . point only to the present protection of the court from actual interference, and not to postponed retribution for lack of respect for its dignity;—not to moving to indicate its independence after enduring the newspaper's attacks for nearly six months, as the court did in this case."[25] Acts could constitute contempt only if they were "so near as actually to obstruct—and not merely near enough to threaten a possible obstruction."[26] Holmes reviewed the news and commentary published by the newspaper and concluded that he could not "find there anything that obstructed the administration of justice in any sense that I possibly can give to those words."[27] And even though in this case Holmes was interpreting the words of a federal statute, his decision coincided with his theory of liability. Contempts were harms; they could be punished regardless of the intent of the agent. But the act had to be actually harmful as defined by the judgment of the rational and prudent person. A tendency of harm or a proximity to harm was not enough. Only if a speaker engaged in harmful speech was the harsh external standard of liability to be applied. Verbal acts that had only a tendency to cause harm or that were only proximate to a harm did not incur liability on this branch of the theory. An act was a contempt only if it "actually obstructed" the administration of justice.

These same principles were applied to those who disobeyed judicial decrees. Holmes said that he "would go as far as any man in favor of the sharpest and most summary enforcement of order in court and obedience to decrees."[28] This was true even if the particular decree

enjoined a person from speaking. The First Amendment protected neither "a man in falsely shouting fire in a theater, and causing a panic
[nor] . . . a man from an injunction against uttering words that may
have all the effect of force."[29] These kinds of acts were objective harms
and therefore, assuming cognizance of surroundings, the agent was liable
regardless of his or her foresight, intention, or motive. Even the person
who meant the shout of "fire" as a joke, not intending or foreseeing the
resulting panic, was liable, because that person did something harmful
knowing facts that would have warned an average person of danger.
Similarly, disobedience of an injunction not only undermined the authority of courts—an obvious harm—but also harmed the individual or
interest that the injunction was meant to protect. Therefore, even if the
injunction restrained a person from using words, it was valid because
"words may have all the effect of force."

Holmes cited *Gompers v. Bucks Stove and Range Company*[30] in
support of his claim that speech alone could constitute a harmful act
subject to liability on ordinary principles. In the majority opinion in this
case, Justice Lamar had held that words could have "a force not inhering
in the words themselves," and if so, they exceed "any possible right of
speech which a single individual may have. Under such circumstances
they become what have been called 'verbal acts,' and as such subject to
injunction as the use of any other force whereby property is unlawfully
damaged."[31] Therefore Holmes understood contempt of court as he did
libel: both were harmful acts subject to liability regardless of the foresight, intent, or motive of the agent. Since policy considerations did not
justify any type of privilege for contempts, the agent's purpose had a
very neglibible role to play. Perhaps a speaker's intent could reveal his
or her knowledge of the circumstances of the act, but knowledge, not
intent or foresight, was the crucial factor. If it could be shown, from
whatever source, that the agent knew enough to warn an average person
of danger, he or she was liable.

Attempt and Conspiracy

A manifestly harmful speech act was not necessary for liability. Holmes
at times imposed liability on nonharmful acts when the agent's intent
was unlawful (see chap. 2). If harm was intended, a person was liable
for doing something that was sufficiently proximate to a harm to qualify

as an attempt or conspiring with others to obtain an unlawful objective. Applying the same theory to speech, he divided culpable speech into harmful speech and speech intended to cause future harm. The constitutional power of government to punish speech was understood in the same way. As he said in *Abrams v. United States,* "the United States constitutionally may punish speech that produces *or* is intended to produce a clear and imminent danger that it will bring about forthwith certain substantive evils that the United States may constitutionally seek to prevent" (emphasis mine).[32] The "or" was meant to be taken in an exclusive sense. He restated the same idea on the following page: "It is only the present danger of immediate evil *or* an intent to bring it about that warrants Congress in setting a limit to the expression of opinion where private rights are not concerned" (emphasis mine).[33] His theory of free speech therefore had two independent branches of liability. The first branch has already been investigated. The second branch is larger, more complicated, and requires a consideration of the famous free speech cases: *Schenck, Frohwerk, Debs, Abrams,* and *Gitlow.*[34] A consideration of individual cases is the best way to proceed. The conclusion is that Holmes decided these cases depending on how the intent-branch of his theory coincided with the factual circumstances as they were submitted in the records filed with the Supreme Court.

Before we turn to the specifics of each case, a cautionary note is in order. Even if Holmes's votes in favor of conviction in *Schenck, Frohwerk,* and *Debs* were consistent with his theory of legal liability, there is no question that repression thrived between 1917 and 1920. The sad story has been told and told well. In almost numbing detail, Peterson and Fite have recounted how states and the federal government, semi-official local groups, and private vigilantes intimidated, harassed, and even tortured individuals who were only exercising their First Amendment rights.[35] The American Socialist party, the Industrial Workers of the World (IWW), the Nonpartisan League, and other unorthodox groups were all crushed under the combined weight of public and private persecution. The country was suffering from hysteria. It would brook not even moderate criticism of the war effort, and after the war the new "Red Menace" brought on a new cycle of vicious bigotry and suppression.[36] The entire episode is a frightening indication of the fragile nature of free speech.

This enormous constitutional outrage, however, should not determine our interpretation of Holmes's theory of free speech. He did uphold certain convictions, but that hardly means that he endorsed this gross suppression of individual rights. Fairness requires that we consider the cases on their own terms. Even if most of those people who criticized the war were innocently exercising their rights, it is plausible that some, or at least a few, did go over the line as Holmes understood it. Hence the proper question is whether Schenck, Frohwerk, and Debs engaged in speech that was over the line while Abrams and Gitlow did not. If the records and the decisions of these cases can be squared with the theory, then my interpretation of Holmes's doctrine of free speech gains credibility.

Though Holmes's theory of free speech was obviously not to blame for the hysteria that gripped the country during World War I and its aftermath, it should be emphasized that the existence of the hysteria did count for something within his free-speech doctrine. Both unlawful intent and a proximity to harm were required for liability in cases of attempt, but proximity to harm was measured by the seriousness and nearness of the harm, its likelihood, and *the apprehension of the community that the harm would occur.* There is little doubt that the community's apprehension counted for something whether it was justified or not. Thus, assuming a certain "proximity" to harm, an evil-intentioned speaker's liability could depend on a community's hysterical apprehensions.

Notwithstanding the significance of this implication of Holmes's approach, a couple of qualifications are needed. First, there is no reason to think that he would have found the proximity-to-harm requirement satisfied by hysterical apprehension alone. The harm had also to be somewhat serious, close, and likely. In addition, unlawful intent had also to be shown. Nevertheless, it is a noteworthy feature of his theory, one that produces justifiable concern, that hysterical apprehension could tip the scales of liability. He took it into account because the law has to deal with the actual feelings of a community, whatever they might be. The all too likely alternative was vigilantism—a far-worse alternative.[37] But it is a troubling aspect of Holmes's theory, one that does not square well with his own understanding of the harm-prevention purpose of a legal order, that in a particular case an evil-intentioned "sinner" who did something close to a harm, but nothing harmful itself, might be punishable only because of the irrational fears of the community. Perhaps it would only matter in a few cases, but in those cases Holmes's theory gave the community a license to act on its prejudices. I do not believe that any of the following cases turn on this factor, but it should be kept clearly in mind as we consider the cases.

Fox v. Washington. Holmes's first free-speech opinion that relied on the intent-branch of his theory of liability was not delivered after World War I. In 1915 he reviewed a Fourteenth Amendment claim that a state statute violated free speech in *Fox v. Washington.*[38] Fox had printed an article entitled "The Nude and the Prude" in which he extolled the virtues of a society of "Homeites," a society of "free spirits" that had escaped into the woods from the "polluted atmosphere of a priest-ridden, conventional society" and that particularly enjoyed the liberty "to bathe in evening dress, or with merely the clothes nature gave them, just as they chose."[39] He also recounted the efforts of "a few prudes" to suppress the "free spirits" by initiating arrests and convictions for indecent exposure and called on all concerned persons to boycott the prudes until they realized the errors of their ways.

The state of Washington prosecuted Fox under a statute that prohibited printing, publishing, or circulating any material "advocating, encouraging or inciting, or having a tendency to encourage or incite the commission of any crime, breach of peace, or act of violence."[40] Though the language of the statute was very wide, Holmes understood "the state court by implication, at least, to have read the statute as confined to encouraging an actual breach of the law," adding that it was "not likely that the statute will be construed to prevent publications merely because they tend to produce unfavorable opinions of a particular statute or of law in general."[41] Consequently, he reasoned, the objection that the statute violated the freedom of speech protected by the Fourteenth Amendment had to fail because "by indirection, but unmistakably, the article encourages and incites a persistence in what we must assume would be a breach of the state's laws against indecent exposure."[42]

The standards of Holmes's theory of legal liability were clearly an important aspect of his review of the constitutionality of Fox's conviction. "The disrespect for law that was encouraged was disregard of it,— an overt breach and technically criminal act."[43] Since the activities engaged in had long been punishable according to his theory of liability, Holmes judged them outside of constitutional protection. The statute was constitutional, as interpreted, because it "lays hold of encouragements that . . . if directed to a particular person's conduct, generally would make him who uttered them guilty of a misdemeanor if not an accomplice or a principle in the crime encouraged."[44] The argument moves from how Fox's actions fit into Holmes's theory of liability to the conclusion that the conviction was constitutional. When he wrote this opinion, cases of inducements to unlawful activity like *Commonwealth v. Peaslee* (see chap. 2) must have been uppermost in Holmes's mind. Peaslee and Fox were within the reach of the law because they had intentionally induced others to do something unlawful. The fact that Peaslee had induced a particular person while *Fox* dealt "with the publication of them [encouragements of illegal acts] to a wider and less selected audience"[45] was irrelevant. Both satisfied Holmes's criteria of an attempt, and therefore the Constitution did not protect them.

The record of the case suggests that Holmes found *Fox* to be an easy case. First, Fox's language certainly shows that his purpose was to induce others to join the nudists. Not only did he refer to the jailing of a woman convicted of indecent exposure as a "vile" action but added that if "this [jailing] was let go without resistance the program of the prudes would be easy." He continued:

The lines will be drawn and those who profess to believe in freedom will be put to the test of practice. There is no possible grounds on which a libertarian can escape taking part in the effort to protect the freedom of the [nudist] Home. There is no halfway. Those who refuse to aid the defense are aiding the other side. For those who want liberty and will not fight for it are parasites and do not deserve freedom. Those who are indifferent to the invasion, who can see an innocent woman torn from the side of her children and packed off to jail and are not moved to action, cannot be counted among the rebels of authority. Their place is with the enemy.[46]

Whether this language could have been uttered by a person not intending others to commit indecent exposure is an interesting question, but the jury could certainly have reasonably concluded that Fox's language revealed an unlawful intent. Since the jury was instructed that they could find Fox guilty only if they found that his purpose was unlawful,[47] there is every reason to believe that this requirement of Holmes's clear and present danger doctrine was satisfied.[48]

Second, Fox's speech-activity had also to be proximate to the harm that he desired to accomplish before Holmes would impose liability according to the attempt-branch of his theory. But here too the evidence against Fox was substantial. Even though Holmes expressed misgivings about the prosecution itself,[49] there was no question that indecent exposure was a harm within the constitutional power of Washington to prohibit, and that acts of indecent exposure were occurring at the time that Fox published his article. The harm may not have been too serious, but in the circumstances it was imminent and likely. Indeed, at the trial, over the objections of Fox's lawyer, evidence was introduced that showed that incidents of indecent exposure increased after Fox's article.[50] Therefore, though not necessary for liability according to Holmes's theory, Fox's speech activity may have in fact caused harm. Nevertheless, whether Fox successfully induced indecent exposure or not, it seems clear that the jury did have sufficient evidence to find a proximity of harm. This, along with unlawful intent, was all that was necessary for liability in a case of attempt.

Fox is important because it shows Holmes using the criteria of the intent branch of his theory in a case involving free speech three years before he came up with his famous phrase "clear and present danger." It therefore focuses attention on the criteria that he used to decide cases of free speech rather than on a rhetorical phrase. The case also indicates how he used his theory of liability to assess the constitutionality of statutes restricting speech. His theory of liability therefore forms a backdrop to his opinions in the World War I cases. It reveals the underlying basis of these more important decisions and thereby their consistency with each other and with Holmes's earlier views.

Third, Fox has some bearing on the relationship between free speech and the liberty protected by the Fourteenth Amendment against state action. Though it is correct that the First Amendment was not explicitly applied against the states until Gitlow v. New York,[51] there were earlier hints that the Supreme Court, or at least certain members of the Court, were moving in this direction. They usually took the form of statements that even if free speech was applied against the states, the defendant's actions would not be protected. This was essentially the view Holmes expressed in Patterson v. Colorado.[52] In Fox, he went slightly further. He interpreted the statute narrowly according to his theory of liability to avoid constitutional doubts.[53] The intimation was that if the statute was "construed to prevent publications merely because they tend to produce unfavorable opinions of a particular statute or of law in general,"[54] it would have had constitutional problems. The conclusion is that, a decade before *Gitlow*, Holmes was seriously considering applying the free speech clause of the First Amendment against state action.

Schenck v. United States. The case of *Schenck v. United States*[55] is at the same time very easy and very difficult to interpret according to Holmes's theory of liability. Schenck and Baer were indicted on three counts of violating the Espionage Act of 1917: conspiracy to cause insubordination in the military and to obstruct recruitment and enlistment; conspiracy to use the mails in violation of the Espionage Act; and the substantive offense of using the mails unlawfully. The evidence used to convict them of all three counts consisted of the following: minutes of a meeting of the executive committee of the Socialist party that outlined the plan and that authorized Schenck, the secretary, to prepare and publish a circular condemning the draft; testimony that Schenck did order the publication of the circulars; a pile of the circulars found at the party headquarters; newspaper clippings (also found at the headquarters) of names of men who had already received their draft notices; the Post Office's discovery of a number of the circulars in the mail posted to men whose names were on the list; and the testimony of several men who had notified the postal authorities that they had received the circulars.[56]

As to the charges of conspiracy, the judge instructed the jury that Schenck and Baer, to be liable, did not have to come to a formal agreement or successfully obtain their unlawful objectives. They only had to act with a common unlawful purpose and do something to accomplish their goal.[57] To evaluate properly the defendants' contention that their purpose had only been to urge the unconstitutionality of the draft law, the jury was advised to consider the fact that the United States was at war and that the circulars were sent to men already drafted.[58] The jury convicted the defendants on all counts, and the judge sentenced them to ten years on each count, though the sentences were to be served concurrently.

The reason why this case seems to have been an easy one is that there was plenty of evidence to warrant the jury's finding that Schenck and Baer had conspired together to obstruct the draft. And since the sentences were concurrent, there does not seem to be much else to argue. The judge's instructions coincided with Holmes's requirements of conspiracy (see chap. 2). The crucial issue was whether the defendants joined a group whose purpose was unlawful. If they did, or, more specifically, if the jury had evidence sufficient to warrant the conclusion that they did, then Holmes, in his own mind, had little choice as an appellate judge but to affirm the conviction.[59]

The real problem with *Schenck* is not why Holmes affirmed the conviction, but why he wrote the opinion that he did. It was his understanding that conspiracy could be established without any proof of either success or proximity to harm. An unlawful agreement was the crux of the offense. But if so, why did Holmes announce the clear-and-present-danger doctrine in *Schenck*? "The question in every case is whether the words used are used in such circumstances and are of such a nature as to create a clear and present danger that they will bring about the substantive evils that Congress has a right to prevent."[60] It is true that Schenck raised the defense of free speech, and for this reason Holmes felt compelled to say "a few words" about it.[61] But the mystery is not why he said "a few words" about free speech, but why he said the words that he did. What did a clear and present danger have to do with a case of conspiracy? According to Holmes's theory of liability, if persons had conspired to do something unlawful, that sufficed for a conviction. No proximity of harm was required.

David Rabban suggests that the language of clear and present danger should be ignored in favor of a sentence that follows later in the opinion. After Holmes said that the existence of war was relevant to the question of Schenck's liability, in "his very next sentence," Rabban argues, he "recurred to the 'bad tendency' doctrine."[62] The sentence is as follows: "If the act (speaking, or circulating a paper), its tendency and the intent with which it is done are the same, we perceive no ground for saying that success alone warrants making the act a crime."[63] In Rabban's opinion, it is "inconceivable that Holmes would use the word 'tendency,' stress the unimportance of a successful act, and rely on cases [primarily *Goldman v. United States*] that did not demonstrate any sensitivity to free speech in order to elaborate a libertarian test designed as a constitutional bar to convictions based on predicting the tendency of speech."[64] The above sentence and the citation of *Goldman v. United States* supposedly show that Holmes in *Schenck* adhered to the bad-tendency test, which imposed liability on speech having a bad tendency regardless of intent or proximity to harm. He adhered to it even if in the same case he, paradoxically, announced the clear-and-present-danger standard.

Rabban is correct that the clear-and-present-danger standard does not fit well with the facts of *Schenck*, but this incongruence does not prove that Holmes was applying a bad-tendency doctrine. First, Holmes used *Goldman* as authority for the uncontroversial conclusion that a conspiracy did not have to be successful to incur liability. The following passage from *Goldman* that Holmes cited[65] makes this clear.

The contention [is] . . . that no crime results from an unlawful conspiracy to bring about an illegal act, joined with the doing of overt acts in furtherance of the conspiracy, unless the conspiracy has accomplished its unlawful purpose by causing the illegal acts to be committed. This, however, disregards the settled doctrine that an unlawful conspiracy . . . is, in and of itself, inherently and substantively a crime, punishable as such irrespective of whether the result of the conspiracy has been to accomplish its illegal end.[66]

But Holmes's opinion that Schenck was guilty even if his conspiracy was unsuccessful does not make him into an adherent of the bad-tendency doctrine. And the sentence that Rabban refers to is of a similar character. If "an act," "its tendency," and "the intent with which it is done" are "the same"—that is, if they are illegal or harmful—then liability could be imposed even if the harm did not occur. But that did not mean that Holmes would impose liability on any speech that had a bad tendency. The reference to an illicit intent makes that interpretation impossible. All that Holmes was saying was that conspiring with others was an act whose tendency and accompanying intent were harmful. Liability could therefore be imposed on persons who conspired to obstruct the draft through speech.

Rabban's account of why Holmes announced the clear-and-present-danger test in a conspiracy case is therefore not persuasive. To say that he never really meant it in the first place does not explain why he said it. A more plausible view is that Holmes treated conspiracy differently when speech was the primary means that conspirators used to obtain their unlawful objective. Perhaps he thought that liability could be imposed, when speech was involved, only if the group's purpose was unlawful and only if the planned speech activity had a reasonable chance of causing the harm. Liability was appropriate in *Schenck* only because the defendants' speech had been effective enough to make the group illegal.

But this explanation also does not ring true. As noted earlier, Holmes saw conspiracy as a "partnership in unlawful purposes."[67] It did "not make the doing of any act other than the act of conspiring a condition of liability."[68] No overt act beyond the conspiracy itself was required by common law, though he respected that additional requirement when added by statute. And even in those cases where an overt act was required, Holmes argued that it did "not matter how remote the act may be from accomplishing the purpose, if done to effect it."[69] Even if the means chosen by the conspirators were perfectly legal, liability would still follow.

No conduct has such an absolute privilege as to justify all possible schemes of which it may be a part. *The most innocent and constitutionally protected* of acts and omissions may be made a step in a criminal plot, and if it is a step in a plot, *neither its innocence nor the Constitution* is sufficient to prevent the punishment of the plot by law. (Emphasis mine)[70]

But if liability follows even if the conspirators tried to accomplish their unlawful end by the most remote and lawful means, then it seems clear that Holmes had no need to introduce the idea of proximity of harm to decide *Schenck*. He himself said that *Goldman v. United States*[71]—an earlier case of conspiracy to obstruct the draft—disposed of Schenck's contention. If the defendants conspired, they were liable whether they engaged in speech or not. That speech acts, as opposed to other types of acts, were laid as overt acts required by the statute was insignificant. Conspirators could not insulate themselves from liability by using speech to obtain their unlawful ends.

A better account of why Holmes proclaimed his clear and present danger doctrine in a conspiracy case emphasizes the context of the decision. Between 9 January 1919 and 10 March 1919, the Supreme Court decided four cases dealing with free speech: *Sugarman v. United States, Schenck v. United States, Frohwerk v. United States,* and *Debs v. United States.*[72] *Schenck* and, as we shall see, *Frohwerk* were essentially cases of conspiracy, which, I argue, had nothing to do with Holmes's requirement of a clear and present danger. *Sugarman* (argued on 9 January 1919 and decided the same day as *Schenck*) as well as *Debs* (argued and decided the same days as *Frohwerk*), however, were different. There were no charges of conspiracy in these cases.

In *Sugarman*, the defendant had given a speech condemning the draft to a Socialist party meeting at which men registered for the draft were present. Though no insubordination in the military or refusal of duty occurred, Sugarman was charged with willfully causing or attempting to cause "insubordination, disloyalty, mutiny, or refusal of duty, in the military or naval forces of the United States."[73] On appeal, he raised the defense of free speech, but Brandeis wrote the opinion dismissing the case for want of jurisdiction. Sugarman's federal claim relied on the trial judge's refusal to give the specific instructions to the jury that he had requested. But Brandeis held that the actual instructions were close enough to those requested that a substantial federal question did not exist. The language that Sugarman wanted was: "and if what he says and publishes has a natural tendency to produce a violation of the law, that is, *to impel the persons addressed to violate the law,* and the person using the language intends that it should produce a violation of law, then the person using the language is subject to punishment" (emphasis mine).[74] All that the judge actually instructed was, "A man has a right to honestly discuss a measure or a law, and to honestly criticize it. But no man may advise another to disobey the law, or to obstruct its execution, without making himself liable to be called to account therefor."[75] The obvious difference between the two instructions—even if the Supreme Court did not think that the difference constituted a substantial federal question—was that the actual instructions permitted conviction even if the unlawful advocacy was impotent, while the requested charge required as an additional consideration some proximity to harm. Sugarman thought he was free of liability unless his speech "impelled" his listener to violate the law.

According to Holmes's theory of liability, since Sugarman was free of any conspiracy, he was liable only if his actions constituted an attempt. Sugarman had to have not only intended his hearers to engage in insubordination and refusal of duty, but his speech had to have been sufficiently proximate to the harm before liability could be imposed. Holmes certainly thought that Sugarman was properly convicted under these criteria. He had spoken to a crowd of up to eight hundred—half of whom were of draft age—and used rather suggestive language.[76] Though Holmes thought that Sugarman had no case, it is intriguing to speculate that Holmes announced his clear-and-present-danger test in a concurrent conspiracy case to get his views of the matter on record and in contrast to Brandeis's.

Certainly Holmes's opinion in *Schenck,* requiring some proximity to harm for liability, fits the facts of *Sugarman* better than it does those of the former case. Again, the cases were argued at the same time and were decided on the same day. Also, the defense's proposed jury instructions in *Sugarman* were closer to the actual requirements of Holmes's clear-and-present-danger doctrine than the instructions that were actually given. Perhaps that fact inclined Holmes to write the opinion that he did in *Schenck*. Moreover, *Debs* was argued approximately two weeks after *Schenck*, but a full month before Brandeis's and Holmes's opinions came down in *Sugarman* and *Schenck*. Holmes therefore had every opportunity and incentive to decide how he was going to assess the constitutionality of speakers who acted alone. His answer, announced in a conspiracy case, was that such defendants were liable only if they were guilty of an attempt: only if their intent was unlawful and only if their speech was sufficiently proximate to the prohibited harm.

Frohwerk v. United States. Holmes's opinion in *Frohwerk v. United States*[77] provides additional support for the above interpretation of *Schenck v. United States*. Frohwerk was convicted of a conspiracy charge and eleven counts of attempts to cause insubordination and refusal of duty, but sentences on the latter counts were to run concurrently with that of the former. Therefore the case was essentially, like *Schenck*, one of conspiracy. And in *Frohwerk*, Holmes cited *Schenck* to support the conclusion "that a person may be convicted of a conspiracy to obstruct recruiting by words of persuasion,"[78] which shows that in his mind *Schenck* was a conspiracy case, relevant to *Frohwerk* for that very reason.

Since *Frohwerk* involved a conspiracy, no actual danger of harm was required. It should therefore not be surprising—even though this fact has drawn some comment[79]—that in his opinion Holmes never referred to the clear-and-present-danger doctrine. The only question was whether Frohwerk joined others for the unlawful purpose of obstructing the draft and causing insubordination in the military. No additional act was needed. A "conspiracy to obstruct recruiting would be criminal even if no means were agreed upon specifically by which to accomplish the intent. It is enough if the parties agreed to set to work for that common purpose."[80] Consequently, it seems clear that Schenck and Frohwerk were subject to punishment on the same branch of Holmes's theory of liability.

Nevertheless, there were important differences between the two cases. While Schenck was a secretary in the Socialist party, Frohwerk "was a poor man, turning out copy for Gleeser, his employer, at less than a day laborer's pay, for Gleeser to use or reject, as he saw fit, in a newspaper of small circulation." And though the evidence tended to show that Schenck deliberately sent his circular to men already drafted, in *Frohwerk* it did "not appear that there was any special effort to reach men who were subject to the draft."[81] Also, the evidence against Schenck consisted of both speech and nonspeech activities. It was in Frohwerk's favor "that the publications set forth as overt acts were the only means, and, when coupled with the joint activity in producing them, the only evidence of the conspiracy alleged."[82] The evidence against Frohwerk was therefore much less substantial than the evidence against Schenck. The Supreme Court perhaps could have overturned the decision on the ground that the evidence of a conspiracy was insufficient for a conviction. But this was not possible since there was no bill of exceptions before the Court. Evidently Frohwerk's trial attorney could not agree with the trial judge on a bill of exceptions. Neither would sign the other's bill. Frohwerk applied to the Supreme Court for a writ of mandamus ordering the judge to sign and send a proper bill of exceptions, but the Court found that no case was made out.[83] Frohwerk was also too poor to pay for a transcript. The end result was that the Court had no way to evaluate the sufficiency of the government's evidence.

In this context, Holmes held that the Court had to "take the case on the record as it is, and on the record it is impossible to say that it might not have been found that the circulation of the paper was in quarters where a little breath would be enough to kindle a flame and that the fact was known and relied upon by those who sent the paper out."[84] He concluded that the Court could not say that there was not enough evidence at least for the conspiracy conviction. If the conspiracy conviction was valid—since all other sentences were to be served concurrently—the case was closed. Later, Holmes was to insist that he had no doubt as to the correctness of the law as applied in *Schenck, Frohwerk,* and *Debs,* which suggests that he may have had doubts about some of the facts.[85] In my judgment, *Frohwerk v. United States* was the case he had reservations about. Nevertheless, it is his sense of the law that is crucial here. In this vein, Holmes, refused to protect conspiracies to obstruct recruiting or to cause insubordination in the military, no matter if the unlawful goals were to be obtained by speech or if there was no likelihood of immediate harm.

Debs v. United States. As mentioned above, *Debs v. United States*[86] was very similar to *Sugarman*. Eugene V. Debs was indicted on ten counts of violating the Espionage Act, convicted of three, and sentenced to serve three concurrent sentences. The government, however, only argued the two attempt convictions before the Supreme Court: an attempt to cause and incite insubordination within the military and an attempt to obstruct recruitment. Hence, if the government could satisfy the Court that Debs was guilty of an attempt, the sentence would stand.

The convictions were based on a speech that Debs gave on 16 June 1918 at the closing session of the Ohio Socialist Convention in Canton, Ohio. The evidence used to convict Debs consisted of: (1) the speech itself, which praised persons who had already been convicted of violating the Espionage Act; (2) the records of the convictions of those individuals whom Debs praised[87]; (3) Deb's admission at the beginning of his speech that "I must be extremely careful, prudent, as to what I say, and even more careful and prudent as to how I say it. I may not be able to say all that I think"[88]; (4) testimony in regard to Deb's endorsement of the St. Louis Anti-War Proclamation that had been approved by an emergency convention of the Socialist party in April 1917[89]; (5) testimony in regard to an antiwar speech that Debs gave in Chicago on 11 August 1918 to a meeting of the state secretaries of the Socialist party[90]; and (6) the existence of a state of war,[91] the size of the crowd (estimated from two hundred to fifteen hundred),[92] the crowd's reaction to Deb's speech,[93] and the fact that no flag flew on the outdoor platform from which Debs spoke.[94]

Most, if not all, of the facts were not in dispute. Indeed, Debs refused to call any witnesses on his behalf. And in his closing argument to the jury, which he delivered himself, he said that if the prosecutors had "known me a little better they might have saved themselves some trouble in procuring evidence to prove certain things against me which I have not the slightest inclination to deny, but rather, upon the other hand, have a very considerable pride in."[95] The issue was not what Debs did or said, but rather whether what he said was protected by free speech.

Debs sincerely thought that he was protected, or at least that he ought to be protected, but the jury decided otherwise. The instructions that the trial judge gave were specific to each of the four counts that went to the jury. For each count, however, including the two attempt charges that were before the Supreme Court, the judge required that the jury find a specific criminal intent and a reasonable likelihood of harm. For example, in regard to the charge of attempting to incite insubordination in the military, the jury could convict only if Debs acted with the specific and criminal intent either "to cause or attempt to cause or incite such insubordination, disloyalty, mutiny or refusal of duty."[96] The judge also told the jury that Deb's speech had to be in such circumstances that "the natural or reasonably probable consequences thereof would be to cause or incite insubordination, disloyalty, mutiny, or refusal of duty among the persons hearing and listening thereto,"[97] though no actual insubordination had to occur.[98] These requirements reappeared in the judge's explanation of each of the other three counts.[99]

Also, Debs's endorsement of the St. Louis Anti-War Proclamation and the content of his speech in Chicago were relevant, the judge insisted, only to the question of intent. The jury first had to find that Debs "uttered the [Canton] speech and that the natural and probable effect of the speech was to produce the unlawful result."[100] Only then could they consider the Chicago speech and Debs's position on the St. Louis platform. Debs could be convicted of the attempt charges, if the instructions were followed, only if the jurors were convinced that his purpose was to cause insubordination in the military and obstruction of the system of enlistment and that there was a strong likelihood that his speech would achieve these unlawful results.

The trial judge, however, did discuss the role that legal presumptions could play in the jury's determination of Debs's intent. Paraphrasing the words of a jurist "more learned than he," the judge instructed the jury to "bear in mind that a person is presumed to intend the natural and probable consequences of his words and acts."[101] Further, he asked the jury to consider three questions. Did Debs

intend or expect that his words and acts would have any influence upon or be likely to be adopted and followed by the young men . . . who heard it? Or did he intend or expect that they would not act upon them in accordance with his utterances and address? Ought he not to have reasonably foreseen that the natural and probable consequences of such words and utterances would or might be to cause insubordination, disloyalty, or refusal of duty in the military forces of the United States?[102]

From the point of view of Holmes's criteria of attempt, the judges's reference to the presumption that a person intends the natural and probable consequences of his acts and his question as to whether Debs should have reasonably foreseen the consequences of his speech were very controversial. They gave to the jury the impression that it could convict even if Debs's actual purpose was not to induce unlawful activity. It suggested to the jury that they could convict if he only *expected* unlawful activity, or, even more extreme, if he only *should have expected* unlawful activity. A conviction would thereby be permissible, even though Deb's actual purpose was only to express his opposition to the war and the constitutionality of the draft law.

According to Holmes's approach, this section of the instructions had serious implications concerning the constitutionality of Deb's conviction. Whether Holmes was aware of this passage from the judge's instructions is unknown. But even if he was cognizant of it, it is still true that the instructions at other places repeatedly and clearly required the jury to find a specific criminal intention.[103] If the judge's instructions are to be read in a consistent manner, perhaps the most reasonable interpretation is to say that the judge permitted the jury to use the presumption that a person intends the natural and probable consequences of his or her acts as a starting point of analysis. The jury would then ask what Debs should have foreseen, given the likelihood of harm, as an initial way to assess the actual purpose of his speech. Juries must start somewhere, and the presumption of intent from probable consequences, if it is defeasible, is not inappropriate. If the instructions are read in this way, then the conclusion is that the jury was still instructed that they could not convict unless Debs's purpose was to induce unlawful activity.

Certainly the federal government understood the law to have required actual illegal intent. In its brief to the Supreme Court, the government limited the scope of the statute to intentional obstructions. "It is only wilful obstruction which the statute seeks to reach and the court so told the jury in this case."[104] Further, the defense never objected to the portion of the judge's instructions dealing with legal presumptions nor was the matter raised in its brief to the Supreme Court. An intriguing question is what would have been Holmes's response if Debs had argued that the instructions improperly permitted the jury to presume unlawful intent.

The primary reason why the defense did not bring up this matter is that they thought and argued that Debs's speech was protected regardless of his purpose, which suggests that his purpose may well have been to induce unlawful activity. Debs also made a point, both at the trial and in his brief to the Supreme Court, that he did not want to get off on technicalities or by denying what he had done.[105] His brief argued that "when we deal with a charge of crime founded upon the use of words to influence the conduct of others, the intent must relate itself definitely to these words and instruments of action, not with secret purposes locked within the breast of the defendant and divulged only by exhibiting his prior conduct."[106] The contention by the defense seems to have been that Debs's speech was protected as long as he did not explicitly advocate unlawful action. He was liable only if his words were "definitely" related to an illegal intent. A secret illegal purpose, locked within Debs's breast, was irrelevant, even if it could be established from his prior conduct. Judge Learned Hand's decision in *United States v. Masses*[107] was cited in support of the defense's view, and the rule of the appellate court that had reversed Hand's decision[108] was characterized as "unsatisfactory."[109] It is therefore fair to say that the defense admitted that Debs's purpose was illegal, but insisted that he was yet protected because he did not literally advocate illegality.

The government's brief conceded that Debs was free "unless the words or utterances by which the expression or advocacy is contained shall have been *willfully intended* by the person making them to commit the acts forbidden by this law" (emphasis mine).[110] It then concluded that Debs "could not complain" about the jury's finding of unlawful intent.[111] The United States was also quick to point out the reasons why Hand's opinion had been overruled. A rule limiting liability to literal advocacy of illegality would render "the Nation powerless to punish any incitement to lawlessness, however intentional and however effective, so long as it is concealed in veiled, indirect, or rhetorical language."[112] Since the defendants in fact agreed that incitement of unlawful activity was outside of constitutional protection, their only mistake was to believe that indirect incitement was not incitement. But once indirect incitement was placed outside of constitutional protection, the only issue on appeal—the government insisted that it was not a constitutional matter—was whether the evidence was sufficient to justify the jury's determination that Debs, by indirect means, incited military personnel to commit insubordination and citizens not to register for the draft or volunteer for the armed forces.[113] The government was sure that the evidence presented at the trial was sufficient.

Holmes, in his opinion for the Supreme Court, agreed with the government. Indeed, given the record of the case and his criteria of attempt, it must have been an easy case.[114] The jury was warranted, in his judgment, in

finding that one purpose of the speech, whether incidental or not does not matter, was to oppose not only war in general, but this war, and that the opposition was so expressed that its natural and intended effect would be to obstruct recruiting. If that was intended, and if, in all the circumstances, that would be its probable effect, it would not be protected by reason of its being part of a general program and expression of a general and conscientious belief.[115]

Holmes simply rejected the defense's argument that indirect incitement was protected. The purpose of the speaker and the probability of harm were far more important than the language that the speaker used. He even went so far as to congratulate the judge, since "the jury were most carefully instructed that they could not find the defendant guilty for advocacy of any of his opinions unless the words used had as their natural tendency and *reasonably probable effect* to obstruct the recruiting service, etc., and unless the defendant had the *specific intent* to do so in his mind" (emphasis mine).[116] Deb's actual unlawful purpose and the likelihood that his speech would cause harm (as measured by the nearness and greatness of the harm and the apprehension felt by the community) was enough to constitute an attempt. Accordingly, his speech was outside constitutional protection.

Rabban tries to explain away the references in *Debs* to actual intent by claiming that Holmes was using legal presumptions. Even though Debs's brief avoided the issue of intent and even though the government was confident that there was plenty of evidence of actual illicit intent, it is argued that Holmes still relied on legal presumptions to decide the matter. "Holmes stated that evaluating the tendency of language as evidence of the speaker's intent is a principle 'too well established and too manifestly good sense to need citation of the books'."[117] But Holmes said nothing of the sort. In the case of harmful activity, legal presumptions were generally used to infer intent and foresight, but attempts required an actual unlawful purpose.

The "well established practice" and "sensible principle" that Holmes mentioned was not that illegal intent could be presumed from a bad tendency. His point was rather that the law, to ascertain the *actual* purpose of Debs's speech, could admit into evidence a proclamation that Debs endorsed an hour before his Canton speech and referred to in his closing remarks to the jury at his trial. Since this proclamation recommended "continuous, active, and public opposition to the war, through demonstrations, mass petitions, and all other means within our power," Holmes argued that it was relevant to the question of Deb's actual intent. "Evidence that the defendant accepted this view and this declaration of his duties at the time that he made his speech is evidence that if in that speech he used words tending to obstruct the recruiting service, he *meant* that they should have that effect" (emphasis mine).[118] Hence the passage from the opinion that Rabban uses to establish that Holmes adhered to a bad-tendency test, which ignores the speaker's intent, in fact shows the exact opposite. If a defendant makes it clear that he or she endorsed certain ideas and conceptions of duty, then the law can take these ideas and conceptions into account to determine the actual purpose of the defendant's speech activity.[119] The only possible inference from Holmes's words, in contrast to the requirements of the bad-tendency doctrine, was that liability could be imposed on a speaker only if he or she intentionally incited illegal activity.

Rabban also disputes whether Holmes required any proximity of harm before he imposed liability in *Debs*. This strong conclusion rests on very weak evidence: the fact that the phrase "clear and present danger" did not appear explicitly in Holmes's opinion. It is, however, a mistake to place so much significance on the presence or absence of a rhetorical formula. Holmes did say that Debs's speech activity fell outside the Constitution if he intended to obstruct the draft "and if, in all the circumstances, that would be its *probable* effect."[120] Debs could not be found guilty "unless the words used had as their natural tendency and *reasonably probable effect* to obstruct the recruiting service" (emphasis mine).[121] Certainly these linguistic formulations of Holmes's basic requirement of a proximity to harm in cases of illegal advocacy are just as weighty as "clear and present danger." The opinion gives every indication that Holmes affirmed the conviction only because the jury's finding of proximity of harm was reasonable. Thus, in *Debs* he did not apply a bad-tendency test.[122]

Abrams v. United States. Jacob Abrams, along with three other anarchists and a socialist, were indicted with four counts of conspiring to violate the Espionage Act in *Abrams v. United States*.[123] The charges were that they conspired to publish and distribute: (1) language about the form of government of the United States that was "disloyal, scurrilous and abusive"; (2) language "intended to bring the form of government of the United States into contempt"; (3) language "intended to incite, provoke, and encourage resistance to the United States" in its war with Germany; and (4) language that advocated "curtailment of production of things and products, to wit, ordnance and ammunition, necessary and essential to the prosecution of the war."[124] The evidence presented by the government consisted of two circulars, one in Yiddish and the other in English, and the printing and distribution of these circulars in circles where there was some chance of causing opposition to the American government's policy of intervention in Russia and harm to the war effort against Germany.[125]

The main issue at the trial was one of intent. The defendants argued that they had only criticized the personnel and policy of Wilson's administration, not the form of government, and that they had no intention of encouraging resistance to the United States or hindering the war effort against Germany. To substantiate their claims, they tried to introduce evidence from Americans who were willing to testify, from their personal experience, that the new Bolshevik government was the natural ally of the United States against Germany.[126] If this testimony were accepted, then the defendants' criticism of Wilson's policy of intervention in the Russian Revolution was not intended to hinder the war effort. If Wilson understood the international situation, he would have supported the Bolsheviks to further, not to hinder, the successful prosecution of the war. Abrams's intention in publishing and distributing the leaflet was therefore perfectly lawful. He wanted to help the American war effort by correcting a flawed foreign policy.

The defense's strategy failed, however, because the trial judge ruled that any such testimony was immaterial. Judge Clayton held that a person could not violate a statute and then justify it by claiming a "wisdom superior" to that of the United States.[127] But this reasoning misstated the defense's argument. It was not that the "unlawful acts" of the defendants were justified by "superior wisdom," but rather that there were no unlawful acts since the illicit intent required by the statute was not present.[128] The only option left was to have all the defendants testify as to their reasons for distributing the circulars. Each said that they intended to stop the American intervention in Russia and all but one expressed hope that Germany would lose the war.[129]

Judge Clayton's charge to the jury may help to explain why the jury voted to convict even though the defendants testified that their purpose was not to hinder the war. Clayton distinguished between motive and intention: "A motive is that which leads a person to do a certain act. The intention is a design, or plan, or purpose to use a particular means to effect a certain definite result."[130] He then advised the jurors that if they believed that the defendants did intentionally place the form of government of the United States into contempt, or urge resistance to the United States, or hinder the war effort by advocating the curtailment of the production of ordnance and ammunition, then "this would constitute criminal intention." This was so even though the jury "may also find that the motives of the defendants were to serve a certain faction in Russia" and that "the defendants were not conscious of doing anything unlawful."[131] According to Clayton's instructions, the jury could convict even if the purpose of the defendants had not been to hinder the war or provoke resistance.

The judge had a few more suggestions for the jury. He directed "that the person charged with any crime or offense is presumed to intend the natural and probable consequences of what he knowingly does."[132] Intention was something other than the defendant's purpose, and it could be established by what was reasonably foreseeable. Even if the defendants did not intend to provoke resistance against the war or to hinder the war effort, and even if they did not foresee the likelihood that the circulation of their leaflets would have these consequences, they were still liable. He also thought it not "amiss" for him "to say that men who are activated by pure and lawful motives as a rule act in the open daylight,"[133] which allowed the jury to make damaging inferences because the defendants published and distributed their leaflets, to some degree, secretly. Finally, the judge had to express his opinion that "Congress did not intend, by the passage of this Act, that a citizen should not faultily say something that, upon second thought, he perhaps would agree he should not have said, and, therefore, he did not say it wilfully."[134] If a person, no matter the purpose, had the misfortune to say something that had the likelihood of provoking resistance or hindering the war, sincere regret would keep that person outside of the statute. This generous qualification had no relevance to the *Abrams* defendants because they did not regret their actions. Instead they thought that their activities were constitutionally protected.

The question of the defendants' intentions and what type of intention was required for constitutional protection was the key to the case on appeal. The defense argued that there was no evidence that the defendants violated the Espionage Act, but if the evidence was sufficient for a conviction, then the act was unconstitutional as applied to the circumstances of this case. Though the defendants' language was "intemperate" and "inflammatory," all that they had done was to engage in "a public discussion of a public policy in reference to a country with which we were not at war and are not at war, and against which country the use of troops has never been legal."[135] Their intent was not unlawful within the meaning of the statute. Even the call for a strike was within the bounds of public discourse. "The defendants did not urge resistance to a law, they called for an act which would call forcibly to the Government's attention that the public were against its action and its policy of intervention in Russia."[136] But if the Court found that there was enough evidence for a conviction, then the law was unconstitutional. A "man who points out wherein the country is making a blunder, or forgetting its ideals and justice, should not be jailed even in war time, even if perchance he is wrong in his belief, or cannot convince a majority that he is right."[137] In these words, later echoed in Holmes's dissent, the defendants' brief endorsed the view that the constitution gave absolute protection to those whose intention was only to criticize existing policy or governmental officials.

The majority of the Supreme Court, however, assessed the intent of the defendants in a way more reminiscent of Judge Clayton's charge to the jury. They had no qualms about determining the defendants' intent by legal presumptions, by what a reasonable person should have foreseen.[138] There was sufficient evidence that the circulars would likely produce resistance to the United States and curtailment of the production of things necessary to the war. The jury could therefore find that the defendants acted with the intent to hinder the war effort because they should have foreseen these harmful results. The major implication of the majority opinion was that the actual purpose of the defendants was immaterial to whether or not a criminal conspiracy existed.

This was the contention that Holmes could not accept. In his dissent, he admitted that the law often imposed liability for intentional crimes on defendants who only foresaw or who only should have foreseen the harm.[139] His general theory of liability required the use of such presumptions in case of harmful activity, even harmful speech activity. But the right to associate was privileged; it could be withdrawn only if the actual purpose of the combination was unlawful—only if the actual purpose was to hinder the war effort against Germany. But the state had not introduced any evidence of such an unlawful purpose. The prosecution had claimed only that the defendants foresaw that their activities would hinder the war effort or that they should have foreseen this result. In the Court's majority opinion, this was a sufficient basis for a conspiracy conviction. Holmes disagreed. His theory of legal liability gave him no choice. It was unconstitutional to punish a person for conspiracy without sufficient evidence of an unlawful purpose.

Holmes dressed up this conclusion in the garb of statutory construction,[140] but only for the sake of appearances. He argued that if the statute's reference to "intent" was not interpreted as "actual purpose," then the statute would lead to absurd results.

A patriot might think that we were wasting money on aeroplanes, or making more cannon of a certain kind than we needed, and might advocate curtailment with success; yet, even if it turned out that the curtailment hindered and was thought by other minds to have been obviously likely to hinder the United States in the prosecution of the war, no one would hold such conduct a crime.[141]

But Holmes admitted that this example did not answer all the relevant questions,[142] presumably because the cases were not exactly analogous. The patriot did not know that his or her actions would hinder the war effort, but it had to have been obvious to Abrams and his associates that strikes in key industries would have had a detrimental impact. Holmes therefore never really explained why the statute could not have been interpreted in a way that would have imposed liability on Abrams and let the patriot off. Commitment to deeper principles had to be the reason why he did not interpret the Espionage Act in a way that would have imposed liability on an organization whose members only foresaw the harms that their actions would inflict on others. But this deeper principle was as old as his opinion in *Vegelahn v. Guntner*.[143] Just as a worker had the right to form a union, even though the worker foresaw the harm inflicted on the employer, so also Abrams had the right to associate with others for the purpose of ending the intervention in Russia, even though he foresaw the harm inflicted on the war effort. But if a worker's or Abrams's intention was malicious or unlawful, the privilege was withdrawn. An unlawful purpose made the union or the association a conspiracy outside of constitutional protection.

Holmes also considered whether the defendants' speech activities constituted a criminal attempt. He argued the issue in terms of his traditional standards: unlawful intent and proximity to harm. In regard to the latter requirement, Holmes claimed no one could believe that "the surreptitious publishing of a silly leaflet by an unknown man, without more, would present any immediate danger."[144] But Holmes did add that publishing "those opinions for the very purpose of obstructing . . . might indicate greater danger, and at any rate would have the quality of an attempt."[145] An "actual intent in the sense that I have explained is necessary to constitute an attempt, where a further act of the same individual is required to complete the substantive crime." It is necessary in this type of case, when an additional act is needed to produce the harm, "because if that intent is not present, the actor's aim may be accomplished without bringing about the evils sought to be checked." Since an "intent to prevent interference with the revolution in Russia might have been satisfied without any hindrance to carrying on the war"[146] against Germany, such an intent could not function as the basis for imposing liability on the defendants. Even if there was a strong likelihood that their speech activities would cause unlawful acts, which there was not, they were clear of liability since their motives were clean. In contrast to Debs, who tried to obstruct the draft, these defendants were not trying to obtain an unlawful result.

Gitlow v. New York. In *Gitlow v. New York,*[147] the defendant was indicted and convicted on two counts of advocating criminal anarchy. The first count alleged that he had advocated the duty, necessity, and propriety of overthrowing organized government; the second that he had published and circulated the same. The facts were once again not in dispute.[148] Gitlow was a part-owner and business manager of a paper called *The Revolutionary Age,* and he was directly involved with the publication and circulation of sixteen thousand copies of the *Manifesto* of the Left Wing of the Socialist party. This *Manifesto* not only reviewed the growth of socialism, but condemned the parliamentary democratic state, called for its destruction by "mass strikes" and "revolutionary mass action," cited the recent strikes in Seattle and Winnipeg as examples to follow, and demanded a dictatorship of the proletariat that would coerce and suppress the bourgeoisie.[149]

The jury was advised that they were to determine if the purpose of the defendant was to describe, explain, and predict historical events or to advocate the overthrow of organized government. Only if Gitlow's purpose was to advocate the overthrow of government was he guilty. Further, in their efforts to discern the defendant's intention, the jury was instructed that they had to take the entire article into consideration and give to the words their "obvious" and "common" meaning.[150] Gitlow, however, could be found guilty even though he did not "point out with particularity the exact method of force and violence that he intended to use, or the exact time, when he intended to put his purpose into effect."[151] Liability was appropriate even if his unlawful goal was in the distant future. With these instructions the jury convicted Gitlow, and he was sentenced to no less than five and no more than ten years.

Since there was sufficient evidence for the jury to find that Gitlow's purpose was to produce a state of criminal anarchy, the basis for Gitlow's appeal was ultimately narrowed to a single simple question. Could a person whose purpose was unlawful be constitutionally convicted of advocating criminal anarchy if there was no likelihood that his or her speech activities would cause harm? Judge Laughlin of New York's appellate division had no doubt that a state could punish such a person. After citing Holmes's opinion in favor of the opposing view, he argued "that the common law theory of proximate causal connection between the acts prohibited and the danger apprehended therefrom . . . has no application here."[152] Laughlin's reasoning reappeared in New York's brief to the Supreme Court. Though citizens had the indisputable right of free speech, the state reserved "the right to hold the citizen liable for his abuse of the right granted."[153] Advocacy of criminal anarchy was, like criminal libel, perjury, and political electioneering within a specified distance of a polling place, an inherently harmful act.[154] Therefore, just as a state can prohibit libel, perjury, and certain types of political engineering, so also the state could make advocacy of criminal anarchy a crime, "irrespective of whether the danger of resulting injury therefrom is imminent or remote." New York based "this belief upon the fundamental principle that the right of the individual to speak freely does not extend so far as to render him immune from punishment if he says that which is inherently inimical to the public welfare."[155] In the opinion of New York, "Criminal anarchy is a dangerous doctrine at any time."[156]

The state also argued that liability could be imposed on the advocacy of criminal anarchy even if the speaker did not intend the unlawful result. The "moment he *advocates* the duty, necessity or propriety of practicing the doctrine [of anarchy], he does what the law prohibits; and he is guilty of a crime even if he does not himself believe in the doctrine advocated."[157] Put in its simplest form, the rule proposed by the state was one of strict liability. Anyone who advocated anarchy was liable no matter the purpose, the likelihood of harm, or the circumstances of the act.

The majority of the Supreme Court affirmed the conviction but would not go as far as the state's brief suggested. Unlawful purpose on the part of the speaker advocating anarchy was necessary for liability. After all, Justice Sanford argued, the statute punishes "advocacy" of anarchy, which implies that the speaker's purpose must be to achieve that end,[158] and the jury in this case had been instructed accordingly. The real issue was whether the state could punish irrespective of any substantive harm. On this basic point, the Court agreed with the state's claim that it could punish "utterances inimical to the public welfare."[159] The state's decision that advocacy of criminal anarchy was a type of "utterance inimical to the public welfare" was not an unreasonable exercise of the state's police power.[160] "Such utterances, by their very nature, involve danger to the public peace and to the security of the state. They threaten breaches of the peace and ultimate revolution. And the immediate danger is none the less real and substantial because the effect of a given utterance cannot be accurately foreseen."[161] The state could not "reasonably be required to defer the adoption of measures for its own peace and safety until the revolutionary utterances lead to actual disturbances of the public peace or imminent and immediate danger of its own destruction; but it may, in the exercise of its judgment, suppress the threatened danger in its incipiency."[162] Therefore the Court's answer to the basic question of *Gitlow* was that a person who advocated anarchy with an unlawful purpose could be punished. No likelihood of actual harm was required because the legislature had judged the utterance to be harmful per se.

Holmes dissented. He rejected the state's and the majority's contention that advocacy of criminal anarchy was harmful per se. He reached this conclusion even though he himself recognized that certain speech acts, subject to his external standard of liability, constituted harms in themselves: libel, contempt of court, falsely shouting "fire" in a theater. Moreover, his general view was that judges should defer to legislative determinations of policy. It is therefore puzzling why Holmes did not defer to a legislative finding that advocacy of criminal anarchy was harmful to the state. Why could the legislature at its discretion not add to the category of harmful speech acts, just as it had the authority to place speech once thought to be harmful—for example, criminal libel— beyond criminal liability?

In his majority opinion, Justice Sanford made exactly this point when he argued that clear and present danger was only applicable if the relevant statute prohibited certain acts (obstruction of the draft, military insubordination) "without any reference to language."[163] With such a law, he continued, "it must necessarily be found, as an original question, without any previous determination by the legislative body, whether the specific language used involved such likelihood of bringing about the substantive evil as to deprive it of the constitutional protection."[164] But this requirement had "no application" to cases like *Gitlow*, "where the legislative body itself has previously determined the danger of substantive evil arising from utterances of a specified character."[165] Sanford was simply saying that reasonable exercises of the state's police power were constitutional, that harmful speech acts were within the police power, and that advocacy of anarchy was sufficiently dangerous to be considered a harmful speech act.

Holmes refused to go along with Justice Sanford's argument. He generally deferred to the legislature, but not always. According to him, judicial decision making, including constitutional adjudication, required the drawing of legal lines. Legal distinctions, as he was fond of saying, were matters of degree, but this was no excuse for not drawing them. If constitutional rights and the idea of limited legislative powers were to mean anything, then at some point judges had to step in. For this reason, Holmes supported the police power of states to cut down the economic value of private property without compensation, but there was a limit.[166] In the case of free speech, there is no reason to think that Holmes would not have given the states some reasonable discretion as to what forms of speech were inherently harmful. But here too there was a limit. A balance had to be maintained by judges between individual rights and legislative authority. Walter Nelles, who wrote Gitlow's brief, argued that a state that punished language independently of circumstances went too far.

> But the measure of its [the state's] right to protect itself is to be determined by a balancing of the right against the citizen's right to express himself upon matters of government. The state may, in a word, protect itself against danger of forcible overthrow or breach of the peace, and may punish speech the circumstances of whose utterances are such as to involve a causal relation with subsequent evil, consummated, attempted, or likely. But a statute which takes no account of circumstances fails, and fails almost as a matter of definition, when put to the basic balancing test. For such a statute may be applied and in the instant case was applied to a situation involving no element of public danger. In its relation to such a situation the statute is a mere invasion of an express constitutional right.[167]

Holmes agreed wholeheartedly with this characterization. The law's purpose was to punish harmful acts, not sinners. A person who advocated criminal anarchy in circumstances where no harm could occur may be an evil person, but that person had done nothing harmful. Impotent advocacy of anarchy could not therefore be punishable in a society that adhered to free speech.

But even if Gitlow's speech activity was not a harmful act, it could still be the basis for liability if it satisfied the criteria of the intent-branch of Holmes's theory of liability. Certainly the jury had sufficient evidence to find that Gitlow acted with unlawful intent. He would therefore have been liable if he had conspired with others to accomplish his unlawful objective or if his speech was sufficiently proximate to a harm to constitute an attempt. Since Gitlow was never charged with conspiracy, it is an intriguing question what Holmes's reaction would have been to a conspiracy charge. Conspiracy required no proximity to harm. Gitlow was also never charged with an attempt though Holmes thought it appropriate to add that

> If the publication of this document had been laid as an attempt to induce an uprising against government at once, and not at some indefinite time in the future, it would have presented a different question. The object would have been one with which the law might deal, subject to the doubt whether there was any danger that the publication could produce any result; or, in other words, whether it was not futile and too remote from possible consequences. But the indictment alleges the publication and nothing more.[168]

An attempt could not be made out if the harm was too remote. Individual advocacy of revolution and anarchy was protected if the danger of an uprising was not imminent.

Summary

Holmes understood speech activity according to the three categories of his theory of legal liability: harmful acts, attempts, and abuses of privileges. Harmful acts were treated especially harshly. If a rational and prudent person, knowing what the agent knew of the circumstances of an act, would judge the speaker's act to be harmful in itself, the speaker was liable no matter the intent or foresight. Libel and contempt of court were examples of such harmful acts, while Gitlow's advocacy of anarchy was not. However, certain harmful speech acts were privileged by the law. Examples would include the right to criticize public officials and the right to associate. The latter privilege was withdrawn, however, if the purpose of the combination was unlawful. The convictions in *Schenck* and *Frohwerk* rested on this basis, while Holmes dissented in *Abrams* because he could find no unlawful purpose. In the case of a single speaker, unlawful intent was similarly requisite for an attempt conviction, but a clear and present danger had also to be shown. Such a danger existed in *Debs* but not in *Gitlow*.

Notes

1. Holmes, "Primitive Notions in Modern Law," *American Law Review* 10 (April 1876), in *The Formative Essays of Justice Holmes,* ed. Frederic Rogers Kellogg (Westport, Conn.: Greenwood Press, 1984), 129 n. 2. Also see Holmes, "Privilege, Malice, and Intent" *Harvard Law Review* 8 (1894), in Holmes, *Collected Legal Papers* (New York: Peter Smith, 1952), 118.
2. Holmes, *The Common Law* (Cambridge: Belknap Press, 1963), 110.
3. *Burt v. Advertiser Newspaper Co.*, 154 Mass. 238 (1891).
4. Id. at 245.
5. Id.
6. 159 Mass. 293 (1893).
7. Id. at 302.
8. Id. at 301.
9. *Cowley v. Pulsifer*, 137 Mass. 392 (1884).
10. *Burt v. Advertiser Newspaper Co.*, 154 Mass. 238 (1891).

11. Id. at 242.
12. *Gandia v. Pettingill,* 222 U.S. 452 (1911).
13. Id. at 457.
14. Id. at 458.
15. Though I do not think that Holmes's general understanding of libel and privilege changed, I do think it is readily obvious that he gradually widened the privileges against libel during his judicial career.
16. 205 U.S. 454 (1907).
17. *People v. New-Times Publishing Company,* 35 Colo. 253, 257–351 (1906). For a more extensive discussion of *Patterson,* see David S. Bogen, "The Free Speech Metamorphosis of Mr. Justice Holmes," *Hofstra Law Review* 11 (1982): 125–31.
18. *Patterson v. Colorado,* 205 U.S. 454, 462 (1907).
19. Id. at 459 and 461.
20. *Telegram Newspaper Co. v. Commonwealth,* 172 Mass. 296 (1899).
21. Id. at 299.
22. Id. at 300.
23. *Toledo Newspaper Co. v. United States,* 247 U.S. 402 (1918).
24. Id. at 423–25.
25. Id. at 423.
26. Id.
27. Id. at 425.
28. Id.
29. *Schenck v. United States,* 249 U.S. 47, 52 (1919).
30. 221 U.S. 418 (1910).
31. Id. at 439.
32. *Abrams v. United States,* 250 U.S. 616, 627 (1919).
33. Id. at 628.
34. *Schenck v. United States,* 249 U.S. 47 (1919); *Frohwerk v. United States,* 249 U.S. 204 (1919); *Debs v. United States,* 249 U.S. 211 (1919); *Abrams v. United States,* 250 U.S. 616 (1919); *Gitlow v. New York,* 268 U.S. 652 (1925).
35. H. C. Peterson and Gilbert C. Fite, *Opponents of War, 1917–1918* (Madison: University of Wisconsin, 1957; Westport, Conn.: Greenwood Press, 1986).
36. See Richard Polenberg, *Fighting Faiths: The Abrams Case, The Supreme Court, and Free Speech* (New York: Penguin Books, 1987); Paul L. Murphy, *World War I and the Origin of Civil Liberties in the United States* (New York: Norton, 1979); Robert K. Murray, *Red Scare: A Study of National Hysteria, 1919–1920* (Minneapolis: University of Minnesota, 1955).
37. See Holmes, *The Common Law,* 36: "If people would gratify the passion of revenge outside of the law, if the law did not help them, the law has no choice but to satisfy the craving itself, and thus avoid the greater evil of private retribution. At the same time, this passion is not one which we encourage, either as private individuals or as law-makers."

38. 236 U.S. 273 (1915).
39. Id. at 276.
40. Id. at 275.
41. Id. at 277.
42. Id.
43. Id.
44. Id.
45. Id. at 277–78.
46. Fox's article is printed in the Brief for Plaintiff In Error at 2–4, *Fox*.
47. It is true that at the Supreme Court of Washington Fox argued that "the element of intent was eliminated by the trial court's instructions to the jury." But this claim was unsubstantiated. The trial judge did say that the state did not have to prove "that the defendant possessed a criminal intent in editing the printed matter set out in the information," but added that the defendant had to have acted willfully, which meant "purposely and intentionally, with a design and hope to accomplish the evil result." For Fox's objection as to intent, see Record at 25, *Fox*. For the trial judge's instructions requiring an "evil purpose," see id. at 50.
48. Fox, in his appeal to the Supreme Court of Washington, justified the requirement of illegal intent by citing Holmes's language in *Swift v. United States* and *Commonwealth v. Peaslee* (see id. at 25). Such citations suggest that at this time it was generally understood that Holmes required actual illegal intent in cases of illegal inducements. But see David Rabban, "The First Amendment in Its Forgotten Years," *Yale Law Journal* 90 (1981): 533–36; idem, "The Emergence of Modern First Amendment Doctrine," *University of Chicago Law Review* 40 (Fall 1983): 1259. Rabban argues that, despite these references to illegal intent, Holmes applied the bad-tendency doctrine in *Fox*.
49. *Fox v. Washington*, 236 U.S. 273, 278 (1915).
50. Record at 20, *Fox*. Edward S. Corwin argued that in *Fox* Holmes implied that "incitement to crime" was "sufficient" for liability "without reference to its actual consequences." See his "Bowing Out 'Clear and Present Danger,'" *Notre Dame Lawyer* 27 (1952): 327. Rabban accepts Corwin's interpretation. See Rabban, "The First Amendment in Its Forgotten Years," 585; idem, "The Emergence of Modern First Amendment Doctrine," 1259 n. 318. In my judgment, the record of the case can not justify this interpretation.
51. 268 U.S. 652 (1925).
52. 205 U.S. 454, 462 (1907).
53. *Fox v. Washington*, 236 U.S. 273, 277 (1915).
54. Id.
55. 249 U.S. 47 (1919).
56. See Record at 17–62, *Schenck*.
57. Id. at 64–65.
58. Id. at 66.

59. Corwin also believed that *Schenck* was not a difficult case for Holmes, but on a different ground. He thought that the case was "Indistinguishable" from *Fox* and that Holmes applied the bad-tendency doctrine in both. See his "Bowing Out 'Clear and Present Danger'," 329. The bad-tendency doctrine, popular throughout legal circles in the early part of the twentieth century (see chap. 5 below), imposed liability on speech if it had a tendency to cause harm; illicit intent or a proximity to harm was not required. But I have already shown how Holmes required an actual unlawful intent and a proximity of harm in *Fox,* and therefore Corwin's argument that the two cases were "indistinguishable" cannot support his interpretation that Holmes adhered to the bad-tendency doctrine. But Corwin's initial assumption that the cases were similar was false. He overlooked the crucial issue that Schenck conspired with others to obstruct the draft while Fox acted alone. Therefore, at least according to Holmes's theory of legal liability, these two cases were very different. Only in *Fox,* only in the case of illegal advocacy, was it necessary to show a proximity to harm.

One reason why Corwin wanted to treat *Fox* and *Schenck* as analogous cases was because his goal was to undermine Holmes's dissent in *Abrams v. United States.* The whole point of his article, written at the time of the Smith Act prosecutions in the 1950s, was to "bow out" Holmes's clear-and-present-danger standard. As early as 1920, he had criticized Holmes's *Abrams* dissent since it required "direct intentional incitement" and a "reasonable likelihood of harm." See his "Freedom of Speech and Press under the First Amendment: A Resume," *Yale Law Journal* 30 (1920): 54–55. Accordingly, he tried to justify the bad-tendency doctrine by showing that Holmes himself honored it in all of his opinions prior to *Abrams.* The irony is evident. Corwin came to his conclusion that Holmes was an adherent of the bad tendency doctrine because he was fond of the very doctrine for which Holmes is now criticized. See Rabban, "The First Amendment in Its Forgotten Years," 585 n. 396; idem, "The Emergence of Modern First Amendment Doctrine," 1259 n. 318.
60. *Schenck v. United States,* 249 U.S. 49, 52 (1919).
61. Id.
62. Rabban, "The Emergence of Modern First Amendment Doctrine," 1261. Also see idem, "The First Amendment in its Forgotten Years," 585.
63. *Schenck v. United States,* 249 U.S. 47, 52 (1919).
64. Rabban, "The Emergence of Modern First Amendment Doctrine," 1261.
65. See *Schenck v. United States,* 249 U.S. 47, 52 (1919).
66. *Goldman v. United States,* 245 U.S. 474, 477 (1918).
67. *United States v. Kissel,* 218 U.S. 601, 608 (1910). See also *Hyde v. United States,* 225 U.S. 347, 388 (1912).
68. *Nash v. United States,* 229 U.S. 373, 378 (1913).
69. *Hyde v. United States,* 225 U.S. 347, 388 (1912).
70. *Aikens v. Wisconsin,* 195 U.S. 194, 206 (1904). See also *Drew v. Thaw,* 235 U.S. 432, 438 (1914); *Swift v. United States,* 196 U.S. 375, 396 (1905).

71. See *Schenck v. United States*, 249 U.S. 47, 52 (1919); *Goldman v. United States*, 245 U.S. 474 (1918).
72. 249 U.S. 182 (1919); 249 U.S. 47 (1919); 249 U.S. 204 (1919); 249 U.S. 211 (1919).
73. *Sugarman v. United States*, 249 U.S. 182, 183 (1919).
74. Id. at 184–85.
75. Id. at 185.
76. "This is not the first time that conscription was ever tried in this country; they tried conscription during the Civil War. How did it work out? There was a small town near Augusta, Me., which said 'We will not be conscripted.' What did they do? They seceded from the Union. Not one man from that community was drafted during the Civil War, and the reason they were not drafted was because they stuck together. That is an example of what you people can do by sticking together." "Well, if you people all stick together, like those 5,000 Socialists down in St. Paul, the chances are that the Government will not want you, and you will go right along running your farm and raising your pigs as you are doing today" (id. at 4 and 6).
77. 249 U.S. 204 (1919).
78. Id. at 206.
79. See Rabban, "The Emergence of Modern First Amendment Doctrine," 1261. Rabban argues that the absence of any reference to "clear and present danger" in *Frohwerk* indicates that Holmes was an adherent of the bad-tendency doctrine, the doctrine that speech was still punishable if it only had a bad tendency to cause harm. This is an odd argument since Rabban earlier, as we have seen, dismisses the significance of such language in *Schenck*. How can the abscence of certain language be so important if its existence elsewhere can be so easily ignored? Rabban also makes much of Holmes's claim that Frohwerk had used "language that might be taken to convey an innuendo of a different sort." The hint is that Holmes was willing to allow liability to depend on "an innuendo," which would tend to support Rabban's interpretation that Holmes liked the bad-tendency standard. The article containing the "innuendo" that Holmes referred to, however was only one of twelve articles that Frohwerk had written. Moreover, the article containing the innuendo went on to say that no one should find a draftee guilty if he followed the instinct of self-preservation, that a draftee was more sinned against than sinned (even if he refused to serve), and that those who voted for the war were more guilty than those who resisted the draft. Accordingly, Rabban's conclusion that Holmes based Frohwerk's liability on an innuendo is something of an overstatement. In any case, the quotation had nothing to do with the bad-tendency doctrine. Holmes's analysis of the articles was to determine if there was sufficient evidence of the combination's unlawful purpose—the essence of conspiracy. But the bad tendency doctrine ignores the intent of the speaker. Therefore Holmes was not applying this doctrine, even if he was trying to decipher Frohwerk's intent by way of an innuendo.

80. *Frohwerk V. United States,* 249 U.S. 204, 209 (1919).
81. Id. at 208.
82. Id. at 206–7.
83. *Re Frohwerk* 248 U.S. 540 (1918).
84. *Frohwerk V. United States,* 249 U.S. 204, 209 (1919). Rabban argues that Holmes's references to "a little breath," "a flame," "to kindle" show that a bad tendency was enough for him to impose liability on speech. Something small would be enough for liability. But this is a misreading of the metaphor; it turns it upside down. Holmes wrote these words because he had to assume, since he had no record of the testimony, the strongest possible case against Frohwerk, that he circulated his articles in the worst sort of circumstances. This is why Holmes used the metaphor of a "little breath." It was not to show how little of a tendency could trigger liability, but how dangerous the context of Frohwerk's speech activity could have been. If Frohwerk alone distributed the articles with the intent to obstruct the draft, he would have been guilty under the clear-and-present-danger doctrine, not the bad-tendency test. But since one of the charges was that Frohwerk had conspired with others, there was no need to establish a proximity of harm in the particular case. The conspirators' actual purpose was the key. Had the conspirators "known about" and "relied upon" the potential of draft resistance in the "quarters" in which they circulated their articles? That was the essential question of the case. And since it concerned Frohwerk's actual intent, the above passage had nothing to do with the bad-tendency test.
85. *Abrams v. United States,* 250 U.S. 616, 627 (1919).
86. 249 U.S. 211 (1919).
87. The convicted persons whom Debs praised in his speech were Charles E. Ruthenberg, Alfred Wagenknecht, Charles Baker, Kate Richards O'Hare, and Rose Pastor Stokes. See Deb's speech in *The Writings and Speeches of Eugene Debs,* ed. Arthur M. Schlesinger, Jr., (New York: Hermitage Press, 1948), 417–33.
88. Record at 31, *Debs.*
89. Clyde P. Miller, a reporter for the Cleveland Plain Dealer at the time of the speech, testified that Debs, immediately before the speech, had told him that he supported the "spirit and substance" of the St. Louis Proclamation, even though he favored a "restatement" of it. See Record at 200-203, *Debs.* After Debs was arrested, he also told Miller that he would not repudiate the St. Louis Proclamation and that he would "die" for the principles found therein. See Record at 300-301, *Debs.*
90. Joseph Triner, a special agent for the United States Naval Intelligence Office, was in the audience and testified to the nature of Deb's Chicago speech. See Record at 304-310, *Debs.*
91. Record at 322-323, *Debs.*
92. Id. at 242, 195.
93. Edward H. Evans testified that Deb's speech produced "considerable enthusiasm" (see Record at 314–15, *Debs*).

94. The prosecution was not above trying to make inferences as to Debs's intent from the fact that no flag was present (see Record at 253, *Debs*).

95. Record at 352, *Debs*. The prosecutor, Mr. Wertz, characterized Debs's closing remarks as "more in the nature of a confession" (see Record at 369, *Debs*).

96. Id. at 413–14.

97. Id. at 416.

98. Id. at 414.

99. Id. at 418–26.

100. Id. at 435.

101. Id. at 433.

102. Id.

103. Id. at 441. Also see id. at 418–26.

104. Brief for the United States at 89–90, *Debs*. In his instructions to the jury, Judge Westenhaver defined "wilful" as "purposely, knowingly, or intentionally, as can be distinguished from accidentally or inadvertently" (see Record at 415, *Debs*).

105. See Record at 339–41, 352–53, *Debs*, and Brief for the Plaintiff at 32, *Debs*.

106. Brief for the Plaintiff at 45–46, *Debs*.

107. *Masses Publishing Co. v. Patten*, 244 Fed. 535 (S.D. N.Y. 1917).

108. *Masses Publishing Co. v. Patten*, 246 Fed. 24 (2nd Cir. 1917).

109. Brief for the Plaintiff, at 70, *Debs*.

110. Brief of Defendant in Error at 75, *Debs*.

111. Id.

112. Brief for the United States at 72, *Debs*.

113. Id. at 77–78.

114. Harry Kalven criticized Holmes decision in *Debs* because he treated the case as "a routine criminal appeal." See his "Professor Ernst Freund and *Debs v. United States*," *University of Chicago Law Review* 40 (1973): 238. Others have endorsed this criticism. See Gerald Gunther, "Learned Hand and the Origins of Modern First Amendment Doctrine: Some Fragments of History," *Stanford Law Review* 27 (February 1975): 736 n. 83; Rabban, "The First Amendment in Its Forgotten Years," 585 and notes; idem, "The Emergence of Modern First Amendment Doctrine," 1259 n. 317. Even if Kalven and the others are correct, and even if Holmes did decide the case as a "routine appeal," it does not justify the conclusion that he decided the case according to the more restrictive bad-tendency test. Indeed, one could argue that applying traditional criteria of criminal liability to speech, if it proves anything, establishes that Holmes had a moderately protective standard. New statutes punishing speech activity would be interpreted to apply only to acts that satisfied traditional criteria of criminal liability. It bears special mention that early proponents of free speech almost universally agreed that the best protection for free speech was to rely on traditional categories of liability. A speaker was liable only

if he was guilty as a *principal*, an *accomplice*, an *accessory*, or a *coconspirator*. As we shall see (in chap. 5), Zechariah Chafee, Jr., argued along these lines. In fact, Seymour Stedman's brief on behalf of Debs argued in favor of a free-speech test that rested on his interpretation of traditional common-law criteria: "It is our contention that the rule as stated by Judge Hand is the correct rule, and that the test for criminal responsibility for expressions leading up to insubordination, etc. is the *common law liability as an accessory* created by urging violation of law upon others" (emphasis mine; see Brief for Plaintiff in Error at 76, *Debs*). If the defendant himself wanted traditional criminal-law criteria applied to his speech activity, in other words, if he wanted the Supreme Court to treat his case as a "routine criminal appeal," then it is difficult to argue that Holmes was hostile to free speech because he gave the defendant what he wanted.

115. *Debs v. United States*, 249 U.S. 211, 214–215 (1919).
116. Id. at 216.
117. Rabban, "The Emergence of Modern First Amendment Doctrine," 1264.
118. *Debs v. United States*, 249 U.S. 211, 216 (1919).
119. In a footnote, Rabban refers to Ray Ginger's biography of Debs and says the following: "In his biographer's opinion, Debs intended his speech not simply 'to arouse resentment and opposition to the war,' but also 'to taunt the federal authorities into placing him on trial' " (see his "The Emergence of Modern First Amendment Doctrine," 1264 n. 355). It is difficult to see how Debs "taunted" the federal authorities unless he intended to obstruct the draft. See also Ray Ginger, *Eugene Debs: A Biography* (New York: Collier Books, 1966), 372.
120. *Debs v. United States*, 249 U.S. 211, 215 (1919).
121. Id. at 216.
122. One might argue that no matter what Holmes said in his opinion, he had to have applied a bad-tendency test because Debs in fact neither intended illegality nor created a serious danger of draft obstruction. This argument is difficult to criticize because I, compared to the jury at Deb's trial, have no special insight into his mind or any worthwhile way to assess the chances that his Canton speech would have obstructed the draft. Moreover, one must avoid the argument that moves from the fact that Debs would not be convicted in the 1990s to the conclusion that Holmes did not apply his clear-and-present-danger doctrine to the case. Such anachronistic assumptions are bound to lead to distorted interpretations of Holmes's thought. David Bogen has suggested some of the reasons why Deb's speech might have posed a danger: (1) Deb's political prominence would have increased the chances of obstruction; (2) the existence of the war; (3) the fragile nature of the draft at this time (see Bogen, "The Free Speech Metamorphosis of Mr. Justice Holmes," 170–71).
123. 250 U.S. 616 (1919).
124. Id. at 617.

125. Record at 237, *Abrams*.
126. Raymond Robins, an American Red Cross official who functioned as the liaison between the American ambassador in Russia and the defacto Soviet government, and Albert Williams, a journalist from the *New York Evening Post*, were apparently willing to testify that the Bolsheviks were the natural allies of the United States (see Record at 114–55, *Abrams*). Though Judge Clayton upheld the objection to the introduction of this testimony, he allowed Harry Weinberger, the defense attorney, to ask the questions. From the nature of the questions asked, it seems clear that Weinberger's expectation was that the witnesses would testify in the direction outlined above. Also, Weinberger explicitly claimed that the facts contained in the circulars were true (see Record at 138, *Abrams*).
127. Record at 116, *Abrams*.
128. An argument subsidiary to the main one presented above was that President Wilson had no authority to send troops to Russia—even if that policy made sense—without congressional approval, a declaration of war, or both (see Record at 119, 132, *Abrams*). But again Judge Clayton would allow no testimony as to the constitutionality of President Wilson's actions (see Record at 132, 137, 157, *Abrams*).
129. Record at 168–230. Molly Steiner testified that she only wanted to help Russia. She expressed indifference as to who won the war (Record at 221–22, *Abrams*).
130. Record at 237–38, *Abrams*.
131. Id.
132. Id. at 237.
133. Id. at 237. At the same place, Clayton also told the jury to use its "common sense"—its "out-of-doors sense"—to decide if the manner by which the defendants distributed the circulars indicated unlawful intent.
134. Id. at 232.
135. Brief for Plaintiff in Error at 19, *Abrams*.
136. Id. at 24.
137. Id. at 47.
138. "It will not do to say . . . that the only intent of these defendants was to prevent injury to the Russian cause. Men must be held to have intended, and to be accountable for, the effects which their acts were likely to produce. Even if their primary purpose and intent was to aid the cause of the Russian Revolution, the plan of action which they adopted necessarily involved, before it could be realized, defeat of the war program of the United States" (*Abrams v. United States*, 250 U.S. 616, 621 [1919]).
139. "I am aware, of course, that the word 'intent' as vaguely used in ordinary legal discussion means no more than knowledge at the time of the act that the consequences said to be intended will ensue. Even less than that will satisfy the general principle of civil and criminal liability. A man may have to pay damages, may be sent to prison, at common law might be hanged,

if at the time of his act he knew facts from which common experience showed that the consequences would follow, whether he individually could foresee them or not" (id. at 626–27).

140. Holmes cautioned that "when words are used exactly, a deed is not done with intent to produce a consequence unless that consequence is the aim of the deed. It may be obvious, and obvious to the actor, that the consequence will follow, . . . but he does not do the act with intent to produce it [the consequence] unless the aim to produce it is the proximate motive of the specific act" (id. at 627).

141. Id.

142. See id.

143. 168 Mass. 92 (1896).

144. *Abrams v. United States,* 250 U.S. 616, 629 (1919). Rabban believes that certain language from Holmes's dissent in *Abrams* shows that he had undergone a conversion in favor of free speech. While Holmes had used "clear and present danger" prior to *Abrams,* in this dissent he switched to a "clear and imminent" standard. Punishment was appropriate only if speech would produce "forthwith" "certain" harms that the government "constitutionally" may "seek" to prevent. For these and other changes in Holmes's terminology, see Rabban, "Emergence of First Amendment Doctrine," 1306–9. However, it is doubtful whether these changes in rhetoric can bear the weight of the thesis that Holmes underwent an intellectual conversion. Rabban's claim that the appearance of a "clear and imminent" standard is especially significant is undermined, to some extent, by Holmes's use of "imminent" in 1918 in *Toledo Newspaper Company v. United States,* 247 U.S. 402, 423 (1918). In the same vein, Rabban's conclusion that Holmes did not distinguish between "public" and "private" speech until *Abrams* conflicts with Holmes's 1912 pronouncement that citizens had a "serious interest" in activities of "public officers" and that "anything bearing on such action was a legitimate subject of statement and comment" (*Gandia v. Pettingill,* 222 U.S. 452, 457 [1912]). Perhaps Holmes did not protect as much "public" speech as we would today, but he certainly was aware before 1919 of the distinction—which was already commonplace in the nineteenth century.

Rabban argues, at a more abstract level, that only with Holmes's *Abrams* dissent did he begin "to doubt 'the very foundations' " of his own conduct. Only then did he acknowledge "that 'the best test of truth' is not 'the majority vote of that nation that can lick all others,' but 'the power of thought to get itself accepted in the competition of the market' " (see his "Emergence of Modern First Amendment Doctrine," 1310). But Holmes's skepticism was not some new infatuation but an integral part of his epistemological view of the world that was formed during the 1870s. The metaphor of a marketplace of ideas, a notion that Holmes obviously inherited from J. S. Mill, was a part of his world-view long before 1919. In 1913 he said explicitly that law embodied the "beliefs that have triumphed in the battle of ideas" (from a speech Holmes gave at a dinner of the Harvard Law School Association of New York, 15 February 1913, reprinted in Holmes, *Collected Legal Papers* (New York: Peter Smith, 1952), 294–95. And this metaphor did not conflict with Holmes's definition of truth as "a majority of a nation that can lick all others." Even though in 1918 he tried to distance himself from this early definition, he still thought it was "correct in so far as it implied that our test of truth is a reference to either a present or an imagined future majority in favor of our view" (see Holmes, "Natural Law," *Harvard Law Review* 32 [1918], in *Collected Legal Papers*, 310). The main point is that there is little positive evidence that Holmes underwent an intellectual conversion. Changes in style, metaphor, or rhetoric are not enough. In my judgment, Rabban has not established that Holmes's *Abrams* dissent was anything more than a powerfully eloquent restatement of what he had believed all along.

145. *Abrams V. United States*, 250 U.S. 616, 629 (1919).
146. Id.
147. 268 U.S. 652 (1925).
148. Darrow, Gitlow's attorney, conceded all the crucial facts (see Record at 171, *Gitlow*).
149. Id. at 656, note.
150. Id. at 148–49.
151. Id. at 155–56.
152. Record at 230–31, *Gitlow*.
153. Brief for Defendant in Error at 10, *Gitlow*.
154. Id.
155. Id. at 14.
156. Id.
157. Id. at 17.
158. *Gitlow v. New York*, 268 U.S. 652, 665 (1925).
159. Id. at 667.
160. Id. at 668.
161. Id. at 669.
162. Id.
163. Id. at 670.
164. Id. at 671.
165. Id.
166. *Pennsylvania Coal Co. v. Mahon*, 260 U.S. 393 (1922).
167. Brief for the Plaintiff in Error, at 101–2, *Gitlow*.
168. Id. at 673.

4. Other Important Cases

SEVERAL OTHER CASES deserve consideration, though in them Holmes only concurred in the result, joined Brandeis's dissent, or wrote a very short dissent. These decisions help justify the interpretation presented in chapters 2 and 3. The more cases that can reasonably be fitted into his theory of liability, the more secure is the conclusion that Holmes decided free-speech cases depending on whether they involved harmful speech acts, attempts, or conspiracies. It is also true that indictments other than those encountered in the major free-speech cases were brought under the Espionage Act. For example, publishing false statements with unlawful intent was a popular charge that merits some attention. It would be helpful to review how Holmes reacted to these convictions even if he did not write an opinion. He also assessed the constitutionality of sanctions on speech that did not consist of civil and criminal liability. How did he determine, for instance, whether a state could discharge an employee for his or her speech activity? According to the preceding account, it might seem that he would have had difficulty perceiving this question as a matter of free speech. Since his theory of liability defined the scope of free speech, sanctions that did not impose liability would seem to fall outside of the guarantee. But Holmes widened, perhaps in an ambivalent way, the scope of his theory of free speech to include these types of cases, even though his basic underlying theory remained the same. This chapter also introduces the issue of how Holmes, in his role as an appellate judge in a federal system, decided if the evidence of a crime involving speech activity was sufficient for a conviction.

Attempts

Some of the cases in which Holmes did not write an opinion included the standard charges of attempting to obstruct the draft and to cause insubordination in the military. He apparently reviewed these convictions according to his general criteria of attempt: unlawful intent plus a proximity to harm. In *Pierce v. United States*,[1] for example, the defendants were convicted of an attempt to cause insubordination in the military by distributing a circular entitled *The Price We Pay*. The majority upheld the conviction, even though the defendants did not circulate the pamphlet until after Judge Rose had directed an acquittal in a different prosecution for distributing the same circular, and even though the defendants testified that their purpose was only to promote socialism. The contents of the circular alone were enough for the jury to infer unlawful intent and to find a bad tendency. And if the probable effect of the circular "was at all disputable, at least the jury fairly might believe that, under the circumstances existing, it would have a tendency to cause insubordination."[2] A jury was to decide if the contents of the circular had a bad tendency that indicated an unlawful intent. If there was any evidence underlying the jury's verdict, the majority would uphold the conviction. A tendency to cause insubordination was enough for liability.

Holmes, who concurred in Brandeis's dissent, seems to have doubted whether there was sufficient evidence to sustain a jury's finding of either unlawful intent or proximity to harm. In *Schenck* and *Debs*, there was corroborative evidence of unlawful intent beyond the contents of the publication or speech. Minutes of meetings, incriminating newspaper clippings, and admissions made to newspaper reporters were introduced at these trials to establish the defendants' unlawful intent. At Pierce's trial, no such evidence was presented,[3] and the government's brief to the Supreme Court insisted that no evidence beyond the contents of the publication was necessary to prove unlawful intent.[4] In my judgment, Holmes refused to affirm the conviction because the evidence of unlawful intent was insufficient to uphold an attempt conviction. His rule may have been that the publication itself was not sufficient to establish unlawful intent unless it unambiguously advocated draft obstruction or insubordination. If the publication or speech was ambiguous, then the government needed corroborative evidence of unlawful intent.

There was also no evidence introduced at the trial concerning the likelihood of harm, whether of obstruction to the draft or insubordination in the military. The government even conceded that the defendants made no special effort to distribute the circular to potential draftees or to members of the military.[5] The government was relying on the assumption that a bad tendency—which was inferred, along with unlawful intent, from the contents of the publication—was enough to constitute an attempt. Holmes, true to his theory, disagreed and joined Brandeis's dissent accordingly.[6] A bad tendency of a speech was not sufficient to show either unlawful intent or a proximity to harm. Other corroborative evidence, both of intent and immediate harmfulness, was required.

In *Schaefer v. United States*,[7] the majority upheld a conviction of attempting to obstruct the draft on reasoning identical to that found in *Pierce*. In *Schaefer*, an editor of the German Newspaper published in Philadelphia was convicted of attempting to obstruct the draft on evidence that he altered, in small ways, the stories that he took from other newspapers and published in his *Tagenblatt*. The government's contention was that the alterations—whether they consisted of comments, omissions, or mistranslations—indicated an unlawful intent and had a tendency to harm the recruitment service. In the words of the majority opinion, the effect of the articles "on the persons affected could not be shown, nor was it necessary. The tendency of the articles and their efficacy were enough."[8] Liability for an attempt could be imposed on anyone who engaged in speech activity that had a tendency to cause harm.

Holmes disagreed and once again joined Brandeis in dissent. As Brandeis put it, "no jury acting in calmness could reasonably say that any of the publications set forth in the indictment was of such a character or was made in circumstances as to create a clear and present danger . . . that they would obstruct recruiting."[9] The evidence of unlawful intent consisted only of the editorial changes made to the articles before publication. Brandeis admitted that other evidence might have been enough to show that the paper "was circulated under circumstances which gave it a peculiar significance or effect." But "no such evidence was introduced by the government."[10] He therefore concluded, along with Holmes, that the evidence was insufficient for a conviction. In cases involving ambiguous publications, in which unlawful intent was not explicit, evidence independent of the speech activity had to be produced to establish unlawful intent. Only then could a person be guilty of an attempt, but some real proximity to harm also had to be shown.

A case that is analogous in some respects to the indictments discussed above is *Gilbert v. Minnesota*.[11] Though Gilbert was charged with violating a Minnesota statute that prohibited the advocacy of either nonenlistment in the military forces or nonsupport of the American war effort, the trial judges's instructions to the jury reduced the issue to one of attempt. The jury was instructed to decide not only if Gilbert used the language alleged in the indictment, but also whether the language constituted "advocacy" or "teaching."[12] The judge then told the jury that explicit "advocacy" or "teaching" was unnecessary: "the statute would be violated if the natural and reasonable effect of the words spoken is to teach or advocate that citizens"[13] should neither enlist nor support the war. The Minnesota Supreme Court, which upheld the conviction, referred to the same standard,[14] and Minnesota's brief to the United States Supreme Court argued that:

If the natural and reasonable effect of his utterances be to encourage resistance to the law requiring military service . . . and the words are used in an endeavor to persuade resistance to such a requirement, it is immaterial that the duty to resist is not mentioned or the interest of the persons addressed in resistance is not suggested.[15]

This language, of course, came close to Holmes's standard of unlawful intent plus proximity to harm. A person engaged in an "endeavor" to persuade resistance was culpable only if the "natural and reasonable effect" of the speech was to harm enlistment or the war effort. Consequently, given the nature of the legal standard used in the case, it is not surprising that Holmes concurred in the Court's decision upholding the conviction even though Brandeis dissented.

There is only one major difficulty with Holmes's decision in *Gilbert*. Though the Minnesota brief at one place argued that the defendant's speech had to be part of an "endeavor" to persuade resistance, on the very next page the state's attorneys argued that the "statute is a police regulation and under it the doing of the forbidden act is a criminal offense regardless of intent."[16] The Minnesota Supreme Court had perhaps forced the state's attorneys to make this argument when it denied that illegal intent was necessary.[17] In a petition for a rehearing, Gilbert claimed that the court's position was wrong: intent was the crux of the offense. If a teacher read Gilbert's speech to a class for an educational purpose, the court's rule meant that the teacher would nonetheless be liable, which was clearly inappropriate.[18] Nevertheless, the Minnesota court denied the petition, which raises the question: Why did Holmes

uphold the conviction if Gilbert was *possibly* convicted of a crime analogous to attempt without a finding of unlawful intent?

Though answers to this question are necessarily speculative, a few
things can be said. Holmes may well have thought that the language of
the statute itself made it clear to the jury that they could not convict
without finding an unlawful intent. Since the statute referred to teaching
and advocacy, it is arguable that the trial judge's failure to explain
carefully this requirement to the jury was not prejudicial to Gilbert. The
more important consideration, since the words of the statute did not
make this obvious, was to instruct the jury that they could convict
Gilbert only if the "natural and reasonable effect" of his speech was to
obstruct the recruitment service or the war effort. Would the trial judge
have added the requirement of proximity to harm unless he assumed
that only those with unlawful intent were liable? It is conceivable that
the judge wanted to punish those who unintentionally created a real
danger to the war effort, but not likely. The chances that anyone would
"unintentionally" create a real likelihood of nonenlistment or nonsupport of the war effort were very small. The judge may well have ignored
this possibility altogether. Thus, the jury may well have understood that
illegal intent was required, but focused on the necessity of a likelihood
of harm because that was the controversial issue.

Certain testimony at the trial was very damaging to the defense's
contention that Gilbert's intent was lawful. Three witnesses for the state
testified that the defendant said, in response to a heckler's claim that his
speech was seditious, "You may say this is sedition, but, if this is sedition
make the most of it."[19] Another witness claimed that Gilbert had re-
marked that a Secret Service agent, who had been following him around,
would not catch him since he was "so smooth."[20] Both of these statements, much like those that Debs had made, go to the issue of Gilbert's
intent. Though the defense denied that Gilbert had made these statements, Holmes had reason to believe that there was sufficient evidence
for the jury to decide the matter the other way.

Gilbert's attorneys, in their brief to the Supreme Court, did not refer
to the innocent character of their client's intent. Though they had focused on this issue of intent at the state level, the emphasis disappeared
immediately thereafter. In front of the United States Supreme Court,
their entire argument concerned whether free speech was an inherent
right applicable against state action and whether the federal government

had exclusive authority over the recruitment system and the war effort.[21] If the defense attorneys understood their client's purpose to have been innocent, they made a serious mistake in not bringing it to the attention of the Supreme Court. Perhaps they simply thought that the issue of Gilbert's intent was a lost cause.

At the trial, there was also testimony introduced that had a direct bearing on the likelihood of harm. There was no indication that Gilbert's speech actually induced anyone not to enlist or to oppose the war effort,[22] but there was plenty of testimony that the crowd was becoming unruly and perhaps riotous. Though once again the facts were in dispute, with the defense's witness claiming that the audience was calm, three witnesses for the state testified that they either uttered threats against Gilbert themselves or heard others make them. Several persons in the audience apparently suggested that Gilbert should be thrown in the river or driven down the street. There were also calls to hang him from a tree.[23] Holmes might have concluded that the circumstances were so threatening that Gilbert's speech was harmful per se. If he understood the case in this manner, then Holmes would have applied his external standard of liability. Gilbert knew facts that would have warned a rational and prudent person of the danger of further speech. He was thus beyond constitutional protection.

Even if these alternative explanations of Holmes's decision in *Gilbert* are plausible, they do not explain why he refused to join the majority opinion and only concurred in the result. The answer to this question lies within the majority opinion itself. Though Justice McKenna referred to Holmes's clear and present danger doctrine, his purpose was only to show that the right of free speech was not absolute. In no way did he endorse the view that a likelihood of harm was necessary before liability could be imposed on nonharmful speech. At most, McKenna was willing to say that the Court, in regard to free speech, had "distinguished times and occasions."[24] But the existence of war and Gilbert's unlawful purpose were evidently enough to place him beyond free speech.

Holmes could not join such an opinion. In his view, Gilbert was liable only because there was sufficient evidence that in the circumstances of the case he was guilty of an attempt or of engaging in speech that was harmful per se. Perhaps Holmes did not write a concurring opinion because his view of the basis of the defendant's liability did not square well with the charges laid against Gilbert in the indictment. But if he would have written an opinion, his rationale would have been far more narrowly drawn to the facts of the case than the majority's. It would have focused on why a jury could reasonably find that Gilbert's speech constituted an attempt or a harmful act.

Conspiracies

Holmes affirmed conspiracy convictions in *Schenck* because there was sufficient evidence of an unlawful agreement above and beyond the contents of the circular itself. The government had, for example, introduced into evidence the minutes of the meeting at which plans were made to obstruct the draft and the newspaper clippings of the names of persons recently drafted to whom the circulars were to be sent. There was evidence independent of the published circular that the defendants had associated together for an unlawful purpose. In *Frohwerk,* Holmes upheld the conviction, not because there was clear evidence in support of the government's indictment, but because he had no record of the evidence at all. In the conspiracy convictions examined below, his position varied with the kind and amount of evidence against the defendant and with whether the case originated in a state or federal court. The latter point was at times crucial, because the law that spelled out the jurisdiction of the Supreme Court did not give it as much latitude if the case came from a state rather than a lower federal court. In a case from a state, the Court could not at will overturn findings of simple facts.

In *Schaefer v. United States,* the majority upheld the conviction of three of the defendants for conspiracy: (*a*) to make false reports with the intent to interfere in the war effort and to promote the success of the enemies of the United States; (*b*) to cause insubordination in the military; and (*c*) to obstruct recruitment. The convictions of Schaefer and Vogel, the president and treasurer of the company that published the *Tagenblatt,* were overturned because of insufficient evidence that they were in any way responsible for the publications. In contrast, the conspiracy convictions of the editors and the business manager of the paper were upheld. The only evidence against the three men—Werner, Darkow, and Lemke—was that they had changed the articles. This was not enough for Holmes and Brandeis: "there was no evidence of conspiracy except the cooperation of editors and business manager in issuing the publications complained of."[25] Ambiguous speech activity was not enough evidence of a conspiracy even if the individuals had cooperated in some endeavor. If the speech's meaning was unclear, unlawful intent had to be shown independently.

The same situation reappeared in *Pierce v. United States.* Here the government explicitly argued that no other evidence of conspiracy other than the fact that the defendants had distributed the pamphlet was necessary.[26] And the trial judge permitted the jury to find an unlawful agreement even though the defendants had waited to distribute the pamphlet until they had a very good reason—Judge Rose's opinion acquitting different defendants for distributing the same circular—to believe that their actions were legal.[27] Brandeis and Holmes once again refused to find conspiracy merely because some people engaged in speech activity. As Brandeis said, "No evidence of intent . . . [to cause insubordination] was introduced unless it be found in the leaflet itself."[28] But the leaflet itself did not clearly indicate an unlawful purpose; its meaning was at best ambiguous. The conclusion is that Holmes and Brandeis would support conspiracy convictions only if there was more evidence of an agreed unlawful purpose than the publication complained of. The government's burden of establishing that an unlawful agreement had taken place was not met by the publication of an ambiguous leaflet.

Whitney v. California[29] was also a case of conspiracy. Though Whitney was indicted on five counts under California's Criminal Syndicalism law, she was only convicted of organizing and being a member of a syndicalist organization—a crime closely analogous to conspiracy.[30] It is true that at the trial the defense objected that there was no charge of conspiracy.[31] But on appeal this contention disappeared in favor of the claim that the indictment failed to identify which group, to which Whitney belonged, constituted a conspiracy. The California District Court of Appeal responded that the state had made it clear during *voir dire* (jury selection) and its opening statement that the illegal conspiratorial party to which Whitney belonged was the Oakland branch of the Communist Labor party of California.[32] Membership in that group justified Whitney's conviction.

In her brief to the United States Supreme Court, Whitney did not dispute California's claim that at bottom the case was one of conspiracy. Her main argument was rather that the district court of appeal's conclusion, that the Oakland branch of the Communist Labor party was a criminal conspiracy, was impossible. This group had never met formally after the state convention in 1919, and so the constitution of the Communist Labor party of California was never ratified.[33] Since the Oakland branch of the Communist Labor party did not formally exist, it could not be the basis of a conspiracy conviction. Even if the local had withdrawn from the Socialist party and had sent delegates to the Communist Labor party state convention, the defense claimed that it did not exist.

The defense also maintained that other organizations and meetings—the national convention of the American Socialist party in 1918, at which time the left-wing faction left to form the national Communist Labor party of America; the state convention of the Communist Labor party of California in 1919; a couple of meetings of the executive committee of the Communist Labor party of California that Whitney attended; and the IWW—were not, for various reasons, suitable bases for Whitney's conspiracy conviction.[34] Consequently, by the time the case reached the Supreme Court, there was no question that it was a case of conspiracy. In his majority opinion, Justice Sanford stated that the "essence of the offense denounced by the act is the combining with others in an association for accomplishment of the desired ends through the advocacy and use of criminal and unlawful methods. It partakes of the nature of a criminal conspiracy." And since there was no doubt that "united and joint action involves greater danger to the public peace and security than the isolated utterances and acts of individuals," it was "clear" that California's Criminal Syndicalism law was a reasonable exercise of the police power and not a violation of any right of free speech, assembly, or association.[35]

The majority's basic conclusion was that membership in a political party that advocated violence, no matter if there was neither a likelihood of harm nor any unlawful agreement to commit a specific illegal act, was enough to constitute a criminal conspiracy.[36] It was for this reason that Holmes and Brandeis refused to join the majority opinion. As Brandeis put it,

The felony which the statute created is a crime very unlike the old felony of conspiracy or the old misdemeanor of unlawful assembly. The mere act of assisting in forming a society for teaching syndicalism, of becoming a member of it, or of assembling with others for that purpose is given the dynamic quality of crime. There is guilt although the society may not contemplate immediate promulgation of the doctrine. . . . The novelty in the prohibition introduced is that the statute aims, not at the practice of criminal syndicalism, nor even directly at the preaching of it, but at association with those who propose to preach it.[37]

Brandeis simply refused "to assent to the suggestion in the majority opinion" that individuals had no right to form a political party "to advocate the desirability of a proletarian revolution by mass action at some date necessarily far in the future."[38] The crime of conspiracy was stretched too far, resulting in a violation of the rights of assembly and association.

Nevertheless, though Brandeis and Holmes implied that California's syndicalism law was unconstitutionally overbroad, they concurred in Whitney's conviction. Evidently, neither of them could accept Whitney's argument that the law was unconstitutionally applied to her.[39] They rejected this argument because they believed that the jury had sufficient evidence to convict her of conspiracy to commit specific illegal acts. Liability was properly imposed, in their view, because of her association with others for this purpose, not because of her association with others for the purpose of advocating some distant revolution. Testimony was introduced "which tended to establish the existence of a conspiracy on the part of members of the Industrial Workers of the World, to commit present serious crimes; and likewise to show that such a conspiracy would be furthered by the activity of the society of which Miss Whitney was a member."[40] The law may have been overbroad, but if the jury's findings of fact were respected, Whitney was outside of constitutional protection.

The witness at the trial who testified that Whitney was implicated in various conspiracies was John Dimond. He was a former secretary of the IWW local at Fresno who admitted that he had associated with the *cats*—the political terrorists of the organization. Dimond not only described acts of violence that members of the IWW committed for the purpose, among others, of forcing the state to release two convicted murderers, but also testified that he knew Whitney, that he saw her meet with other members of the IWW, and that she had circulated defense letters and an accompanying circular for the purpose of seeking the release of the "political prisoners."[41] When this testimony was combined with Whitney's support for a resolution at the convention of the Communist Labor party of California that called on the masses to use "their collective power to force the unconditional release of each and every one now serving a sentence as a political or class war prisoner,"[42] Brandeis and Holmes may well have concluded that there was sufficient evidence for a jury to find that Whitney was a member of a conspiracy to force the release of prisoners through violent crimes. Whitney's actions, as the jury found them, were thus beyond the constitutional right of association. There was no constitutional right to engage in criminal conspiracy.

Since there was some testimony that Whitney was involved in a conspiracy, Holmes and Brandeis could not overturn the conviction. The jurisdiction of the Supreme Court gave them no choice. The case was before the Court on a writ of error from a state, and therefore the factual findings could be reviewed only if

(1) a federal right has been denied as the result of a finding shown by the record to be without evidence to support it;
(2) where a conclusion of law as to federal right and finding of fact are so intermingled as to make it necessary, in order to pass upon the federal question, to analyze the facts.[43]

But neither of these exceptions applied in *Whitney*. There was certainly some evidence of a conspiracy and no federal right was intermingled with a finding of fact. All the crucial findings, which is often the case with conspiracies, were completely factual in character. Did an association have a criminal purpose? Was Whitney a member? What was her intent?[44] Whitney could only argue that there was no evidence to support her conviction, which conflicted with the record of the case. No matter how meager the evidence was, there was some testimony lying behind the jury's verdict. Accordingly, it may have been the rules governing the Court's jurisdiction that convinced Holmes and Brandeis that the Supreme Court had a negligible role to play in reviewing conspiracy cases coming from state courts. The free speech clause did not widen the Supreme Court's authority to second guess a state's findings of simple facts.

To some extent, however, Brandeis was willing to review a conspiracy case coming from a state if the defendant argued that there was no clear and present danger of harm: an obvious intermingling of fact and law. Even if Whitney was engaged in a conspiracy, Brandeis said, "it must remain open to a defendant to present the issue whether there actually did exist at the time a clear danger; whether the danger, if any, was imminent; and whether the evil apprehended was one so substantial as to justify the stringent restriction interposed by the legislature."[45] Whitney should have, but had not, raised this issue either at her trial or on appeal in the California courts. If she had done so, Brandeis reasoned, the issue would have been saved for review by the Supreme Court. As it was, the case was from a state court by way of a writ of error, and the Court only had jurisdiction over specific federal rights that were " 'specially set up' and denied by the [lower] court."[46] Since Whitney had failed to raise the issue of a clear, present, and substantial danger in California's courts, Brandeis thought it was inappropriate for him to examine the issue. He did note, however, that there was some testimony that tended to support an assessment that specific illegal acts were likely.[47]

Holmes's decision to join Brandeis's concurrence in *Whitney* is consistent with his general theory of free speech. Conspiracies were outside of constitutional protection, and the jury had heard evidence that linked Whitney to such a group. Yet it is somewhat surprising that he did not write his own concurrence. He could not join the majority opinion because he thought that the right to create a political party that advocated violent revolution in the distant future was privileged. Mere membership in a political party was not sufficient to constitute a criminal conspiracy unless the group's purpose was to engage in specific illegal acts.

I do not see, however, how Holmes could have agreed with the way Brandeis confused the clear-and-present-danger doctrine with conspiracy and the right of association. In his other writings and decisions, Holmes made it very clear that an unlawful agreement was a sufficient basis for liability no matter how remote or unlikely the specific illegal act was. The harmful purpose of the agreement was enough to withdraw the right of individuals to associate with one another. Hence, even if Whitney's counsel had followed Brandeis's recommendation by denying that there was a clear and present danger, there is some reason to believe that even then Holmes would have concurred with the result in *Whitney*. If the issue had been raised, it would have been within the Court's jurisdiction, but Holmes would have thought that the likelihood of harm was irrelevant in a case of conspiracy.

The companion cases of *Fiske v. Kansas*[48] and *Burns v. United States*[49] help clarify the Court's role in reviewing conspiracy cases. *Fiske* was a unanimous decision overturning a conviction under a criminal syndicalism statute, while *Burns* affirmed such a conviction, though Brandeis dissented. *Burns* was quite analogous to *Whitney*. The same California criminal syndicalism statute was involved, but the case arose in federal court because the offense was committed in Yosemite National Park. Federal law provided that if an act done in the park violated the laws of California, the defendant would be "subject to the same punishment as the laws of California prescribe for a like offense."[50]

Burns was charged, on the basis of his activities in the IWW, with being a member of an organization that advocated criminal syndicalism and with helping to organize the same. There was no doubt that Burns belonged to the IWW. His membership and printed material that was in his possession at the time of his arrest were introduced into evidence. In the Supreme Court's judgment, the printed material established that the IWW "advocated, taught, and aided various acts of 'sabotage' that are plainly within the meaning of the [criminal syndicalism] act."[51] The statute itself only prohibited advocacy of *sabotage* that was intended to cause physical damage or injury to physical property. Any kind of advocacy that was intended only to reduce an employer's profits was outside the statute. Though the trial judge had instructed the jury that the advocacy of any act that intentionally reduced profits was sabotage, the majority thought the error was nonprejudicial to the defendant. The opinion noted that the trial judge twice defined sabotage in the language of the statute, and that his instructions generally required advocacy of willful destruction of property or other criminal acts.[52]

In my opinion, Holmes joined the majority opinion in *Burns,* rather than concur in the result as he had done in *Whitney,* because Justice Butler's opinion in *Burns* was drawn far more narrowly than Justice Sanford's *Whitney.* While Sanford favored imposing liability on a person who joined a political party that advocated a revolution in the distant future, Butler confined his *opinion* to the current criminal activities and plans of the IWW or of informal groups within the wider organization. Based on the evidence introduced at the trial, he listed the types of illegal acts that the IWW advocated in its literature.

Some examples are: Injuring machinery when employed to use it, putting emery dust in lubricating oil, damaging materials when using them in manufacture or otherwise, scattering foul seeds in fields, driving tacks and nails in grape vines and fruit trees to kill them, using acid to destroy guy wires holding up the poles provided to support growing vines, putting pieces of wire and the like among vines to destroy machines used to gather crops, scattering matches and using chemicals to start fires to destroy property of employers.[53]

It seems that the IWW (or small groups within it) was not only advocating destruction of property, but was in fact planning and participating in such illegal activities. It is therefore not surprising that Holmes believed that the jury had sufficient evidence to convict Burns of conspiracy. He joined the majority opinion accordingly.

The puzzle of this case is not so much why Holmes was with the majority but why Brandeis dissented. Since it is fairly clear that Burns was more deeply immersed in the illegal activities of the IWW than Whitney, how could he affirm Whitney's conviction but vote to reverse Burns's? One plausible explanation is that the rules of the Supreme Court's jurisdiction determined Brandeis's decisions in the two cases. In contrast to *Whitney, Burns* was before the Court on a writ of error from a lower federal court. Brandeis therefore insisted that all the "alleged errors at the trial which were properly excepted to are therefore before us." [54] He then focused on an objection that Burn's attorney had made to the relevancy of certain testimony. A witness had testified about an IWW member's speech that advocated loading ships in a way that created more work. The defense claimed that such testimony was immaterial, because advocacy of activity that was only meant to reduce an employer's profits was outside of the statute. The trial judge overruled the objection, claiming that any deliberate attempt to reduce the profits of the employer was an injury within the act.[55]

Brandeis was willing to reverse Burn's conviction on the ground that the judge's ruling was prejudicial error.[56] His vote to reverse was therefore based on the right of a fair trial, not free speech. He took this step even though Burns had not objected to the admission of such evidence in his brief to the Supreme Court, and even though there was plenty of evidence indicating that the IWW had advocated other types of violent illegal acts that were clearly within the meaning of the statute. The more incriminating evidence was set aside because, in his opinion, it "related, in the main, to acts of individuals," [57] not to the organization of the IWW. Also, erroneous rulings at a trial were presumptively prejudicial.[58] It therefore did not matter if the other evidence was clear and convincing. The main point, however, is that Brandeis thought that the Supreme Court should exercise its power to review cases coming from lower federal courts "to correct errors committed below, although objection was not taken there."[59] It was for this reason that he dissented in *Burns.*

Brandeis's dissent in *Burns* provides additional evidence that the Supreme Court's rules of jurisdiction explain his concurrence in *Whitney v. United States.* If the rules involving a writ of error from a state court had permitted him "to correct errors committed below although objection was not taken there," then Brandeis, in all likelihood, would have overturned Whitney's conviction on the ground that the state had not shown a clear and present danger. The fact that Whitney had not argued this point before the Supreme Court would have been irrelevant, as it was in *Burns.* But since the rules governing cases coming from state courts on a writ of error confined the Court's jurisdiction to claims "specially set up," Brandeis concurred in Whitney's conviction. If these rules of jurisdiction are kept in mind, then Brandeis's opinions in *Whitney* and *Burns* appear to be consistent.

Fiske v. Kansas shows that there was a limit beyond which the Supreme Court would not tolerate the suppression of political association by way of conspiracy statutes. In this case, Kansas had imposed liability not because Fiske had conspired to commit illegal acts or to advocate specific illegal acts. What was at issue was whether his membership in the IWW alone was sufficient to justify a conviction. The state said membership alone was enough, and Fiske was convicted on the ground that he invited new members to read the preamble of the constitution of the IWW. Though the preamble did not in any explicit way advocate violence, Kansas courts upheld the conviction. No other evidence, whether of the nature of the activity advocated by the IWW or of Fiske's involvement in it, was introduced. The state maintained that the language of the preamble was "equivocal," capable of conveying a "sinister" intent, and that was enough to justify the conviction.[60]

Though Fiske had links to the IWW, a unanimous Supreme Court overturned the conviction. Even if Fiske was an organizer in the same group to which Burns and Whitney had belonged, the state had failed to provide independent evidence of either the illegal character of the IWW or of Fiske's knowledge and support of any specific illegal activity. Yet *Fiske v. Kansas,* like *Whitney,* was before the Court on a writ of error from a state court. It might therefore seem that the Court would have been obliged to defer to the state's findings of conspiracy. In *Fiske,* however, the Court exercised one of the exceptions (noted above) to the rule that facts were beyond its jurisdiction in a case coming from a state court by way of a writ of error. It said that "this Court will review the findings of facts by a State court where a federal right has been denied as the result of a finding shown by the record to be *without* evidence to support it." (Emphasis mine).[61] There was some evidence of a conspiracy introduced in *Burns* and *Whitney,* but only the preamble of the IWW's constitution in *Fiske.* A unanimous Court agreed that Fisk's rights were violated because there was no evidence to substantiate the state's case.

The general point is that the rules governing the Supreme Court's jurisdiction had a crucial impact on how it decided cases of criminal syndicalism. A case of conspiracy coming from a state court by way of a writ of error was likely to be upheld. It was for this reason that Holmes was inclined to uphold convictions if there was some evidence that an individual belonged to a group whose purpose was to engage in specific illegal acts. This was especially true if there was corroborative evidence, beyond the defendant's speech activity, of the speaker's illegal purpose. The factual character of conspiracy (since a clear and present danger did not have to be shown) and the Court's rules of jurisdiction gave the Supreme Court a negligible role to play in cases of criminal syndicalism. As an appellate judge, Holmes was predisposed to defer to a lower court's findings of simple fact. But in conspiracy cases coming from state courts by way of a writ of error, the rules controlling the Supreme Court's jurisdiction gave him no choice but to affirm convictions unless there was no evidence supporting the verdict.

False Reports and Statements

A new type of issue that came before the Court in 1919–20 was the publication of false reports or statements with unlawful intent. The Espionage Act punished such falsehoods if the intent was to interfere with the military forces or to promote the success of the enemies of the United States. Two of the five defendants in *Schaefer v. United States*[62] faced indictments of this character, and the Supreme Court's decision to uphold the convictions on these counts was especially tragic. The defendants were editors of a Philadelphia newspaper, the *Tagenblatt,* and they were responsible for taking articles from other newspapers, translating them into German if necessary, and publishing them in the *Tagenblatt* with small alterations. Were such alterations "false reports" or "false statements" in the sense of the Espionage Act? The various ways in which the trial judge, government attorneys, and the Supreme Court answered this question indicate that the defendants never were treated fairly.

The trial judge, against the defense's objections, instructed the jury that "the substantial thing which you are to pass upon is, was the report or statement that they put out false? Was it wilfully and knowingly false?"[63] Since the judge advised the jury to use their general knowledge to decide if the articles were false or not,[64] it is fairly clear that he ignored the altered character of the articles[65] and focused instead on the actual falsity of what was written. At the trial, if the defendants were guilty, they were guilty because they uttered actual falsehoods, not because they altered articles taken from other newspapers. With these instructions, the defendants were convicted of intentionally making false statements.

On appeal the defense contended that liability could not be based on the falsity of the defendants' statements, since such charges were not laid in the indictment.[66] It would appear that the government found this argument persuasive, since it reversed course and argued that the Espionage Act prohibited "false reports" as well as "false statements." The latter referred to lies about external reality; the former to altered reports of someone else's characterization of reality.

If the newspapers falsify the matter received by them so as to make a false report thereof to their readers, one of the important sources of public information is made an obstruction, instead of an aid, to the ascertainment of truth. Whether the false "report" is true as a matter of fact, or is nearer the truth than the facts as ascertained by the reporter is immaterial, since the reader is entitled to make up his own mind as to this.[67]

Accordingly, "false reports" were to be punished even if the altered report was closer to the truth than the original. This was the government's new position, even though the jury never examined whether there were any discrepancies between the *Tagenblatt* articles and the originals. The defendants were guilty, not because they had uttered falsehoods, but because they had falsely reported what other newspapers had written.

The majority of the Court could not accept the government's argument. The implication that a newspaper could be liable even though the alterations it made to the original article were in fact justifiable corrections was too much for them. Instead, returning to the trial judge's theory of the case, the majority preferred to think that the "gist of the case" was whether the dispatches were "received and then changed to express falsehood."[68] The Court came down on this side of the issue even though the trial court heard no evidence as to the actual truth or falsity of what the *Tagenblatt* published, and even though the original indictments had only alleged acts of alteration, not acts of publishing falsehoods.

That Holmes joined Brandeis in dissent is not surprising. It was a clear issue of statutory construction. By that part of the Espionage Act that punished false reports and statements, Brandeis argued, "Congress sought thereby to protect the American people from being wilfully misled to the detriment of their cause by one actuated by the intention to further the cause of the enemy. . . . Such is the kind of false statement, and the only kind which, under any rational construction, is made criminal by the act."[69] It was thus irrelevant that the defendants altered the original stories. They were guilty only if they published falsehoods with the intent of helping Germany. But since the indictment did not allege that the defendants had willfully published falsehoods, and since no evidence of the publication's truth or falsity (apart from general knowledge) was introduced at the trial, there was no basis for a conviction.

The more difficult case concerning the constitutional issue of punishing false statements arose in 1920 in *Pierce v. United States*.[70] The government maintained that the defendants had circulated a pamphlet (*The Price We Pay*) that contained obvious falsehoods.[71] They were accordingly charged with, among other things, distributing false statements with the intent to interfere with the war effort.[72] The government conceded that the defendants could be convicted on this count only if the statements were of fact; only if they were false; only if the speaker knew them to be false or recklessly disregarded their truth or falsity; and only if the defendants acted with the required unlawful intent.[73]

The government, however, argued, and the majority of the Court agreed, that it was usually within the province of the jury to decide if a statement was one of fact and if it was false.[74] The evidence presented by the government to prove the falsity of the defendants' statements was therefore relevant but hardly necessary. "Common knowledge . . . would have sufficed to show at least that the statements as to the causes that led to the entry of the United States into the war against Germany were grossly false; and such common knowledge went to prove also that the defendants knew they were untrue."[75] The objection that the statements were not factual in nature (in that they were not meant to be taken literally) was dismissed by the majority. As a matter of law, it could not be said that a considerable number of readers would not have taken the statements "in a literal sense and take them seriously."[76]

Brandeis's dissent denied that the defendants were properly convicted of making false statements with unlawful intent. Even though he accepted generally the government's criteria in the case, he added another consideration and reduced the role of the jury. As the government had argued, the statement had to be factual in character, false, and known to be false. But these issues, in the opinion of Brandeis and Holmes, were not to be left entirely to a jury. The court should have decided whether the statements were factual claims, expressions of opinion, comment, or interpretation of the facts. On this point, Brandeis concluded, "All the alleged false statements were an interpretation and discussion of public facts of public interest. . . . There is no reason to believe that Congress, in prohibiting a special class of false statements, intended to interfere with what was obviously comment as distinguished from a statement."[77]

Holmes's opinion in *Gandia v. Pettingill*[78] was cited to support this position, which suggests that he had played a role in shaping Brandeis's approach. In this earlier libel case, Holmes had argued that any comment on the actions of a public officer was privileged unless the publisher's motive was malicious. And the question whether a particular statement was comment or a statement of fact was one for the judge, not the jury. Holmes and Brandeis interpreted the provision of the Espionage Act referring to "false reports" and "false statements" in a similar fashion. It only applied to false statements of fact, and the judge, not the jury, was to decide if a publication was of such a character that a jury should determine its truth or falsity.

But even if the statements were factual in nature, which Holmes and Brandeis denied, and even if the statements were false, there was no evidence that the defendants knew them to be false. They denied the majority's assertion that the jury could move from common knowledge to the conclusion that the defendants must have known that what they published was false. But the more important point is to see how Brandeis and Holmes emphasized, in cases involving liability for false reports or statements, the importance of unlawful intent and the necessity of a clear and present danger. The majority merely assumed that the false statements were published with the intent to interfere with the war effort and denied that any likelihood of harm had to be shown before liability could be imposed.[79] In contrast, Brandeis and Holmes took the unlawful-intent requirement much more seriously. The state's only evidence of unlawful intent was the tendency of the contents of the publication, which was insufficient in their opinion to establish unlawful intent when the publication was at all ambiguous. It should also be remembered that the defendants did not distribute the leaflet until after a federal judge had ruled that it was legal to do so. The contents of a leaflet that a federal judge had already ruled innocuous were clearly not sufficient, in the opinion of Holmes and Brandeis, to establish unlawful intent.

Brandeis's and Holmes's dissent added, beyond unlawful intent, another requirement before liability could be imposed: "the nature of the words used and the circumstances under which they were used showed affirmatively that they did not 'create a clear and present danger' that thereby the operations or success of our military and naval forces would be interfered with."[80] This passage from Brandeis's dissent once again suggests Holmes's influence. The literal words of the statute imposed liability on willful harmless falsehoods if uttered with the intent to interfere with the war effort. This result conflicted with Holmes's general approach to liability: if they were harmless, the law should leave evil-intentioned people alone. He therefore interpolated the additional requirement of a clear and present danger into the statute to square it with his doctrine of attempt. If a person intentionally created a likelihood of immediate harm to the war effort, that person committed an attempt whether his or her objective was gained by uttering truths or falsehoods.

Sanctions Other Than Legal Liability

There are a number of Holmes's opinions that deserve attention even though they fall outside of his strict theory of free speech. These cases were not clearly within his theory because they did not involve legal liability, at least not in its usual sense. For example, could a state dismiss a police officer who engaged in speech and associational activities that were prohibited by police regulations? While a judge on the Massachusetts Supreme Court, Holmes addressed this issue in *McAuliffe v. New*

Bedford.[81] A police officer was found by the mayor of New Bedford to have solicited money and aid for political purposes and to have been a member of a political committee. Both of these activities conflicted with police regulations, and he was discharged accordingly.

Holmes gave the short answer to the officer's claim that the applicable regulation violated his right of free speech: "The petitioner may have a constitutional right to talk politics, but he has no constitutional right to be a policeman."[82] The case did not concern the constitutional right of free speech because public employment was a privilege, not a right. Since removal from public service was not equivalent to legal liability, the police officer was not protected by the right of free speech. As this book has argued throughout, Holmes's theory of legal liability defined the scope of free speech. It was thus hard for him to perceive a case as one of free speech if legal liability was not involved.

Holmes's opinion in *McAuliffe* might seem to our generation to be extremely insensitive to the value of free speech. It should be noted, however, that even today public employment does justify "reasonable" regulations limiting a public employee's right of free speech.[83] And though his aphorism denying any constitutional right to be a police officer was stated in absolute terms, Holmes's actual ruling was qualified. He said that "on the same principle" that permitted a private employer to offer employment on the condition that the employee suspend, presumably during the hours of employment, constitutional rights of free speech and idleness, "the city may impose any *reasonable* condition [including ones that did control leisure time] upon holding offices within its control" (emphasis mine).[84] Hence, even if his theoretical perspective inclined him to overlook the free speech values that were lurking in the case, Holmes was sufficiently sensitive to say that any restriction of a public employee's right of free speech had to be reasonable—a conclusion not far removed from contemporary law.

Another early case that reveals how Holmes's theory of liability restricted the scope of his theory of free speech was *Commonwealth v. Davis*.[85] Can the city of Boston punish public speaking on the Boston Common without a permit? Even though a small fine was involved, the case was outside of Holmes's theory of liability since it concerned the special regulations an owner—the city—could make in regard to the use of its property. The public was as free as any private landowner to restrict the use of public lands. "For the Legislature absolutely or conditionally to forbid public speaking in a highway or public park is no more an infringement of the rights of a member of the public than for the owner of a private house to forbid it in his house."[86] Davis may have a constitutional right to speak, but he does not have a constitutional right to speak on public property.

Here again, as in *McAuliffe*, Holmes failed to see the issue as one of free speech. He even described the argument that the case involved free speech as one implying "the same kind of fallacy that was dealt with in *McAuliffe v. New Bedford.* . . . It assumes that the ordinance is directed against free speech . . . whereas in fact it is directed toward the modes in which Boston Common may be used."[87] It is therefore obvious that the two early Massachusetts cases were, in Holmes's own mind, of the same character. Reasonable regulations of public employment or the use of public lands raised no constitutional issue of free speech because they were outside of his theory of liability. In the former case, no liability was involved, and in the latter, the rules violated were those of a landowner, even if the landowner in this particular case, the state, had the power to impose fines for any infraction. This special kind of liability was completely independent of Holmes's theory of legal liability. Accordingly, he had difficulty conceiving the case as one of free speech.

The general principle of *Commonwealth v. Davis* is indisputable. Cities and states can require permits to use public lands if the licensing statutes are "properly drawn" to limit discretion of municipal officials.[88] History, however, has rejected Holmes's claim that a state could *absolutely* forbid public speaking. Today, there is a general recognition that citizens have a constitutional right of access; states and cities are obliged to give citizens a public forum, including at least public parks and streets, even though reasonable regulations of the forum are still constitutional.[89] Holmes, in contrast, gave the city much more latitude to do with its property as it willed. The only possible restriction hinted at in his *Davis* opinion was that cities or states could not discriminate among types of speech, applying different regulations to them. Against the objection that the ordinance requiring a permit to use the Boston Common was "directed essentially against free preaching of the Gospel in public places, as certain Western ordinances seemingly general have been held to be directed against the Chinese," Holmes replied that he had "no reason to believe, and do not believe, that this ordinance was passed for any other than its ostensible purpose, namely, as a proper regulation of the use of public grounds."[90] Since the rules were impartial as to types of speech and rested on the state's special power as a property owner, no constitutional claim of free speech was involved.

In 1921, Holmes considered a case analogous to the preceding ones, even though he dissented from the majority opinion denying the free-speech claim.[91] Burleson, the postmaster general, had revoked from the *Milwaukee Leader,* a newspaper published by the Social Democratic party, its second-class postage rate on the ground that articles published in it violated the Espionage Act. To avoid the more expensive rate classifications, the paper sued, arguing that the government's action violated free speech. In response, Burleson claimed that his actions were authorized by the Espionage Act, which declared that any publications that violated the act were "non-mailable," and by the Classification Act of 1879, which required that periodicals or newspapers receive the second-class rate only if they were "regularly issued" and "published for the dissemination of information of a public character."[92] The government argued that issues containing the illegal "non-mailable" articles were full of lies and distortions. They could not be counted as "regular issues," and they showed that the paper was not being "published for the dissemination of information." If so, the government reasoned, the *Leader* was neither "regularly issued" nor was it published for "the dissemination of information." It was therefore not entitled to the second-class rate.[93] The government assured the Court that the *Milwaukee Leader* could immediately apply for a new second-class permit, and that one would be immediately granted if recent issues of the newspaper did not conflict with the Espionage Act.[94] Nonetheless, the Classification Act gave the government the right to revoke the privileged rate because the Espionage Act made certain material nonmailable.

The majority of the court accepted this argument, but Holmes and Brandeis dissented. Holmes's dissent is puzzling because his opinions in his earlier Massachusetts cases suggest that he would have been with the majority. After all, if a person had a constitutional right to talk politics but not to be a police officer, then how could a newspaper be entitled to a subsidized rate of postage, especially if the newspaper was violating the Espionage Act. Certainly a right to a subsidized rate of postage was as much a privilege as public employment. If the former was consti-tutionally subject to reasonable regulations, so also was the latter. Seditious newspapers could be excluded from the mail, just as the police officer who talked politics could be excluded from public employment.

Such an argument must have seemed powerful to Holmes. He began his dissent with the observation, "At first it seemed to me that if a publisher should announce in terms that he proposed to print treason, and should demand a second class rate, it must be that the Postmaster General would have authority to refuse it.[95] But he came down on the other side because Brandeis had convinced him that the statutes referred to by Burleson did not authorize his actions. The relevant statutes permitted the postmaster general to return to the sender any specific items that were nonmailable, whether because they were obscene materials, lottery tickets, or publications in violation of the Espionage Act. But the postmaster general had no statutory authority to deny to a newspaper a subsidized rate of postage.

Despite what the government had argued, the *Milwaukee Leader* was still entitled, in Brandeis's opinion to the second-class rate because it was "regularly issued," even if some of the issues were nonmailable. And it was published for "the dissemination of information," even if some of the information was false.[96] The case was one of statutory construction,[97] and according to Holmes and Brandeis, the government's interpretation of the law was bad. There was therefore no inherent incongruity between Holmes's early Massachusetts cases and his *Burleson* dissent. The owners of the *Milwaukee Leader* had a constitutional right to publish their newspaper; they did not have a constitutional right to a subsidized rate of postage. The latter was a statutory right subject to Congress's discretion.

However, certain features of his dissent do not square well with the above conclusion that Holmes believed that the *Milwaukee Leader* had no constitutional right to a subsidized rate of postage. It is true that he did say, "The United States may give up the Postoffice when it sees fit," which coincides perfectly with what he had said earlier about the state's power to forbid all public speaking in parks or on highways. But then he added that while the government carries the mail

the use of the mails is almost as much a part of free speech as the right to use our tongues; and it would take very strong language to convince me that Congress ever intended to give such a practically despotic power to any one man. There is no pretense that it has done so. Therefore I do not consider the limits of its constitutional power.[98]

Coming from Holmes, this hint that such a statute—one that gave the postmaster general discretionary authority to decide if the views of particular citizens were entitled to a governmental privilege—was unconstitutional is surprising. Had he changed his mind, was he inconsistent, or is the above quote in some way reconcilable with what he had said in the earlier cases?

Holmes had hinted in *Davis* that if the permit requirement was directed at a certain type of speech, it might be unlawful. Perhaps he would have come down on the other side in *Davis* if the ordinance gave one official the authority to decide arbitrarily who could speak on the Boston Common and who could not. But even so, his claim that the "use of the mails is almost as much a part of free speech as the right to use our tongues" reveals a shift in attitude. Since the use of the mails was a privilege, a service provided by the government, the early Holmes would have had difficulty even conceiving of it as an issue of free speech. In his early period, his theory of liability had exclusively defined the scope of the right of free speech, and a revocation of a subsidized mail rate would have fallen outside of constitutional protection. At some point, Holmes had become more sensitive to free speech. Whether he gradually or suddenly came to this appreciation is not known. What is clear is that by 1919 he upheld free-speech claims, even if sanctions other than civil or criminal liability were being applied.

Holmes's dissent in *United States v. Schwimmer*[99] confirms, in a very eloquent way, the conclusion that he widened the scope of his theory of free speech beyond the core criteria of his theory of liability. A federal district court had denied Schwimmer citizenship because she was "not attached to the principles of the Constitution of the United States and not well disposed to the good order and happiness of the same."[100] The evidence for this judgment was that Schwimmer, though willing to take the oath of allegiance, would neither swear to her willingness to fight to defend the country nor refrain from persuading others of the validity of her views.[101] The majority upheld the lower court's decision on the ground that Congress had absolute control over naturalization,[102] that the statute justified examining the applicant's willingness to fight and her disposition to hinder others from the performance of their obligations,[103] and that in this case there was sufficient evidence to support the lower court's finding that Schwimmer did not meet the standards of the statute.

Since a grant of citizenship was a privilege, having nothing to do with liability, it could be supposed that Holmes would find the majority's reasoning persuasive. He had, after all, written in an analogous case, "It is admitted that sovereign states have inherent power to deport aliens, and seemingly that Congress is not deprived of this power by the Constitution of the United States."[104] But if Congress can at its discretion establish conditions for the privilege of residing in the United States, then why does it not have power to deny the privilege of citizenship to those residents that fail to satisfy its qualifications? Schwimmer, the argument would go, may have a right to be a pacifist, but she has no constitutional right to be an American pacifist.

But the surprise is that Holmes dissented in the case. And his reasoning rested heavily on the idea that

if there is any principle of the Constitution that more imperatively calls for attachment than any other it is the principle of free thought—not free thought for those who agree with us but freedom for the thought that we hate. I think that we should adhere to that principle with regard to admission into, as well as to life within, this country.[105]

How far Holmes would have been willing to push this doctrine is impossible to say. He did note that Schwimmer held "none of the now-dread creeds, but thoroughly believes in organized government and prefers that of the United States to any other in the world,"[106] which suggests that he still might have thought that Congress had the power to deny citizenship to anarchists and communists. In his fashion, he probably thought the issue was one of degree, and that Schwimmer's beliefs— quite similar to the Quakers' who "have done their share to make the country what it is"[107]—were not pernicious enough to justify a denial of citizenship. And since Schwimmer was a woman over fifty years of age who would not have been "allowed to bear arms if she wanted to," it was a nice case for Holmes to cut into Congress's power over naturalization. It raises the question, despite what he said about Congress's "inherent" power to deport aliens, whether he would have in 1929 allowed Congress to deport aliens who were merely propagating pacifism. It is anyone's guess how he would have responded to such a case. However, his dissent in *Schwimmer* shows conclusively that Holmes widened constitutional protection beyond his traditional theory of free speech. Free speech protected speakers not only from civil and criminal liability, but also, to an unclear degree, from a loss of privileges.

Summary

An examination of the cases in which Holmes did not write a major opinion or dissent has provided a deeper understanding of how he applied his theory of speech to different types of prosecutions and extended his commitment to free speech beyond the limits of his basic approach. If the publication was ambiguous, he insisted on evidence of unlawful intent beyond the tendency of the contents of the publication itself. In the case of attempts, he also gave the state the burden of proving that a speech act posed a clear and present danger. Whether what the speaker said was false or true, the state could impose liability only if there was unlawful intent and a real proximity of harm. In cases of conspiracy, however, he abandoned the latter requirement. All that had to be shown was that there was some evidence for a jury to conclude that persons had combined to reach a specific illegal objective. If there was such evidence independent of the ambiguous speech activity itself, Holmes would generally affirm convictions, especially if the case came from a state court on a writ of error. The rules that defined the Supreme Court's jurisdiction gave him less discretion in such a case than one that came from a lower federal court. Though this was his basic approach to cases of free speech, there is some evidence that he became more willing to uphold free speech claims against a government's desire to withdraw or withhold a privilege. This new branch of Holmes's theory did not conflict in any way with his more basic theory, but rather complemented it. Its significance in the development of his thought, however, cannot be denied.

Notes

1. 252 U.S. 239 (1920).
2. Id. at 249.
3. In his dissent, Brandeis made this point explicitly in reference to the attempt charge (see id. at 272).
4. Brief on the Behalf of the United States at 8, *Pierce*.
5. See *Pierce v. United States*, 252 U.S. 239, 248 (1920).
6. Brandeis also discussed the absence of a clear and present danger in regard to the attempt charge (id. at 272–73).
7. 251 U.S. 466 (1920).

8. Id. at 479.
9. Id. at 483. Also at 486.
10. Id. at 484.
11. 254 U.S. 325 (1920).
12. Gilbert gave a speech before a crowd of approximately two hundred persons in which he said, "We are going over to Europe to make the world safe for democracy, but I tell you we had better make America safe for democracy first. You say, what is the matter with our democracy? I tell you what is the matter with it: Have you had anything to say as to who should be President? Have you had anything to say as to who should be governor of this state? Have you had anything to say as to whether we should go into this war? You know you have not. If this is such a good democracy, for Heaven's sake, why should we not vote on conscription of men? We were stampeded into this war by newspaper rot to pull England's chestnuts out of the fire for her. I tell you, if they conscripted wealth like they have conscripted men, this war would not last over forty-eight hours" (see *Gilbert v. Minnesota,* 254 U.S. 325, 327 [1920]). Note that the judge's instruction to the jury that they must find that Gilbert "advocated" or "taught" implied that liability could be imposed only if Gilbert's intention had been to obstruct recruitment or the war effort.
13. Record at 236, *Gilbert.*
14. Id. at 286.
15. Brief for Defendant in Error at 19, *Gilbert.*
16. Id. at 20.
17. See Record at 285–86, *Gilbert.*
18. Id.
19. Record at 11, 56, 132, *Gilbert.*
20. Id. at 37.
21. See Brief for the Plaintiff in Error, *Gilbert.*
22. There was evidence that there was at least one person subject to the draft in the crowd of 150–200 persons. See Record at 112, *Gilbert.*
23. Id. at 123.
24. *Gilbert v. Minnesota,* 254 U.S. 325, 332 (1920).
25. *Schaefer v. United States,* 251 U.S. 466, 483 (1920).
26. Brief on Behalf of the United States, at 7–8, *Pierce.*
27. Id. at 10.
28. *Pierce v. United States,* 252 U.S. 239, 272 (1920).
29. 274 U.S. 359 (1927).
30. Id. at 360.
31. Record at 276, 288, *Whitney.*
32. See the Appendix to the Appellant's Petition for a Hearing by the California Supreme Court at ii, *Whitney.*
33. Brief for Plaintiff in Error at 20, *Whitney.* The defense's claim on appeal was that the failure of the state to identify the organization in the indictment was a violation of due process (id. at 24, 35).

34. Whitney was not at the national convention in 1918; she attended the state convention of California but supported the use of political measures to take power; no evidence whatever was presented of Whitney's role at the meetings of the executive committee; and she was not a member of the IWW (see id. at 39–49).

35. *Whitney v. California*, 274 U.S. 357, 371–72 (1927).

36. Also, the evidence substantiating the claim that the party advocated violence could be rather oblique. The fact that the Communist Labor party of California voted down a resolution in favor of political action (one that Whitney herself supported) and endorsed the national platform of the party was thought to be crucial. The national platform stated that the Communist Labor party of America adhered to the Communist Manifesto of the Third International, commended the work of the IWW, and applauded the Seattle and Winnipeg strikes. The state accordingly argued that the statements, propaganda, and activities of the Third International and the IWW could be introduced as evidence of the character of the local organization to which, it was alleged, Whitney belonged. For the defense's objection to the introduction of this evidence, see Record at 276–280, Appellant's Petition for a Hearing by the California Supreme Court at 2–5, Brief for the Plaintiff in Error at 15–16, *Whitney*. For the state's view that such evidence was relevant to deciding the nature and character of the Oakland branch of the Communist Labor party of California, see the trial judge's instructions, Record at 46, District Court of Appeal's opinion, Appendix to Appellant's Petition for a Hearing by the California Supreme Court at IV–V, and Brief of Defendant in Error at 3–5, *Whitney*.

37. *Whitney v. California*, 274 U.S. 357, 372–73 (1927).

38. Id. at 379.

39. See Supplementary Brief for Plaintiff in Error at 18, *Whitney*.

40. *Whitney v. United States*, 274 U.S. 357, 379 (1927).

41. Record at 274, 281–85, *Whitney*.

42. Record at 310, *Whitney*. But Whitney denied that she was advocating the use of violence to release the prisoners.

43. *Aetna Life Ins. Co. v. Dunken*, 266 U.S. 389, 394 (1924), cited in Supplementary Brief for Plaintiff in Error at 26, *Whitney*.

44. These were the three issues of the case according to the state, and each issue was one of fact that was outside the jurisdiction of the Supreme Court. See Brief of Defendant in Error at 29, *Whitney*. The defense argued time and time again that the state had failed to show unlawful intent on the part of Whitney and that without such a showing she could not be convicted of conspiracy. See, for example, Brief for Plaintiff in Error at 25, *Whitney*. The trial judge had instructed the jury that they must find unlawful intent, but "that the law presumes that every man intends the natural consequences of his acts" (Record at 40, *Whitney*). Though the trial judge conceded that the presumption was rebuttable, he hinted that the jury could find unlawful

intent from the fact that Whitney voluntarily joined the Communist Labor party. The District Court of Appeal went further: not only was the claim that Whitney had no unlawful intent described as "past belief," but also the Court stated it was "one of the conclusive presumptions of our law that a guilty intent is presumed from the deliberate commission of an unlawful act (see the Opinion, Appendix to Appellant's Petition for a Hearing by the Supreme Court at V, *Whitney*). This was a harsh rule, at least according to Holmes's notion of conspiracy, because the voluntary joining of the Communist Labor party was unlawful only if Whitney was engaged in a conspiracy, only if her purpose was unlawful. The fact that Holmes ignored the issue of specific intent in *Whitney* is an issue that needs explanation. In my judgment, the answer is that *Whitney* was a case of conspiracy from a state court on a writ of error and Holmes considered the crucial facts to be issues outside of his jurisdiction.

45. *Whitney v. California,* 274 U.S. 357, 379 (1927).
46. *Seabord A. L. R. Co. v. Duvall,* 225 U.S. 477, 487 (1912), cited by Brandeis, *Whitney v. California,* 274 U.S. 359, 380 (1927). See also cases cited by the majority opinion, id. at 362–63.
47. See *Whitney v. California,* 274 U.S. 359, 379 (1927).
48. 274 U.S. 380 (1927).
49. 274 U.S. 328 (1927).
50. Id. at 330.
51. Id. at 333.
52. Id. at 331–36.
53. Id. at 333.
54. Id. at 337.
55. Id. at 339.
56. Id. at 337.
57. Id. at 340.
58. Id.
59. Id. at 341.
60. *Fiske v. Kansas,* 274 U.S. 380, 382–85 (1927).
61. Id. at 385.
62. 251 U.S. 466 (1920).
63. Record at 752, *Schaefer.*
64. Id. at 743.
65. The key alterations that were the basis of the conviction were discussed by Brandeis in his dissent. In brief, they were: (1) adding a sentence to a story concerning America's ability to export foodstuffs; (2) omitting a sentence from a story concerning the Russian defense against German aggression; (3) translating the word *breadlines* from a speech by Senator La Follette into *brot-riots,* which meant *bread-riots* (see Brandeis's dissent, *Schaefer v. United States,* 251 U.S. 466, 486–94 [1920]). In regard to the last example, the defendant testified that there was no exact German equivalent for the

expression *breadlines*. Since a literal translation would have given German readers the impression of lines of bread, he had no choice but to use the term *brot-riots* (see Record at 529–31, *Schaefer*).

66. See Brief of Plaintiffs in Error at 16, *Schaefer*.

67. Brief for the United States at 18, *Schaefer*.

68. *Schaefer v. United States*, 251 U.S. 466, 473 (1920). The Court's response to the article "For the Fourth of July," published in the *Tagenblatt* on 4 July 1917, indicates that the majority had adopted the trial judge's view of the case. The article was a sufficient basis for liability, not because it was altered, but because the alterations were false. "And its statements were deliberate and wilfully false, the purpose being to represent that the war was not demanded by the people, but was the result of the machinations of executive power" (id. at 481).

69. Id. at 492–93.

70. 252 U.S. 239 (1920).

71. The following excerpts from the circular were false according to the government: (1) "In to your homes the recruiting officers are coming. They will take your sons of military age and impress them into the Army. . . . And still the recruiting officers will come; seizing age after age, mounting up to the elder ones and taking the younger ones as they grow to soldier size" (the government argued that recruitment officers only deal with enlistment and have nothing to do with impressment); (2) "The Attorney General of the United States is so busy sending to prison men who do not stand up when the Star Spangled Banner is played, that he has not time to protect the food supply from gamblers" (the government argued that only citizens in the military had a duty to stand during any performance of the National Anthem and that the attorney general had no responsibility to enforce this duty); (3) "Our entry into it [the war] was determined by the certainty that if the Allies do not win, J. P. Morgan's loans to the Allies will be repudiated, and those Americans who bit on his promises would be hooked" (the government argued that the President's address to Congress on 2 April 1917 contradicted the defendant's assertions and that the President's statement of the true grounds of the war were presumptively correct). See Brandeis's dissent, *Pierce v. United States*, 252 U.S. 239, 264–69 (1920). It should be pointed out that the government on appeal dropped the contention that the first assertion listed above was within the statute (see Brief on the Behalf of the United States at 14, *Pierce*).

72. See the third count of the indictment, *Pierce v. United States* (1920).

73. Brief on the Behalf of the United States, at 12, *Pierce*.

74. Id. at 15.

75. *Pierce v. United States*, 252 U.S. 239, 251 (1920).

76. Id.

77. Id. at 269.

78. 222 U.S. 452 (1912).

79. *Pierce v. United States*, 252 U.S. 239, 251 (1920).

80. Id. at 271.
81. 155 Mass. 216 (1892).
82. Id. at 220.
83. See *United Public Workers v. Mitchell*, 330 U.S. 75 (1947); *CSC v. Letter Carriers*, 413 U.S. 548 (1973); *Broadrick v. Oklahoma*, 413 U.S. 601 (1973). For further cases and discussion and criticism, see William W. Van Alstyne, "The Demise of the Right-Privilege Distinction in Constitutional Law," *Harvard Law Review* 81 (May 1868): 1439.
84. *McAuliffe v. New Bedford*, 155 Mass. 216, 220 (1892).
85. 162 Mass. 510 (1895).
86. Id. at 511.
87. Id.
88. See *Cox v. Louisiana*, 379 U.S. 536 (1965); *Cox v. New Hampshire*, 312 U.S. 569 (1941). For general discussion, see Blasi, "Prior Restraints on Demonstrations," *Michigan Law Review* 68 (August 1970): 1482–1574.
89. "See *Shuttlesworth v. City of Birmingham*, 394 U.S. 147, 152 (1969); *Gregory v. City of Chicago*, 394 U.S. 111, 112 (1969); *Cox v. New Hampshire*, 312 U.S. 569, 574 (1941); *Hague v. Comm. for Indus. Org.*, 307 U.S. 496, 515 (1939). Access to traditional public forums include public libraries, grounds of a jail, public buses, public theaters, military bases, public fairgrounds, and home letter boxes. See *Brown v. Louisiana*, 383 U.S. 131 (1966); *Adderly v. Florida*, 385 U.S. 39 (1966); *Lehman v. Shaker Heights*, 418 U.S. 298 (1974); *Southeastern Promotions, Ltd. v. Conrad*, 420 U.S. 546 (1975); *Greer v. Spock*, 424 U.S. 828 (1976); *Heffron v. Int' Soc. for Krishna Consc.*, 452 U.S. 640 (1981); *U.S. Postal Service v. Greenburgh Civic Assns.*, 453 U.S. 114 (1981). There is a parallel argument that citizens have a constitutional right to use forums that are privately owned: shopping centers and broadcasting media. See *Amalgamated Food Employees v. Logan Valley Plaza*, 391 U.S. 308 (1968); *Lloyd Corp. v. Tanner*, 407 U.S. 551 (1972); *Hudgens v. NLRB*, 424 U.S. 507 (1976); *Pruneyard Shopping Center v. Rolins*, 447 U.S. 74 (1980); *Red Lion Broadcasting Co. v. FCC*, 395 U.S. 367 (1969); *CBS, Inc. v. Democratic Nat. Comm.*, 412 U.S. 94 (1973).
90. *Commonwealth v. Davis*, 162 Mass. 510, 512 (1895). The United States Supreme Court upheld Holmes's decision. The record indicated that Davis had not requested a permit and that no person who requested a permit had been refused. See Michael T. Gibson, "The Supreme Court and Freedom of Expression from 1791 to 1917," *Fordham Law Review* 55 (1986): 317.
91. *United States ex rel M. S. D. Pub. Co. v. Burleson*, 255 U.S. 407 (1921).
92. See Brief for the Defendant in Error at 16–17, *Burleson*.
93. Id. at 22–28.
94. Id. at 17.
95. *United States ex rel. M. S. D. Pub. Co. v. Burleson*, 255 U.S. 407, 436–37 (1921).
96. See Brandeis's dissent, Id. at 421–28.

97. Id. at 417.
98. Id. at 437.
99. 279 U.S. 644 (1929).
100. Id. at 646.
101. Id. at 647–49.
102. Id. at 649.
103. Id. at 651.
104. *Tiaco v. Forbes*, 228 U.S. 549, 556 (1913).
105. *United States v. Schwimmer*, 279 U.S. 644, 654–55 (1929).
106. Id. at 654.
107. Id. at 655.

5. Holmes and His Peers

Many critics of Holmes's theory of free speech rest their conclusions on a comparison of his ideas to those of his contemporaries.[1] The underlying assumption is that the best way to measure anyone's commitment to free speech is to pay attention to historical context. This approach, of course, is far better than the anachronistic alternative that faults a jurist because he or she fails to come up to today's standards of free speech. The comparative method, however, does not insure success. Valid interpretations of the jurist's theory of free speech as well as those of his peers must be obtained. I have set forth my interpretation of Holmes's theory in the last three chapters. I now turn to his contemporaries. Did they have recognizable, coherent theories of free speech? Were their theories, in general, more or less protective of free speech than Holmes's? My belief is that historians of free speech have looked on the contemporaries, in direct contrast to the way that they have examined Holmes, with a far too uncritical eye. The main purpose of this chapter is therefore to restore some balance to our understanding of free speech during its formative era. There is reason to conclude that Holmes, when compared to his peers, was a moderate and a coherent defender of free speech.

Judge Learned Hand

Judge Learned Hand's contribution to the development of free-speech doctrine deserves special consideration. He is thought to have not only formulated a distinctive constitutional test of free speech, but also to have persuaded Holmes to "put some teeth into the clear and present danger formula."[2] In regard to the first point, Hand's reputation depends, to a great extent, on whether he was the first to adopt a "word-oriented" test of free speech—one that limited liability to *direct literal incitement* of unlawful action.[3] But there is a potential problem here. The danger is that a fondness for a certain type of free-speech test may well distort our understanding of Hand's doctrine. If a word-oriented test is admired, and if Hand is thought to have formulated it, there is a tendency to overestimate the protective character of his theory. A better way to proceed is to examine his free speech opinions without any predispositions.

A few observations concerning Hand's later academic and judicial career provide a context to assess the relative contributions that he and Holmes made to free speech during its formative era. In his Oliver Wendell Holmes Lecture of 1958, it is well known that Hand expressed doubt concerning the entire doctrine of judicial review and added that he did "not think that the interests mentioned in the First Amendment are entitled in point of constitutional consideration to a measure of protection different from other interests."[4] Thus, a court should defer to a legislature, even if the relevant statute restrained speech, if the latter acted "impartially"[5] by considering the interests of those effected. That was all that Hand required of the legislature. If the legislature considered the interests of all involved but still decided to suppress the speech in question, judges were to defer. The guarantee of free speech therefore did not require any special protection be given to speech, only that the legislature not act arbitrarily. Hand came to this conclusion because he was more sensitive than most to the policy-making character of judicial review. His basic aim was therefore to let the impartial legislature have its way.

In this same lecture, Hand denigrated Holmes's clear-and-present-danger test on the ground that it required an immediate evil before liability could be imposed on speech.[6] The requirement of an immediate harm went too far in the direction of judicial policy making. Congress was to decide if an immediate evil was or was not necessary for liability, not a judge or a court. He cited Paul Freund's comment that the clear-and-present-danger formula should not disguise that the judiciary, when applying the formula to invalidate a law, was second-guessing a legislature's policy-decision.[7] For Hand, the implication was that if a legislature impartially decided that advocacy of revolution should be repressed, judges should obediently defer, even if there was no likelihood of immediate harm.

Because advocacy of revolution "proceeded from an unlawful purpose," Hand also claimed that it did "not therefore fall within any interest that the amendment is designed to protect,"[8] which shows that he was not in favor of a word-oriented test in 1958. Advocacy of revolution was outside of the First Amendment because of its illegal purpose, not because the speaker literally incited revolution. He also predicted the demise of the clear-and-present-danger doctrine, adding that he could not "help thinking that for once Homer nodded."[9] His general doctrine of judicial deference to legislative will should not hide this more revealing feature of Hand's attitude toward free speech. In 1958 he personally favored such repression. He was not just willing to defer to a legislative determination that all advocacy of revolution should be punished. Repression of advocacy of revolution made good sense; it was a wise policy.

Any evaluation of Hand's theory of free speech, whether in regard to its consistency or its viability, must consider his 1950 opinion in *Dennis v. United States.*[10] In this case, he set to one side the issue of incitement to riot: liability for such utterances was clearly indicated.[11] The more troubling matter was the utterance that was "at once an effort to affect the hearers' belief and a call upon them to act when they have been convinced."[12] Was a speaker who preached the virtues of revolution in the distant future liable? Hand began his discussion with an aside: if the question was a new one, "it might have been held that the Amendment did not protect utterances, when they had this double aspect: i.e., when persuasion and instigation were inseparably confused."[13] This was the preferable course because political speech would then have been treated consistently with other types of speech that incurred liability whenever the utterance was "coupled with appeals to unlawful means."[14] His example was of a speaker who advocated that a school obtain funds by fraud. Such a person was liable no matter the likelihood of harm.[15]

Hand asked, why should a person who advocated revolution not be treated in the same way? Consistency demanded equal treatment. Unfortunately, in his opinion, this option was precluded by legal precedents. He indicated his view of these precedents by noting, "The Supreme Court has certainly evinced a tenderness towards political utterances since the first World War."[16] Such a characterization of earlier free-speech cases leaves the impression that in 1950 Hand would have had little mercy for revolutionary speech. It suggests that he was already of the opinion, which he explicitly endorsed in his 1958 lecture, that revolutionary speech should be placed completely outside of constitutional protection.

Since this was his perspective, it should cause no surprise that in *Dennis,* Hand interpreted the legal precedents mentioned above in a way hostile to the advocacy of revolution. This is especially obvious in the way Holmes's clear-and-present-danger doctrine was distorted. Cardozo's dissent in *Herndon v Georgia*[17] was cited to establish "that the rule of 'clear and present danger' might be properly limited to situations in which the words were not themselves those of direct instigation."[18] Direct calls for illegal action, even if they were for a distant revolution, were a sufficient basis for liability, while "indirect" calls[19] would be punishable only if they constituted a clear and present danger. This adaptation of the test was a clear departure from Holmes's theory of free speech. Apart from criminal conspiracy, a clear and present danger was always required. It did not matter whether the utterance directly or indirectly advocated unlawful action.

Hand not only narrowed the scope of Holmes's clear-and-present-danger doctrine by restricting it to indirect incitement, he also revamped it. To determine whether a clear and present danger existed, the judge was to "ask whether the gravity of the 'evil,' discounted by its improbability, justifies such invasion of free speech as is necessary to avoid the danger."[20] This formulation of Holmes's test implied that a harm could be so serious that liability was incurred even though the harm was improbable and remote. After subtracting the improbability from the seriousness of the harm advocated, a judge could still find that the remainder justified punishing speech. In *Dennis,* Hand reasoned exactly in this way. A communist revolution, despite its unlikelihood and remoteness, was such a serious harm that liability could be imposed on those who indirectly advocated it.

Hand's proposed test was obviously an interpretation of Holmes's clear-and-present-danger doctrine in name only. Since the danger neither had to be clear nor present, the test was in fact more similar to the bad-tendency doctrine than to Holmes's' standard.[21] Adherents of the former doctrine hold that speech was culpable if it had some tendency to cause harm, no matter how improbable or remote the harm was. If there was a difference between Hand's test in *Dennis* and the bad-tendency doctrine, it was that the speaker's actual purpose had also to be unlawful.

Adherents of the bad-tendency doctrine were perfectly willing to infer unlawful intent if a speaker should have foreseen that his or her speech had a likelihood of causing harm. It was not necessary for the speaker actually to have intended or foreseen it. There is no reason to believe that Hand was willing to take this step. The step, however, was unnecessary in *Dennis* because there was no doubt, in his mind, that the defendants desired a revolution, even if it was in the distant future.[22]

Hand's justification for modifying Holmes's standard of free speech in cases of unlawful advocacy of revolution was twofold. First, the standard was too "formalistic." The "phrase, 'clear and present danger,' is not a slogan or a shibboleth to be applied as though it carried its own meaning; but that it involves in every case a comparison between interests which are to be appraised qualitatively."[23] But if Hand by this statement meant to criticize Holmes, he was attacking a straw adversary. In cases of criminal attempt, the factors to be considered were the gravity of harm, the proximity of danger, and the apprehension of the community. Certainly these factors required a weighing of interests, which means that the standard was never meant to be applied in any kind of formulaic way. What Holmes never said was that a harm could be so great that advocacy of it was punishable regardless of its remoteness and improbability. This was the real difference between the two theorists. Holmes thought liability for impotent revolutionary utterances went too far in the direction of imposing liability on sinners; Hand did not.

Second, revolutionary advocacy should be punished even if there was no likelihood of immediate harm, Hand explained, because we are not indifferent to future generations.

We have purposely substituted "improbability" for "remoteness," because that must be the right interpretation. Given the same probability, it would be wholly irrational to condone future evils which we should prevent if they were immediate; that could be reconciled only by an indifference to those who come after us.[24]

But Hand himself realized that this argument seriously begged the question. The accuracy of our estimates of the likelihood of harm would vary directly with the harm's remoteness. "We can never forecast with certainty; all prophecy is a guess, but the reliability of a guess decreases with the length of the future which it seeks to penetrate."[25] Both Hand and Holmes agreed that judges had to decide the matter. It was "a responsibility that they cannot avoid. Abdication is as much a failure of duty, as indifference is a failure to protect primal rights."[26] But Hand believed that judges had a duty, if the legislature demanded it, to impose liability on speech even if it was unlikely to cause some remote evil. Indeed, his opinion in *Dennis* gave every impression that the legislature's policy of suppression was the best way to deal with the Communist party, a view which reappeared in his 1958 lecture. Holmes, however, believed that judges should overturn all laws that restricted political speech, even if the speaker intended harm, unless the speech constituted a clear and present danger of a specific criminal act or unless the speaker conspired with others to commit such an act. Neither of these conditions were satisfied in *Dennis*. Accordingly, when compared to the approach of Hand during the 1950s, Holmes's theory was decidedly more speech protective.

Perhaps it is so obvious that Hand underwent some kind of intellectual metamorphosis that nothing is gained by placing much weight on his later opinions and writings.[27] The real issue is how his early views (circa 1917–1920) compare to Holmes's. This may be a reasonable conclusion, but it avoids the issue of the coherence of Hand's theory of free speech and precludes the real possibility that Hand's later views can shed a great deal of light on his earlier ones. A perception, whether justifiable or not, that Holmes was hostile to free speech early in his life has been the basis for calling into question Holmes's commitment to free speech and his role in the development of free-speech doctrine. Should the same standard not be applied to Hand? If it were, our enthusiasm for Hand's contributions to free speech would be dampened, but we would gain a more balanced understanding of the history of this important right.

But were Hand's early views as consistent and speech protective as we have been led to believe? How did they fit with his later pronouncements on the topic? The current understanding is that he formulated a new "incitement" test that was significantly more speech protective than Holmes's theory.[28] The evidence supporting this characterization is neither overwhelming or unambiguous: Hand's opinion in *Masses Publishing Company v. Patten*[29] and his correspondence with Holmes and Zechariah Chafee, Jr. The first problem with the claim that his opinion in *Masses* endorsed a new, word-oriented constitutional test of free speech is that Hand explicitly denied it. The test was not a constitutional standard but a statutory one. The issue was "how far Congress after much discussion has up to the present time seen fit to exercise a power which may extend to measures not yet even considered but necessary to the existence of the state as such."[30] His opinion was therefore not meant to define either the limits of Congress's war power or the right of free speech and press. He even hinted in what ways Congress could, if it wished, exert its power more aggressively. It might "forbid the mails to any matter which tends to discourage the successful prosecution of the war." That such laws might cut into sacred individual rights did not escape Hand's notice. But he insisted, "Fundamental personal rights of the individual must stand in abeyance, even including the right of the freedom of the press."[31]

Hand was therefore not offering a constitutional test under the guise of statutory construction.[32] How could his interpretation of a statute constitute a constitutional limit of legislative power when he implied that Congress could go further? And the view that the standard announced in *Masses* was only a statutory one has the added virtue that it is consistent with the doctrine of judicial deference to legislative will—a doctrine that became increasingly prominent in Hand's legal philosophy. Thus any claim in regard to Hand's constitutional theory of free speech that relies on his opinion in *Masses* has, at best, a shaky foundation.

It is also relatively clear that Hand never even meant his incitement test to function as a comprehensive standard by which to interpret the Espionage Act of 1917. Hand did use some kind of incitement test to determine if the defendants were guilty of "willfully causing insubordination, disloyalty, mutiny, or refusal of duty in the military or naval forces."[33] But in *Masses,* other charges that had nothing to do with incitement were also before him. Did the defendants make "false statements with intent to interfere with the operations or success of the military or naval forces of the United States or to promote the success of its enemies"?[34] In regard to this charge, Hand argued that the applicable statutory provision "properly" included "only a statement of fact which the utterer knows to be false,"[35] concluding that the defendants in this case had no such knowledge. The defendants therefore escaped liability not because their utterance did not constitute incitement, but because the publication dealt with opinion (not fact) that the publisher believed to be true.

The important point is that Hand implied that the converse was also true. If someone actually published a falsehood with the requisite unlawful intent, he or she was liable even if the utterance did not constitute incitement. While Holmes imposed liability in such a case only if there was a clear and present danger, Hand never explicitly endorsed this additional requirement. Perhaps in his early period, if the right case had come along, he would have added this condition of liability for false statements. Yet Hand's policy of judicial deference to legislative will and his insistence that Congress could go farther than the Espionage Act should make us cautious. It is likely that he would have punished harmless false statements if Congress made its will explicit—a position that Holmes never accepted. In any case, Hand's incitement test was an interpretation of only certain provisions of the Espionage Act. It was not a comprehensive statutory test, much less a constitutional standard.

Nevertheless, in regard to those provisions that prohibited causing insubordination or refusal of duty, Hand did adopt an incitement test. "One may not," he insisted, "counsel or advise others to violate the law as it stands,"[36] and he added, "To counsel or advise a man to an act is to urge upon him either that it is his interest or his duty to do it."[37] Gerald Gunther thinks that Hand meant that liability could be imposed only if the speaker's words literally referred to the audience's interest or duty.[38] Evidence in support of this view can be found both in Hand's opinion and in his correspondence with Zechariah Chafee, Jr. In *Masses*, Hand absolved the defendants, even though what they had said had a tendency to encourage the emulation of draft resisters, because in their language there "is not the least implied intonation . . . that others are under a duty to follow"[39] the example of the draft resisters. And in letters to Zechariah Chafee, Jr., he argued for "an absolute and objective test to language"—"a test based upon the nature of the utterance itself."[40] Such a test was preferable because, if intent and likelihood of harm were the criteria, "juries won't much regard the difference between the probable result of the words and the purposes of the utterer."[41] A test that focused on the speaker's language, in his opinion, could better insure that those provisions of the Espionage Act dealing with obstructing the draft and causing insubordination would not be used by juries to suppress speech beyond what Congress had authorized.

Hand's emphasis on the speaker's language, however, should not be read to preclude liability for indirect unlawful advocacy. He admitted that it was "of course" possible for unlawful advocacy to "be accomplished as well by indirection as expressly."[42] A speaker could appeal to duty or interest in an indirect manner. An obvious case in point was Marc Antony's funeral oration. This example showed, as Hand admitted in a later espionage case, that "there may be language . . . which can in fact counsel violence while it even expressly discountenances it."[43] His test was therefore not an exclusively word-oriented test, whether of the Constitution or the provisions of the Espionage Act dealing with obstruction and insubordination. Hand did say that "the literal meaning is the starting point for interpretation." But clearly where he stopped was more important than where he started. And when he said that words were "to be taken, *not literally,* but according to their full import" (emphasis mine),[44] he made it crystal clear that his stopping point was not literal incitement.[45] Thus Hand's test was not exclusively word-oriented.

Hand's more specific discussions of indirect unlawful advocacy were vague and contradictory. At times he implied that the speaker's purpose was the criterion to whether speech constituted indirect incitement, while elsewhere the speech's effects on the audience were emphasized. For example, in a letter to Chafee in which he gave his reaction to *Abrams v. United States,* Hand claimed that Holmes's "distinction seems to me pretty tenuous between the purpose to encourage resistance to the United States and merely to prevent the United States from overthrowing the Bolshevik party."[46] His first impression was that Abrams and his associates were properly convicted, and that the purpose of their speech activity—since they did not explicitly advocate illegality—was a sufficient basis for liability.

In a follow-up letter, Hand changed his mind about the facts of *Abrams,* but not about the proper standard. Even if the defendants should have been freed, he still believed that intent was the crucial issue. A set of jury instructions that he proposed for defendants like those in *Abrams* indicates as much.

I say: "you must find that the defendants *intended* to impede the war, and to do so you must decide either that they had that *purpose,* which in your places I should find that they had not, or that *they knew* that in stopping the production of munitions till the Russian expedition was given up, the war against Germany would inevitably be impeded. If you think that *they understood* that they could not stop munitions here without that result, that knowledge is enough special intent under the statute." (Emphasis mine)[47]

In this passage, Hand not only focused on the speaker's purpose, rather than the words used, but also reduced intent to the defendants' foresight. Even if the speaker did not wish a particular consequence of his speech to occur, he was liable if he foresaw it. In the same letter, immediately following the above set of jury instructions, he asked Chafee, "There, am I orthodox? Does there lurk a heresy somewhere in there? Further I will not go."[48] Words like these suggest that Hand did support liability for cases of indirect advocacy of unlawful action if a speaker foresaw or intended the harmful consequences of his or her actions.

At other places, however, Hand suggests, surprisingly enough, that the speaker's purpose was irrelevant to the existence of indirect illegal advocacy. His opinion in *United States v. Nearing*,[49] a case that came after the reversal of his decision in *Masses*,[50] reveals this contradictory element in his thinking. In this later case, he claimed that common law had limited liability to "counseling" or "advising" illegality, but immediately added that the counseling or advising need not be explicit "since the meaning of words comprises what their hearers understand them to convey."[51] The key issue was therefore neither the literal meanings of the words used nor the purpose of the speaker, but what effect the speaker's utterance had on the audience. Applying this test to the facts of *Nearing*, he concluded that the speech "at common law would not, I think, subject their author to criminal responsibility for the results, *no matter what his intent*" (emphasis mine).[52] If the audience understood the speaker to be counseling illegality, then the speaker was liable no matter the specific intent or the nature of the words used. Explicit advocacy of unlawful action of course always produced the requisite effect and liability followed accordingly. Liability for indirect incitement, conversely, would depend on the audience's reaction. If the audience believed the speaker was advocating illegality, the speaker was liable; if not, then not. But in either case, the crucial factor was the effect of the speech, not its purpose or the words used.

Hand's emphasis in *Nearing* on the effect of a speech was not an isolated slip of the pen. In a letter to Chafee, he returned to the same theme. "I prefer," he insisted, "a test based upon the nature of the utterance itself. If, taken in its setting, *the effect upon the hearers* is only to counsel them to violate the law, it is unconditionally illegal" (emphasis mine).[53] Here again Hand rested liability, not on the words or the purposes of the speaker, but on the effects that a speech had on an audience. But other passages that we have seen suggest that the speaker's purpose was the crucial factor. It is very difficult to fit these various contradictory strands into any kind of a coherent approach. The conclusion may be that Hand never formulated a workable test of indirect illegal advocacy, which would seriously undermine his status as a theorist of free speech.

Since Hand's theory of free speech is not consistent, it is only possible to contrast it to Holmes's approach in a hypothetical way. If Hand's theory is understood as an exclusively word-oriented test, it is not necessarily more protective of speech than Holmes's doctrine.[54] Hand would punish all speakers who literally advocated violence, while Holmes would punish those who spoke with unlawful intent and created a clear and present danger. Even if it is true that a jury, using Holmes's test, would quickly infer unlawful intent from the likelihood of harm,[55] it is important to note that according to Hand no likelihood of harm needed to be established. Impotent advocacy of unlawful action, if it was explicit, was in his opinion outside of constitutional protection.

Consequently, in cases in which unlawful intent was present, Hand would punish explicit illegal advocacy regardless of likelihood of harm, while Holmes would punish speech likely to cause an immediate harm regardless of the words used. How much speech would be protected by either standard would depend on the empirical facts: what types of utterances were made. In 1920 the Justice Department claimed that there were 471 radical periodicals in the United States advocating the violent overthrow of capitalism. Presumably all of them would have been subject to liability according to Hand's principle, but not necessarily according to Holmes's.[56] But even if Hand's word-oriented test was generally more speech protective than I have suggested, his later opinions and writings clearly indicate that he changed his mind. In the 1950s, it was not only constitutional to punish indirect advocacy of revolution, but a wise policy to do so.

If Hand's test was an exclusively word-oriented test, it permitted speakers with unlawful intent to avoid liability simply by choosing the right words. It may have been for this reason that he abandoned this test, if he ever adhered to it in the first place. The problem was what to do with cases of indirect illegal advocacy. If the speaker's purpose was the crucial criterion, Hand once again gave no indication that the utterance had to create a likelihood of immediate harm. A speaker was liable, irrespective of what he or she said, if the jury found that the purpose was unlawful. Also, he reduced the requirement of intent to one of foresight. If a person foresaw the harm, that person intended it even if he or she hoped the consequence would not occur. Clearly this formulation of Hand's standard provided significantly less protection than Holmes's theory, which required that the speaker's actual purpose be unlawful and that a clear and present danger exist.

Conversely, if indirect advocacy of illegality was determined by the speech's effect on the audience, if the crucial issue was not the speaker's purpose but whether the audience would understand the speaker to be counseling illegality, here again the standard provided less protection to speech than Holmes's doctrine. A speaker was punished no matter what the intent if hearers understood the speaker to counsel illegality. Clearly, if a jury could apply Holmes's standard in a repressive way, they would have less trouble repressing speech with Hand's effects-test. It only required the jury to find that the audience understood the speaker to be encouraging illegality. The likelihood of harm and the speaker's purpose were irrelevant. Communists could be punished, regardless of their intent or the likelihood of harm, because their hearers understood them to be advocating unlawful action. With such a test, overly "patriotic" juries would have absolutely no trouble bringing in convictions.

One final source of evidence that should be considered to evaluate if Hand was more sensitive to the value of free speech than Holmes is their correspondence. It is worthwhile to explore this topic separately because Gerald Gunther has argued that it shows that Hand had the greater commitment to free speech.[57] The very first letter of the correspondence, Gunther argues, reveals that Hand "argued the case for protecting the dissenter."[58] A few cautions, however, are in order. Though it is true that in this letter Hand did want to deny a general right to kill merely "because the victims insist upon saying things which look against Provisional Hypothesis Number Twenty-Six,"[59] he also acknowledged parenthetically (which Gunther does not comment on) that the rule applied "except for limited periods and then only when you want to [kill] very much indeed."[60] Hand, in short, did recognize the majority's right to kill a vocal minority in exceptional circumstances. He may have "argued the case for protecting the dissenter," but he did so only with this major qualification.

In his return letter of 24 June, Holmes said that persecutions were like coerced vaccinations, except that with the former "the occasions would be rarer when you cared enough to stop"[61] free expression. He therefore agreed with Hand that, at least in the modern world, the majority would only rarely repress dissent. In Holmes's opinion, however, Hand put too much emphasis on the persecutor's skeptical self-awareness. According to Hand, the persecutor had the "sacred right to kill the other fellow" only if the persecutor was aware that his or her own doctrine might be false. Apparently, it was Hand's belief that a skeptical persecutor operated on a higher moral plane than a dogmatic, self-righteous one. He even hinted that the true skeptic might stay out of the fight entirely.[62]

Holmes disputed both of these propositions. Whether you are a skeptic or a fanatic, "if for any reason you did care enough you wouldn't care a damn for the suggestion that you were acting on a provisional hypothesis and might be wrong. That is the condition of every act."[63] Take for example vaccinations. If they have the power, absolutists (who are absolutely convinced of the program's merits) and skeptics (who may wonder whether the program might in the long run cause more harm than good) compel vaccinations notwithstanding their contrasting opinions of the validity of their beliefs. Accordingly, why was it so important that the persecutor be a skeptic? And the opinionated philosopher who, because of his skepticism, failed to join either side—whether the issue was vaccinations or the suppression of a dogma—was described by Holmes to be the "greatest fool of all." He did not "see that man's destiny is to fight."[64] Every person must take a "place on the one side or the other, if with the added grace of knowing that the Enemy is as good a man as thou [that is, knowing that the Enemy's beliefs arise from contingent experience just as yours do], so much the better, but kill him if thou Canst."[65]

These were the qualifications that Holmes wished to make to Hand's argument. They both agreed that in rare instances humans legitimately kill others merely for what they say. The only difference was that Hand believed that a skeptic either had a better right to kill in such circumstances or that a skeptic could rise above it all. According to Holmes, even the skeptical philosopher must choose between free speech and suppression. Holmes did not especially recommend either option, but only cautioned against passivity and pride. In contrast, Hand closed his letter with the observation, "I am a philosopher and if Man is so poor a creature as not to endure the truth, it is no concern of mine. I didn't make him.[66]

The first caution that comes to mind after reading this interesting exchange of letters is whether it has anything to do with the free-speech clause of the Constitution. Gunther argues that though Hand recognized the "sacred and natural right to kill the other fellow," it was for him "not a right that society and the law could afford to acquiesce in."[67] These two letters therefore contain, in Gunther's judgment, a constitutional defense of free speech. But there is some reason to doubt this conclusion. Though Hand never said that the "right to kill" was a right that "the law could acquiesce in," neither did Holmes. Of course, it is not surprising that both refused to endorse this particular right as a permanent feature of contemporary society. Modern society could not exist as we know it if the law continuously authorized, encouraged, or required the majority to kill vocal minorities. But if neither was referring to an existing legal right, then it is hard to understand Hand's letter as a piece of constitutional analysis. If it is, it is at best an odd piece of work.

A better interpretation is that the Hand-Holmes exchange was concerned with morality, not constitutional law. It is doubtful, for example, whether Hand would have said that the "right not to be killed for one's beliefs" could be suspended "for limited periods" if he was formulating a constitutional right. Constitutional rights are not usually described in this manner. They are thought to have a more durable character. Also, Hand's reference to the "sacred" and "natural" right to kill suggests that he was addressing the moral, not the constitutional, right not to be killed for one's beliefs. And why would Hand refer to himself as a "philosopher" if he was elucidating his responsibilities as a judge under the Constitution of the United States? How could he announce a policy of indifference to people if he was addressing his judicial duty to enforce constitutional rights? These questions make it hard to believe that the letter contains constitutional analysis.

Holmes's response was of the same character, with one minor difference. While Hand referred to the sacred *right* to kill, Holmes generally avoided this term because he accepted "a rough equation between isness and oughtness." He only respected the "rights" that "a given crowd will fight for—which vary from religion to the price of beer."[68] For this reason, his language did not refer to the persecutor's rights, but to whether the persecutor "cared enough" to kill the other fellow. But this stylistic difference has no bearing on the meaning of these letters. The exchange was a philosophical, not legal, discussion of the relationship between epistemology, morality, and toleration. Thus, even if the differences between the two men are not insignificant, they have little or no bearing on the substance of either judge's theory of free speech.

The Holmes-Hand correspondence of 1919 was a different matter, and the tone of these later letters does much to undermine the constitutional significance of the earlier ones. There were five letters exchanged. In the first, Holmes admired the force and form of Hand's opinion in *Masses,* but added that he would have found a different result.[69] He would have upheld the convictions even if the defendants did not try to convince their audience that it was their duty or in their interest to violate the law. If they had intended illegality and produced a likelihood of immediate harm, that was enough to impose liability.

Gerald Gunther argues that in the second letter[70] Hand renewed "his campaign for greater protection of speech" because he was so distressed by Eugene Debs's conviction.[71] But this is a paradoxical claim, since Hand, at the beginning of his letter, said that he had not "a doubt that Debs was guilty under any rule conceivably applicable."[72] Gunther tries to explain away this comment "as an expression of Hand's extraordinary deference to Holmes, as an effort to seem to agree with the result while trying to persuade the master of the error of his reasoning.[73] But this explanation falls short. The entire letter was critical of Holmes's reasoning in *Debs,* so there was no reason for Hand to pull his punch if he in fact disagreed with the conviction. It is more likely, if he in fact had doubts about the decision itself, that he would have indicated the features of the case that made liability inappropriate. He could then have argued that Holmes's theory was flawed because it led to incorrect results. Hand did none of this, presumably because what he said at the beginning of the letter was true. He had no trouble with the conviction itself, but only with Holmes's reasoning in the opinion.

Gunther cannot believe that Hand's affirmation of the conviction was sincere, because "it is impossible to believe that Debs's statements would have been punishable under the direct incitement test of *Masses.*"[74] Since Debs did not literally advocate illegality, Hand could not have favored his conviction. But this argument ignores the possibility of indirect illegal advocacy and assumes that Hand's test was exclusively word-oriented. The reasons why this may not be a good assumption have been discussed above. Hand could well have thought that Debs had indirectly counseled unlawful action, and that he therefore was properly convicted on the incitement test of *Masses*. Accordingly, there is no reason to doubt Hand's endorsement of Debs's conviction, even if he disagreed with the rationale of the opinion.

Hand's criticism of Holmes's reasoning in *Debs* was twofold: based on common-law precedents, reasonable likelihood of harm should not be the standard, but rather whether the words were an incitement. Intent was a dangerous criterion, since juries would too quickly infer the intent from the probable result of the words.

I do not understand that the rule of responsibility for speech has ever been that the result is known as likely to follow. It is not,—I agree it might have been,—a question of responsibility dependent upon reasonable forecast, with an excuse when the words, had another possible effect. The responsibility only began when the words were directly an incitement . . .

Assuming that I am not wrong, then it was a question of extending the responsibility, and that was fairly a matter of better or worse.[75]

Though Hand endorsed once again the incitement test in this passage, it is important to note that he declined to make it a constitutional test. The question whether liability should be expanded was a legislative policy matter. Hand doubted whether the legislature had yet extended liability beyond the common law, but he implied that it could do so at its discretion.

Holmes's response, the third letter of the five letters exchanged during 1919, began with his admission, "I don't quite get your point."[76] Gunther argues that this language is evidence of Holmes's insensitivity and indifference to free speech.[77] But this conclusion seems to be unjustifiably harsh. First, Holmes correctly assumed that Hand agreed with him that words could "constitute an obstruction within the statute, even without proof that the obstruction was successful to the point of preventing recruiting."[78] Second, from Hand's opinion in *Masses* and his letter, Holmes was aware that Hand favored liability for indirect counseling of unlawful action. Consequently, it is not so strange that Holmes expressed some bewilderment at Hand's criticism of the rule of liability stated in *Debs*. If one can assume that Debs had deliberately chosen his words to avoid literal incitement, the rule of liability had to focus on the speaker's intent, the speech's effects, or both. These were the only alternative bases for liability. Hand himself, when he addressed the possibility of indirect advocacy of unlawful action, had shifted the criteria of liability to the speaker's intent or to the effects the speech had on the audience's understanding. Holmes's confusion about Hand's point is therefore quite understandable. In his letter, Hand had in no clear way indicated his position on indirect incitement. Holmes's admission, "I don't see how you differ from the test as stated by me," [79] is therefore not clear evidence that he was insensitive to the value of free speech.

The fourth letter, the last letter that needs to be considered since the fifth was merely Holmes's thank-you note in reply, contained Hand's reaction to Holmes's dissent in *Abrams v. United States*.[80] Here again confusion lurks because Hand wrote, "I also agree with enthusiasm with your analysis of motive & intent about which there has been much too meager discussion in the books."[81] Hand was referring to Holmes's refusal to impose liability in *Abrams* because the defendants' purpose was to oppose the American intervention in the Russian revolution, not the American war effort against Germany. If Hand's test was word-oriented, then why did he not question the relevance of Holmes's analysis of the speakers' intent? He muddied the waters even more by intimating that Holmes in *Abrams* was somehow following his standard:

It was with strong emotion that I read your words, stronger because I had found so little professional support for my own beliefs which would always have been expressed so [presumably as Holmes had done in his *Abrams* dissent] had I the power to express them. I cannot help feeling like thanking you, even though I recall the annoyance it gives me when anyone undertakes to thank me for what I may say in an opinion.[82]

Since Hand believed that Holmes's focus on Abrams's intent coincided with his own views, this passage seems to mean that his theory of free speech focused, at least at times, on the speaker's purpose. This conclusion, however, conflicts with what Hand said elsewhere. The impression is that the ambiguity and contradictory elements of Hand's theory of free speech reappear in his correspondence with Holmes.

Indeed, it was within a week after he expressed his admiration for Holmes's analysis of purpose in *Abrams* that Hand wrote to Zechariah Chafee, Jr., that "the distinction seems to be pretty tenuous between the purpose to encourage resistance to the United States and merely to prevent the United States from overthrowing the Bolshevik party."[83] And in a later letter to Chafee, he reduced intent to foresight of harmful consequences.[84] Even if Abrams's ultimate purpose was to help the

Bolsheviks, he would still be guilty if he foresaw that his speech activities would hinder the war effort against Germany. Though in this letter Hand tried to distance himself from Holmes's *Abrams* dissent, he also said that Holmes's opinion delighted him, and that it was "some comfort to find myself not in a judicial minority of one"[85]—language that suggests, paradoxically enough, that Hand still believed that Holmes was, to some extent, following his approach.

Finally, after Hand had both complimented and criticized Holmes's analysis of intent and his general approach to free speech, he said that he did "not altogether like the way Justice Holmes put the limitation" and that he preferred "an absolute and objective test to language."[86] With such a statement following all that Hand had said earlier in this particular letter and in his earlier letters to Holmes, the general conclusion must be that the Hand-Holmes-Chafee correspondence is a weak basis for making any claims concerning the degree to which the two judges were committed to free speech in 1917–19. Before any such claims can be made, it is first necessary to reconcile Hand's various statements on the subject of free speech. This may well prove to be an impossible task.

One last point concerns Hand's willingness to defer to Congress's decision to deport aliens. In an earlier chapter, we saw that Holmes supported, on the basis of free speech, a constitutional limit of Congress's power to refuse citizenship to a person who preached the virtues of pacifism. Hand never took an analogous step. Committed to his doctrine of judicial deference, he joined an opinion that upheld a deportation of a "philosophical anarchist" who never explicitly advocated violence.[87] A letter from Hand to Chafee reveals the anxiety the case caused. As he put it, "Lord, it will go against the grain if I have to let a man be deported for his opinions."[88] But go against the grain he did, which says a lot about how he understood the judicial function. It may be the case that Hand, as a personal matter, was more committed to the value of toleration and free speech than Holmes was, but that hardly means that in his judicial role he acted on these personal commitments. His doctrine of judicial deference may have kept his personal ideals sharply separated from his institutional responsibilities. It was from this perspective, in the same letter to Chafee, that Hand wrote, "Quite seriously, I don't think we judges could intervene if they deported all aliens who ate with their knives."[89] Judicial deference to legislative will was what Hand understood his job as a judge to be, and he never let his personal values get in the way of it. In the end, he simply valued judicial deference to legislative will more than he did free speech. It is therefore hard to argue that he surpassed Holmes as a defender of free speech.

Justice Brandeis

Louis Brandeis deserves consideration for more than one reason. Certain commentators have argued that it was his influence, not Hand's, that explains why Holmes purportedly adopted a more pro-speech position in *Abrams v. United States*.[90] An alternative account is that he served only as a conduit through which the ideas of Zechariah Chafee, Jr., and Learned Hand induced Holmes to adopt a more protective and sensitive attitude toward free speech.[91] But apart from all the controversy as to who influenced whom, Brandeis's stature in the history of American civil liberties justifies a comparison of his theory of free speech to Holmes's. He was certainly one of Holmes's peers, and a look at his ideas will help us to appreciate the speech-protective character and coherence of Holmes's theory.

It is indisputable that Brandeis would have protected speech that Holmes would have placed outside the Constitution. His dissenting opinion in *Gilbert v. Minnesota*,[92] a case in which Holmes concurred in the result but not in the majority's opinion, is enough to show that he extended constitutional protection to some speech that Holmes did not. But is the opposite also true? From the language of their respective opinions, can it be said that Holmes would have probably protected speech that Brandeis would not have? Did Brandeis ever develop a constitutional test of free speech that he adhered to consistently over time? Did he formulate any new rationales for our societal commitment to free speech? My own tentative view is that Brandeis's contributions to free speech are primarily, though not exclusively, in this latter area.

It seems probable that Brandeis developed his theory of free speech during late 1919. This is so not because he decided against the defendants in the early cases of that year: *Schenck v. United States, Frohwerk v. United States,* and *Debs v. United States.* Holmes also had rejected the free-speech claims raised in these cases, and I have examined the reasons why he, and presumably Brandeis, affirmed these convictions. Conversely, commentators who believe that these early cases were indistinguishable from *Abrams v. United States* and the others that followed must consider the anomaly that Brandeis voted in favor of convictions in them. Though one important study has intimated that Brandeis underwent some kind of transformation,[93] the more plausible account, in my view, emphasizes how the early cases were different from the later ones. The distinctions between *Abrams, Gitlow,* and *Whitney* may no longer be important to our contemporary understanding of free speech, but they were important to Holmes and Brandeis, and that is the relevant consideration here.

Also, Brandeis did not write an opinion that addressed free speech until *Schaefer v. United States,*[94] and he later admitted (sometime between 1921 and 1924) in conversation with Felix Frankfurter that he never had thought "through" the subject until he wrote his dissents in this case and *Pierce v. United States.*[95]

I have never been quite happy about my concurrence in [the] Debs and Schenck cases. I had not then thought the issues of freedom of speech out—I thought at the subject, not through it. Not until I came to write the Pierce and Schaefer dissents did I understand it.[96]

But even if Brandeis did not think through the problems of free speech until late 1919, the language of his dissents in *Pierce* and *Schaefer* suggests that he had not by this time got much beyond Holmes's clear-and-present-danger doctrine. In *Schaefer,* he called Holmes's test a "rule of reason"[97] and argued that the Supreme Court had already "declared" and that Zechariah Chafee had already "shown" that the "test to be applied—as in the case of criminal attempts and incitements—is not the remote or possible effect. There must be the clear and present danger."[98] Brandeis, at least at first, seems to have adhered to Holmes's theory of free speech.

Despite Brandeis's clear references in *Schaefer* to the clear-and-present-danger doctrine, controversy has nevertheless surfaced concerning whether he was really within Holmes's fold at this time. David Rabban has argued that it is significant that in his *Schaefer* dissent, Brandeis said that "this court" had "declared" what Zechariah Chafee, Jr., had "shown." In Rabban's opinion, Brandeis was trying to adapt, under Chafee's influence, Holmes's restrictive standard of free speech into a more speech-protective test.[99] But this argument is not convincing. The conclusion that Brandeis was secretly ushering Chafee's theory into constitutional law cannot rest on the nuances of *declaring* and *showing*. The difference between the two words is just too slender of a reed on which to claim that Brandeis was breaking new ground under the guise of applying Holmes's clear-and-present-danger doctrine. In fact, the language seems entirely explicable in terms of the respective functions of the Supreme Court and a constitutional commentator: the former *declares* the law, the latter tries to *show* whether the declared rule is appropriate or not.

One must also remember that the Supreme Court's rule, to which Brandeis referred in *Schaefer,* was declared in *Schenk* on March 3, 1919. The rule was therefore declared before Chafee had published the article that showed that the clear-and-present-danger test was correct.[100] Hence, it tends to be misleading to argue that Brandeis was "claiming that 'this court has declared' what 'Professor Chafee has shown.' "[101] The chronology of events conflicts with this claim, at least if it is understood to mean that the Court declared what Chafee had already shown. Indeed, Brandeis's point seems to have been the opposite one: "Professor Chafee has shown" what "this court has [already] declared." It is accordingly very difficult to argue that Brandeis's citation of Chafee's article was part of an attempt to alter the Court's rule of clear and present danger. At most it was an attempt to bolster the validity of a rule that the Court had already declared.

Brandeis's reference, in the phrase "this court has declared," to the Court rather than to Holmes also does not show that he was secretly trying to expand the clear-and-present-danger doctrine. A better explanation is that Brandeis in *Schaefer* was reminding the Court that it was not following the test that it had declared only two years earlier.[102] He did not refer to Holmes for the simple reason that his purpose was to indicate the authoritativeness of the rule, not to belittle Holmes's contribution. When there is such a commonsense explanation of Brandeis's language, there is good reason to set aside the more controversial account.

In an analogous vein, Rabban argues that Brandeis's focus in *Schaefer* on the "nature and possible effect of a writing" indicates that he was reaching beyond Holmes's standard to Hand's more speech-protective, word-oriented test.[103] But there is little evidence to support such a conclusion. Even if the question as to whether Hand's test was exclusively one of literal incitement is ignored, Brandeis never said or implied that literal advocacy of unlawful action was a necessary condition of liability. To the contrary, a full quotation of the passage from Brandeis's dissent that Rabban relies on to justify his conclusion indicates that the opposite conclusion has a better foundation.

The nature and possible effect of a writing cannot be properly determined by culling here and there a sentence and presenting it separated from the context. In making such determination, it should be read as a whole; at least, if it is short, like these news items and editorials. Sometimes it is necessary to consider, in connection with it, other evidence which may enlarge or otherwise control its meaning, or which may show that it was circulated under circumstances which gave it a peculiar significance or effect.[104]

Brandeis was saying that in some cases it was "necessary to consider . . . other evidence which may enlarge or otherwise control" the meaning of a piece of writing. Thus it is incorrect to say that he based liability exclusively on the literal words. The language used by the speaker or writer was just one of several factors relevant to the meaning of some discourse. The intent of the individual, the likelihood of harm, and the circumstances of the act were all thought by Brandeis to be relevant factors.

It is true that in *Schaefer* no evidence other than the defendants' writings was introduced by the government. Therefore, as Brandeis put it, "The writings here in question must speak for themselves."[105] Only the writings existed to show unlawful intent and likelihood of harm and, in his opinion, the evidence introduced was insufficient to establish either. Accordingly, the defendants were within their constitutional rights. If other evidence had existed concerning the defendants' intent or the likelihood of harm, however, the dissent implies that it would have been relevant and admissible. Brandeis's focus in *Schaefer* on "the nature and effect of a writing" thus coincided far more with Holmes's clear-and-present-danger test than with any word-oriented standard.

It was only in *Pierce v. United States*[106] that Brandeis made his first real contribution to the development of free-speech doctrine. His contribution was not, however, to alter Holmes's rule of clear and present danger. It was rather to apply the test in a new area—liability for false statements and reports that were made with the intent to aid the enemies of the United States. Though this charge had been in *Schaefer*, Brandeis had dismissed it because the government only showed that Schaefer's articles were not accurate copies of stories published elsewhere. It was obvious to Brandeis that such articles were not "false reports" within the meaning of the statute.[107] In *Pierce,* however, three different types of charges were before the Court: making false statements with the required illicit intent of aiding the enemy; attempting to cause insubordination or obstruction of the draft; and actual obstruction of recruitment.

Brandeis began his analysis with the crucial claim that "the essentials of liability" varied "materially" with these three classes of offenses.[108] Setting aside the third class as irrelevant, he then said

there necessarily arises in every case—whether the offense charged be of the first or of the second—the question whether the words were used "under such circumstances and are of such a nature as to create a clear and present danger" ... and also the question whether the act of uttering or publishing was done wilfully; that is, with the intent to produce the result which the Congress sought to prevent.[109]

Holmes's clear and present danger doctrine was applicable not only to attempts, but also to false statements and reports. Even if a person told a deliberate lie with the purpose of interfering with the American war effort, that person was free of liability unless he or she posed a clear and present danger of obstructing the war. Since the statutory language made no reference to any likelihood of harm (though an intent "to interfere with the operation and success of the military and naval forces" was required), Brandeis's condition was quite significant. He was applying, with Holmes's approval, the clear-and-present-danger doctrine to a new type of case. And the importance of Brandeis's contribution should not be disparaged even if he was still operating within the confines of Holmes's doctrine. By 1920, he had taken a real step, even if it was a step in accordance with, not in opposition to, Holmes's approach.

But soon thereafter Brandeis abandoned Holmes's doctrine for a theory that relied on the war power of Congress. His "metamorphosis" had to have occurred during 1920 because his new approach appeared in his dissent in *Gilbert v. Minnesota,*[110] which was decided 13 December 1920. In this case, the majority upheld, with Holmes concurring only in the result, a state statute that prohibited anyone from advocating that Americans should neither enlist in the armed forces nor aid the war effort. Brandeis dissented on one ground. Though he hinted at the end of his dissent that a state law prohibiting the advocacy of pacifism might violate the Fourteenth Amendment's due process clause, he prefaced this suggestion with the remark that he saw "no occasion to consider"[111] the issue. His actual objection was that the Minnesota law "interfere[d] with

Federal functions and with the rights of a citizen of the United States to discuss them."[112] The state law was defective because Congress had "exclusive power to declare war, to determine to what extent citizens shall aid in its prosecution, and how effective aid may best be secured."[113] Persuant to this power, Congress had expressed its will on the subject in the Espionage Act. In contrast to Minnesota's law, the federal law "did not prohibit the teaching of any doctrine; it prohibited only certain tangible obstructions to the conduct of the existing war with the German empire, committed with criminal intent."[114] Since the defendants were outside of the Espionage Act, at least as Brandeis understood it, they were free of liability.

The majority was puzzled by Brandeis's reasoning because the state of Minnesota had based the statute, not on any war power, but on the state's traditional police power. The Court's view was that no matter what the federal government did, the state could suppress speech that was arguably within the state's police power. The missing premise of Brandeis's argument was the proposition that only the war power was a sufficient basis to restrict political speech.[115] Congress could restrict such speech because it had the war power; states did not and therefore could not restrain it. And since Congress's war power was confined to circumstances of war, it could suppress it only during wartime. In peacetime, free speech was absolute.

That this was Brandeis's position is indicated by a conversation that he had with Frankfurter, a conversation that occurred after *Gilbert* but before *Gitlow v. New York.*

I would have placed the Debs case on the war power—instead of taking Holmes' line about "clear and present danger." Put it frankly on the war power—like [the] Hamilton case (251 U.S.)—and then the scope of espionage legislation would be confined to war. But in peace the protection against restriction of speech would be unabated. You might as well recognize that during a war— [here Frankfurter interrupted with the words "all bets are off"]. Yes, all bets are off. But we would have a clear line to go on. I didn't know enough in the early cases to put it on that ground.[116]

In *Gilbert,* though he used the language of clear and present danger, Brandeis was introducing this new theory: political speech could be suppressed only on the basis of Congress's war power. "To avert a clear and present danger," Congress could "prohibit interference by persuasion with the process of either compulsory or voluntary enlistment. *As an incident of its power to declare war,* it may . . . require from every citizen full support, and may, to avert a clear and present danger, prohibit interference by persuasion with the giving of such support" (emphasis mine).[117] Despite his use of the phrase "clear and present danger," he was abandoning it for another constitutional standard. He wanted a "bright line" and he found it in the war power. Congress could during war, but only during war, suppress political speech.

It is well known that Holmes was unimpressed with Brandeis's reasoning in *Gilbert*.[118] Though in *Gilbert* Brandeis cited an opinion written by Holmes to support his idea of an exclusive federal power over political speech,[119] the two cases were quite different. *Johnson v. Maryland*[120] concerned whether a state could require a federal post office employee to have a state driver's license. Holmes, writing for a unanimous court, denied the state's authority "not upon any consideration of degree, but upon the entire absence of power on the part of the states to touch the instrumentalities of the United States."[121] But in *Gilbert,* the state was not requiring anything of federal officers or employees, but rather of private individuals who found themselves within Minnesota's borders. Nothing in *Johnson* barred state action against private individuals.

More important, Holmes did not accept the idea that political speech was insulated from every governmental power save the war power. Hence he had no sympathy for the conclusion that states were completely barred from controlling political speech. Language that was harmful per se or that constituted an attempt or that abused a privilege was potentially within state control whether the speech was political or not or whether the country was at war or peace. There was also a dark side to Brandeis's theory of free speech. What was the status of political speech during war? Though Holmes willingly conceded that the power of government to suppress speech was greater during war, that was "because war opens dangers that do not exist at other times."[122] But the principle itself, he doggedly insisted, remained the same: "But, as against dangers peculiar to war, as against others, the principle of the right to free speech is always the same."[123] How speech should be handled in wartime had to have been a major point of contention on the Court.[124] It was Holmes's position that speech during war should be treated according to a theory that was applicable in times of peace. This approach was the best way, in his judgment, to preserve liberty in a crisis.

Brandeis's alternative, at least in 1920, was to "cancel all bets" during war. It seems that he meant that the Court should absolutely defer to what Congress thought was necessary for the war effort; any speech concerning the war effort was subject to Congress's discretion. His reference to the "Hamilton case" [125] and language from his dissent suggest as much. In the former case, in which he wrote the majority opinion, the Court upheld the Wartime Prohibition Act even though the fighting was over. Along the way, he observed:

that to Congress, in the exercise of its powers, not least the war power upon which the very life of the nation depends, *a wide latitude of discretion must be accorded;* and that it would require a clear case to justify a court in declaring that such an act, passed for such a purpose, had ceased to have force because the power of Congress no longer continued. (Emphasis mine) [126]

Not only was the war power extensive, but courts were generally to defer to Congress's determination of whether the country was at war. The war-power approach could therefore have suppressive effects, but Brandeis thought it was nonetheless worth the price. It produced a "clear" line.

In his dissent in *Gilbert,* the same theme of Congress's power during wartime reappears.

There are times when those charged with the responsibility of government, faced with clear and present danger, may conclude that suppression of divergent opinion is imperative; because the emergency does not permit reliance upon the slower conquests of error by truth. And in such emergencies the power to suppress exists. But the responsibility for the maintenance of the Army and Navy, for the conduct of the war, and for the preservation of government, both state and Federal, from "malice domestic and foreign levy" rests upon Congress. [127]

No doubt Brandeis understood this plenary war power to be something much more than Congress's power to punish attempts or conspiracies to obstruct the draft. Even if Congress, by the Espionage Act, had only gone so far as to punish these types of attempts and conspiracies, [128] he implied that Congress could go further. In all likelihood, he excluded private speech from Congress's absolute discretion. But during war, it appears that Brandeis would have upheld *any* Congressional restriction of speech related to the war effort. [129]

Brandeis's war-powers approach to free speech was not a flash in the pan. The same standard was used in his dissent in *United States v.*

Burleson.[130] Here the question was whether the postmaster general could deny a subsidized rate of postage to a magazine if several of its issues were nonmailable according to the Espionage Act. The majority upheld the postmaster general's authority, but Brandeis and Holmes dissented, each writing their own opinion. The question hitherto unanswered is why they dissented separately. Both dissents agreed that the Espionage Act never gave the postmaster general the power to deny a newspaper a subsidized rate of postage, even if certain of its issues were nonmailable. The statute, in their view, only permitted the postmaster general to return to the sender all nonmailable material on an issue-by-issue basis.

Why did Brandeis and Holmes dissent separately? The answer is that each Justice tried to fit his judgment into his own theory of free speech. Brandeis claimed that it could not "be stressed too strongly" that the power of the postmaster general

here claimed is *not a war power* . . . To that end [of pursuing the war] Congress conferred upon the Postmaster General the enormous power contained in the Espionage Act, of entirely excluding from the mails any letter, picture, or publication which contained matter violating the broad terms of that act. But it did not confer . . . the vague and absolute authority to deny circulation to any publication which, in his opinion, is likely to violate in the future any postal law. The grant of that power is construed into a postal-rate statute passed forty years ago. . . . If, under the Constitution, administrative officers may, as a mere incident of their *peace-time* administration of their departments, be vested with the power to issue such orders as this, there is little substance in our Bill of Rights. (Emphasis mine) [131]

This quotation repeats the logic of Brandeis's dissent in *Gilbert.* If in peacetime the postal authorities can deny preferred postage rates to newspapers on the ground of the political speech contained therein, then there was no substance to free speech. Accordingly, a statute enacted in peacetime, the one enacted forty years earlier, could not be construed to give to the postmaster general the discretionary power to deny a newspaper a subsidized rate of postage. Based on its war power, Congress had only denied mail service to material that violated the Espionage Act. This was as far as Congress had gone. But the impression left by Brandeis's war-powers approach was that Congress could go further if it wished. During war, "all bets were off."

Though Holmes at the beginning of his dissent admitted that he agreed with the substance of Brandeis's view, he could not accept this rationale. His key objection was that the war power was simply irrelevant to the decision. While Brandeis insisted that it was significant that the Espionage Act was an exercise of war powers and that the earlier postal law was not, Holmes responded that "the regulation of the right to use the mails by the Espionage Act has no peculiarities as a war measure, but is similar to that in earlier cases, such as obscene documents." The implication was that he would be much more willing than Brandeis to allow the government to declare certain material nonmailable even in peacetime. In regard to whether Congress could constitutionally during war give the postmaster general the power to deny the postal service to any "treasonable" or "seditious" newspaper, however, Holmes said "it would take very strong language to convince me that Congress ever intended to give such a practicably despotic power to any one man. There is no pretense that it has done so. Therefore I do not consider the limits of its constitutional power." [132]

What Holmes did not say here was as significant as what he did say. He gave no indication that the constitutionality of such a law would depend on whether the country was at war or whether the law was an exercise of the war power. Indeed, the very way that he presented the constitutional question suggests that he would have denied to Congress the power to delegate to the postmaster general this arbitrary power even if a war was on. Holmes simply could not accept the existence of war as the crucial criterion of constitutionality. It produced a "bright" line, but it was a dangerous one. He wrote his own dissent in *Burleson*, he did not simply concur in Brandeis's dissent as he had done in *Schaefer* and *Pierce*, to distance himself from Brandeis's war-theory of free speech.

It is not clear how long Brandeis entertained his distinctive theory of free speech. Perhaps *Gitlow v. New York* [133] convinced him that his war-power test was unworkable. Certainly he had the opportunity to write his own dissent in *Gitlow*, but instead he concurred in Holmes's dissent that reasserted the clear-and-present-danger test. But certainly Brandeis's concurrence in *Whitney v. California* [134] shows that by 1927 he had abandoned any "absolutist" approach to free speech and returned to some version of the clear and present danger doctrine.

But, although the rights of free speech and assembly are fundamental, *they are not in their nature absolute.* Their exercise is subject to restriction, if the particular restriction proposed is required in order to protect the state from destruction or from serious injury, political, economic, or moral. (Emphasis mine) [135]

Since *Whitney* arose during peacetime and since it was a state prosecution, it is arguable that Brandeis only abandoned half of his absolute rule: certain types of speech were unprotected during peace from both the state and federal governments, but during war "all bets were still off." However, the flavor of his dissent suggests otherwise. He took special pains to describe the judge's duty to decide if the legislature's initial finding of clear and present danger was within constitutional bounds. "But where a statute is valid only in case certain conditions exist, the enactment of the statute cannot alone establish the facts which are essential to its validity."[136] It seems that Brandeis now believed that federal and state judges had the duty to decide if the proximity and likelihood of harm justified the suppression of speech and that judges had this duty whether the country was at war or at peace.

Though Brandeis returned to the clear-and-present-danger doctrine in *Whitney*, it is possible that he revamped the test to make it more speech-protective. David Rabban, arguing along this line, has claimed that Brandeis added new conditions to Holmes's clear-and-present-danger doctrine. Before speech could be punished, in addition to Holmes's requirements, the speech had to satisfy Hand's test of incitement and the harm had to be "immediate" and "grave."[137] Each of these claims deserves consideration.

Rabban's argument that Brandeis, in *Whitney*, "cemented" Hand's word-oriented test to Holmes's clear-and-present-danger doctrine is not convincing.[138] I have already shown that Brandeis's dissent in *Pierce v. United States* provides no support for this conclusion, and the *Whitney* concurrence contains nothing that would indicate that Brandeis changed his mind and adopted a test of literal incitement. In his concurrence, he did cite—a point that Rabban emphasizes—Hand's decision in *Masses Publishing Company v. Patten*, a book by Zechariah Chafee, Jr., and a decision by Judge Amidon.[139] The purpose of Brandeis's reference to these sources, however, was to show, "Every denunciation of existing law tends in some measure to increase the probability that there will be violation of it."[140] An utterance does not lose constitutional protection merely because it increases the probability of illegal action. The doctrine that held that it did—the bad tendency doctrine—was wrong. A mere increase in the probability of harm could not be the test of free speech since that would require punishment of every denunciation of law. Therefore, the point of Brandeis's citation of Hand, Chafee, and Amidon

160 JUSTICE OLIVER WENDELL HOLMES

was in no way to endorse a word-oriented test, but to criticize the bad-tendency doctrine.

Brandeis did say that illegal advocacy was still protected if it fell "short of incitement."[141] But little can be made of the fact that he used the word *incitement*. That alone hardly shows that he was endorsing a word-oriented test. The crucial issue is how he determined whether a particular case of unlawful advocacy constituted incitement.

The wide difference between advocacy and incitement ... must be borne in mind. In order to support a finding of clear and present danger it must be shown either that immediate serious violence was to be expected or was advocated, or that the past conduct furnished reason to believe that such advocacy was then contemplated.[142]

No doubt this passage is vague and ambiguous. Brandeis did not make much progress in clarifying the terms if only because he used the concept of advocacy to explain the difference between advocacy and incitement. Nevertheless, in no way did he suggest that the literal words used by the speaker were the crux of the matter. The passage rather focuses on the purpose of the speaker, rather than the words. Did the speaker *expect* illegal action or was there reason to believe that the speaker *contemplated* unlawful advocacy? Accordingly, Brandeis's formula was much closer to Holmes's standard—clear and present danger plus unlawful intent—than to a word-oriented test. His language might be a little weaker, implying that a speaker who only foresaw the harm was perhaps punishable, but too much should not be made of it. The use of the word *expected* may have been an oversight. After all, Brandeis did concur in Holmes's dissent in *Abrams v. United States,* which argued that Abrams should escape liability since he only foresaw but did not intend the harm. But there is nothing in his *Whitney* concurrence that supports the conclusion that he was in any way in favor of a standard of literal incitement.

Rabban also suggests that Brandeis revised Holmes's doctrine by adding a requirement that the harm be "imminent."[143] But the significance of this revision is unclear, since Holmes already required that the danger be present. Even though Rabban is correct that Brandeis protected speech "unless the incidence of the evil apprehended is so imminent that it may befall before there is opportunity for full discussion,"[144] it is doubtful whether he meant anything more than a present danger. More likely than not, the distinction between an imminent and a present danger is only in the eye of the beholder. It should be recalled that in *Abrams,* Holmes had already said, "Only the emergency that makes it immediately dangerous to leave the correction of evil counsels to time warrants making any exception to"[145] free speech. I do not think that Brandeis's requirement of an imminent harm in *Whitney* adds anything to this earlier formulation.

The more important and credible claim is that Brandeis added something new when he said that the harm not only had to be clear and present but also serious before speech could incur liability.[146] "Prohibition of free speech and assembly is a measure so stringent that it would be inappropriate as the means for averting a relatively trivial harm to society."[147] The significance of this additional requirement, however, depends on how grave the harm had to be. Seriousness of harm was already one of the dimensions Holmes used to measure proximity of harm in cases of attempts, including attempts by way of illegal advocacy. The example discussed by Brandeis in *Whitney* was that of advocacy of trespass. Rabban's claim is that even if such advocacy presented a clear and present danger, it would be protected by Brandeis because the harm was trivial.[148]

Perhaps so, but there is reason for doubt. Brandeis said:

But it is hardly conceivable that this court would hold constitutional a statute which punished as a felony the mere voluntary assembly with a society formed to teach that pedestrians had the moral right to cross unenclosed, unposted, waste lands and to advocate their doing so, even if there was imminent danger that advocacy would lead to a trespass.[149]

What a state could not punish was the formation of a society whose purpose would be to advocate certain relatively harmless forms of trespass. He did not preclude liability if the society's purpose was to advocate trespass on "enclosed," "posted," and "productive" lands. Moreover, what was denied was that liability could be based on the formation of the group alone. Once the society actually started to advocate trespass, perhaps liability could be imposed, even if the trespass that was likely was on unenclosed, unposted, waste lands. The state might, he said, "punish an attempt, a conspiracy, or an incitement to commit the trespass."[150] Consequently, whether Brandeis increased the degree of gravity beyond what Holmes's test required is a close question. The above language suggests that the increase, if there was any at all, was negligible. If so, it is difficult to argue that he revamped Holmes's test in any serious respect.

Brandeis, however, also said, "The fact that speech is likely to result in some violence or in destruction of property is not enough to justify suppression. There must be the probability of serious injury to the state."[151] If he was consistent, this passage might only mean that it was his judgment that trespass was a serious injury to the state. Thus forming a society to advocate certain forms of trespass was protected, but incitement to trespass was punishable if the possibility of trespass was clear and likely. But this explanation is not, of course, very satisfactory. If violence or destruction of property was not a serious enough danger to justify suppression of illegal advocacy, then Brandeis could not have favored, despite what he said, liability for illegal incitement of trespass. In the end, perhaps all that can be said is that he was never very clear about his requirement of a serious harm.

Though my general conclusion is that Brandeis never consistently adhered to a specific constitutional test of free speech, he was certainly sensitive and committed to its value. From my reading of his opinions, he was less interested in theory than in results. And though he switched from one approach to another and back again, and though his theoretical discussions were marked with ambiguity and vagueness, he was the most fervent defender of free speech on the Court of his time.

Brandeis also formulated, in strikingly eloquent language, a novel and historically important rationale for free speech. Holmes had offered a justification of speech that relied on skepticism and the marketplace of ideas. Though some commentators have tried to interpret this rationale to be nonpolitical, even to the point of describing the metaphor as "antipolitical,"[152] he was aware that the marketplace of ideas operated within a political context.

If you have no doubt of your premises or your power . . . you naturally express your wishes in law and sweep away all opposition. . . . But when men have realized that time has upset many fighting faiths, they may come to believe even more than they believe in the very foundations of their own conduct that the ultimate good desired is better reached by free trade in ideas,—that the best test of truth is the power of the thought to get itself accepted in the competition of the market; and that truth is the only ground upon which their wishes safely can be carried out. That at any rate, is the theory of our constitution.[153]

A careful reading of this passage shows that Holmes was not discouraging people from expressing their views in law—people invariably did that—but rather from sweeping away all criticism. The minority that lost the legislative struggle must have the right to convince the majority of the error of its ways. Only then did the majority have any assurance that its "wishes can safely be carried out." Therefore Holmes certainly understood free speech in a political sense, as a precondition of "deliberative politics." As he said in regard to a proletarian revolution: "If, in the long run, the beliefs expressed in proletarian dictatorships are destined to be accepted by the dominant forces of the community, the only meaning of free speech is that they should be given their chance and have their way."[154] Even if in our own age these two rationales of free speech—the marketplace of ideas and speech as a precondition for democratic politics—seem analytically distinct, in his mind they were complementary. Ideas that were victorious in the marketplace were embodied into law, but law's legitimacy depended on whether criticism was permitted.

Brandeis contributed to the philosophy of free speech not by uncovering its relationship to truth or the American political process. Holmes had already done that. Rather, his original theme was the idea that free speech was necessary for people "to develop their faculties" and for "individual happiness."[155] It would be too much to say that this element was predominant in his justification of free speech, since he placed most of his emphasis on the relationship between free speech and politics. Nonetheless, the idea that free speech was valuable at the individual level had not found its way into any Supreme Court opinion until Brandeis's concurrence in *Whitney v. California*. Though he never made it entirely clear how this notion was to be used to define the limit of free speech, certain of his successors have relied heavily on it. The Supreme Court has gradually widened the scope of constitutional protection to fit this new justification. Its significance is therefore indisputable.

Brandeis did not, of course, invent this new rationale for free speech. Zechariah Chafee, Jr. had popularized it in the academic world of the 1920s, and the intellectual origins of it go back to John Stuart Mill and Wilhelm von Humboldt.[156] Nevertheless, Brandeis was responsible for introducing this justification of free speech and individual liberty, which today is at the cutting edge of free-speech litigation, into our constitutional jurisprudence. It is for that contribution that he should be remembered, not for any constitutional test of free speech that Brandeis either formulated or developed.

Zechariah Chafee, Jr.

Another name that figures prominently in the history of free speech doctrine is Zechariah Chafee, Jr. Though at first a relatively unknown law professor at Harvard, he found prominence by defending free speech during and immediately after World War I. *Freedom of Speech*,[157] published in 1920, was his major work, shaping the country's general understanding of free speech for at least a generation.[158] Hence, that Chafee played an important role in deepening and widening the American commitment to free speech is indisputable. On more particular points, however, doubts arise. Did he endorse a definite constitutional test of free speech? Did he endorse the test early enough to shape the doctrine of Holmes? Did he in fact influence Holmes, Hand, or Brandeis? Though others have argued that all of these questions must be answered in the affirmative,[159] there is room for legitimate skepticism. It can be argued that Chafee came to his constitutional theory of free speech slowly and tentatively and that the opinions of Learned Hand and Holmes had more of an influence on Chafee than vice versa.

A couple of months before Holmes's opinion appeared in *Schenck*, Chafee published an article entitled "Freedom of Speech" in *The New Republic*.[160] It is therefore possible that Chafee shaped free-speech doctrine from the very beginning. But any claim that this article had a significant impact on Holmes's approach faces considerable difficulty. First, it is puzzling why Holmes's pro-speech attitude, which on this interpretation did not develop until *Abrams*, did not appear immediately in *Schenck*. Second, the primary purpose of the article was to attack the idea that free speech was limited to protection from prior restraints. According to Chafee, such an understanding of free speech was wrong for two reasons: it would not allow the government to restrain a newspaper from publishing military information, while at the same time it would allow the government to punish a speaker who merely criticized the government's policy. Since the standard of prior restraints was inappropriate, the question was, "Where shall we draw the line?"[161] If the free-speech clause established a limit beyond which Congress could not punish speech, then the crucial issue was the constitutional standard.

Unfortunately, Chafee did little more than make a few suggestions in regard to defining a constitutional test, and those that he did make were not all that consistent. At one point he said that speech should be free unless it was "clearly liable to cause direct and dangerous interference with the conduct of the war." He then commended Judge Hand's approach in *Masses* and endorsed his test of "direct incitement to violent resistance." [162] But of course these two standards of free speech were not identical, and Chafee made no attempt to reconcile them. In a similar vein, though he argued that the original Espionage Act of 1917 was constitutional, he was only willing to say that the more suppressive 1918 amendments "probably" violated free speech. [163] The tone of the entire article reflects the fact that this was Chafee's first real look at free speech. His views had not yet crystallized. It is not surprising that he only got as far as he did. But it is implausible to argue that this article had any serious impact on Holmes's approach to free speech.

In the following year, after Holmes's opinions in *Schenck, Frohwerk,* and *Debs* had appeared, Chafee published a more extensive article on free speech in the *Harvard Law Review*. [164] This article marked an important step in his developing theory of free speech. The new aspects of his approach, however, made it even more difficult for him to put all the pieces together in a coherent way. The resulting ambiguities in the theory make it hard to believe that it was instrumental in forcing Holmes to adopt a pro-speech position.

Chafee began where he had left off the previous year: "where to draw the line?" "It is becoming increasingly important to determine the true limits of freedom of expression, so that speakers and writers may know how much they can properly say, and governments may be sure how much they can lawfully and wisely suppress." [165] He repeated his criticism of Blackstone's definition of free speech and rejected the concept of "abuse of liberty." The latter was not a meaningful criterion to distinguish punishable from nonpunishable speech. [166] But the main purpose of the 1919 article was to attack the idea that punishment of seditious libel was constitutional. Chafee used constitutional history and a functional analysis to criticize the view that government could punish any speech having a remote tendency to cause harm, especially if the speaker's unlawful intent was "constructed" from the possibility of harm. [167]

Chafee's discussion of seditious libel, the bad-tendency doctrine, and constructive intent, which he grouped together, was the core of the article, but it was negative in form. If the ultimate goal was to determine the line of constitutionality beyond which Congress could not go, it was not very helpful. His optimism—revealed in his claim that "our problem of locating the boundary line of free speech is solved"—is therefore difficult to understand. His notion that the boundary line was "fixed close to the point where words will give rise to unlawful acts" hardly "solved" anything. He simply had not defined the limit of free speech with any kind of precision. His admission that he could not "define the right of free speech with the precision of the Rule against Perpetuities or the Rule in Shelley's Case, because it involves national policies which are more flexible than private property," was perfectly understandable. What is not so defensible is his belief that he had established "a workable principle of classification in this method of balancing and this broad test of certain danger."[168] A "broad test of certain danger" provided no guidance to either the citizen or the state. As a test of constitutionality, it produced a "line" that was so wide that it was no longer a line.

One indication that Chafee's criterion of constitutionality had not advanced much beyond what he had written in 1918 was that he repeated his conclusion that the 1918 amendments of the Espionage Act were only "probably" unconstitutional.[169] It is hard to discern why he thought his certain-harm criterion drew a bright line of constitutionality if it produced such ambiguous judgments. It is also unclear how he squared his emphasis on a constitutional test as a major premise with his recognition that any constitutional evaluation of free speech required a balancing of social interests. He criticized Holmes for not coming up with this major premise.

But when we ask where the line actually runs and how they know on which side of it a given utterance belongs, we find no answer in their opinions. Justice Holmes in his Espionage Act decisions had a magnificent opportunity to make articulate for us *that major premise,* under which judges ought to classify words as inside or outside the scope of the First Amendment. He, we hoped, would concentrate his great abilities on fixing the line. Instead, like other judges, he has told us that certain plainly unlawful utterances are, to be sure, unlawful. (Emphasis mine)[170]

It seems that Chafee stressed the importance of the test because he adhered to a deductive model of constitutional adjudication, at least when free speech was involved. The common-law approach, the gradual inclusion and exclusion of concrete cases, was of "very little use for the First Amendment," he argued, because the cases were "too few, too varied in their character, and often too easily solved, to develop any definite boundary between lawful and unlawful speech."[171] His solution was to propose "the major premise," the concept from which correct decisions in free-speech cases could be deduced. Presumably, in 1919 his idea of certain harm was to serve this function.

Holmes, who believed that "general propositions did not decide concrete cases," would not have been impressed with this line of reasoning. There was no way, in his opinion, to define beforehand a crystal clear line of illegality, even if speech was involved. This very issue probably came up in the conversation that Chafee had with Holmes later that year, after Chafee's article had been published. In a letter to Judge Amidon, Chafee reported that Holmes had said that he did "not think it possible to draw any limit to the first amendment but simply to indicate cases on the one side or the other of the line."[172] At the time that he had written his 1919 article, Chafee must have disagreed. Only in this way can his attempt to find a major premise be understood.

But for our immediate purpose, it is more important to see that Chafee himself was not being consistent. In his 1919 article, the same article in which he criticized Holmes for not providing a major premise, he also wrote that it was "useless to define free speech by talk about rights" and that to "find the boundary line of any right, we must get behind rules of law to human facts."[173] Constitutional adjudication required the balancing of social and individual interests "to determine which interest shall be sacrificed under the circumstances and which should be protected and become the foundation of a legal right.[174] But if balancing interests was the essence of the matter, then his call for a major premise in cases of free speech and his criticism of Holmes's opinion in *Debs* conflicted with his own assumptions. Balancing interests was a task requiring the judge to be constantly sensitive to new interests and to changing circumstances. If a judge was balancing interests, he could not decide cases deductively according to a major premise.

It is also puzzling why Chafee thought that his certain-harm standard was different from or superior to Holmes's clear-and-present-danger doctrine. Even though Holmes did not understand his standard as the major premise of a syllogism, he did specify the criteria that judges were to use on a case-by-case basis: unlawful intent, clear and present danger, and conspiracy. It must have been these criteria to which Chafee referred when he said that Holmes had "not left us without some valuable suggestions pointing toward the ultimate solution of the problem of the limits of free speech."[175] The general impression left by his 1919 article, however, was that Holmes's standard was wanting in a serious way. But why? These suggestions were more definite and concrete than Chafee's proposed test of certain harm.

Another source of confusion in Chafee's article was the distinction that he tried to draw between the *limits* of Congress's power over speech and the *policy* of free speech that should be used in statutory construction.[176] Free speech was not just a boundary line to congressional authority, but "an exhortation and a guide for the action of Congress inside that boundary."[177] The whole Bill of Rights was thought to have this dual purpose.

Our Bills of Rights perform a double function. They fix a certain point to halt the government abruptly with a "Thus far and no farther"; but long before that point is reached they urge upon every official of the three branches of the state a constant regard for certain declared fundamental policies of American life.[178]

From this perspective, Chafee applauded the free-speech policy that was implicit in Learned Hand's interpretation of the Espionage Act of 1917. Liability was confined to words that came "close to injurious conduct," or, to put it differently, that urged others "that it is their duty or their interest to resist the law."[179] This test was then equated with the common-law definition of attempt and incitement, both of which required, in Chafee's view, unlawful intent and proximity to harm. Holmes's clear-and-present-danger doctrine was then thrown into the pot because it "substantially agrees with the conclusion reached by Judge Hand." Holmes drew "the boundary line very close to the test of incitement . . . and criminal attempts"[180] at common law. What these passages show is that Chafee's focus in the 1919 article was on the proper interpretation of the Espionage Act of 1917, an interpretation that was sensitive to free speech as a *policy*. His attention was not primarily on the outer limit of Congress's power. He hoped to win the argument by rallying the common law, Hand, and Holmes to his side.

The strategy was unworkable for two reasons. First, the distortions of history and of Hand's and Holmes's approaches probably did not escape the notice of his contemporaries.[181] An exchange of letters later that year between Chafee and Alfred Bettman, who helped to write most of the government's briefs in the free-speech cases of 1918 and 1919, reveals that there was at least one lawyer who remained unconvinced.[182] The second problem is more serious. Chafee, it would appear, confused his own distinction between free speech as a limit and as a policy because the same criteria were used to define both. He never made it clear how his criterion of certain-harm, which was to set the limit of Congress's authority, was different from the principles of liability contained in the Espionage Act, which defined how far Congress had gone to suppress speech given our policy of free speech.

Somewhere in such a range of circumstances is the point where *direct causation begins and speech becomes punishable as incitement under the ordinary standards of statutory construction and the ordinary policy of free speech,* which Judge Hand applied. Congress could push the test of criminality back beyond this point, although eventually it would reach the extreme limit fixed by the First Amendment, beyond which words cannot be restricted for their remote tendency to hinder the war. In other words, the ordinary tests punish agitation just before it begins to boil over; Congress could change those tests and punish it when it gets really hot, but it is unconstitutional to interfere when it is merely warm. (Emphasis mine)[183]

The problem with this quote is that Chafee offers certain harm and direct causation as the standards of the *policy* of free speech, even though (as seen above) he had identified them elsewhere with the *limits* of free speech. But how could "direct-causation of harm" be the correct interpretation of the Espionage Act if the same standard was used to delineate the outermost limit of Congress's authority? How could Congress suppress speech beyond the Espionage Act if the certain-harm test defined the outermost limit of Congress's power?

The basic conclusion is that Chafee had not fully worked out his theory of free speech by the middle of 1919. It did not fit together in a coherent way. He had not yet figured out whether his free-speech test was to operate in a deductive or inductive manner, nor had he clarified how his distinction between the policy and the limit of free speech was related to the various standards of free speech that existed at the time. Nonetheless, by the time Chafee published *Freedom of Speech* in the fall of 1920 the situation had changed greatly. Not only had he abandoned the idea that some test of free speech could define beforehand the limits of free speech,[184] but he also had begun to distinguish between Hand's and Holmes's approaches to free speech.

The first development was possibly the result of Chafee's 1919 conversation with Holmes. Though this event is often used to support the idea that Chafee exerted some influence on Holmes, the greater likelihood is that Holmes convinced Chafee that his search for an ultimate solution, an explicit major premise from which correct decisions in cases involving free speech could be deduced, was a futile quest. In his letter to Judge Amidon that described his meeting with Holmes, Chafee conceded that he himself no longer "anticipate[d]" that "any hard and fast line could be drawn,"[185] an admission that may mark a departure from his earlier views.

Certainly in his book of 1920 there was no longer a sense that he had solved the problem or that a major premise was all that was needed. His book has a more mature flavor, especially in those parts that were not reprints of articles published earlier. Less emphasis was placed on whether a particular law was constitutional or not. More attention was given to the idea that the free-speech clause was essentially an "exhortation." Its most important role concerned how laws that touched on speech should be interpreted, not invalidated.[186] The basic theme of the book was that such suppressive laws were unwise, and that they therefore should be interpreted narrowly in accordance with traditional criteria of criminality.

It is possible that Chafee cast his argument in terms of wisdom and utility for tactical reasons. Perhaps he wanted to reach a popular audience and thought that a nonlegalistic approach would serve these pedagogical goals better than a discussion of legal criteria.[187] But it is also likely that his new orientation reflected a deeper transition in his thinking, that he had in fact become convinced that the policy of free speech was more important than its limits. The reason for such a change of heart is not difficult to discern. By 1920 he had lost confidence in the federal judiciary. Not only had he seen how the war hysteria of 1917–18 had overcome judicial integrity and impartiality at the district court level,[188] but the majority opinions in *Schaefer, Pierce,* and *Abrams* must have been especially disappointing to him.[189] What was the point of trying to define a proper constitutional test if federal judges were so far afield?

Since the federal judiciary had failed him, Chafee turned to Congress.

Only it, he now argued, could "effectively safeguard minority opinion in times of excitement."[190] But since Congress reflected public opinion, the real task was to explain the value of free speech to the American people. The assumption was that if the people were properly educated, Congress would never push its authority to the limit of free speech. This was Chafee's new perspective. It was reflected in his claim that "the proper construction of the Espionage Act of 1917 is far more important than its constitutionality."[191] Though at times in his book, especially in those parts that were merely reprints of former articles, Chafee returned to the idea of drawing the line of constitutionality,[192] the main emphasis of the book was on the value of free speech as a matter of policy.[193]

Also in *Freedom of Speech,* Chafee for the first time drew a clear distinction between Hand's and Holmes's standards of free speech. He now recognized that Hand's test was "an objective test, the nature of the words used,"[194] while Holmes's made "the nature of the words only one element of danger."[195] Accordingly, Hand imposed liability only if the language used by the speaker literally advocated illegality, while Holmes permitted convictions, no matter what language was used, if the speaker intended the harm and the speech posed a clear and present danger.[196] To explain this new sense of the difference between Hand's and Holmes's approaches to free speech, Hand's 1919–20 correspondence with Chafee has crucial significance. In response to the letter in which Hand criticized Holmes's dissent in *Abrams* and endorsed his own objective test, Chafee said that he was "very much interested" in what Hand had said.[197] Such a reaction hints that Chafee was unaware of the differences between Hand's and Holmes's approaches to free speech until 1919.

Another letter from Hand to Chafee convinced Chafee that Hand's approach was superior to Holmes's on the grounds of administrative efficiency.

My own objection to the rule rests in the fact that it exposes all who discuss heated questions to an inquiry before a jury as to their purposes. That inquiry necessarily is of the widest scope and if their general attitude is singular and intrasigent, my own belief is that a jury is an insufficient protection.[198]

That this passage had a great impact on Chafee is fairly clear. In his book he not only repeated the same reasoning, but also used language nearly identical to Hand's. "The trouble with the District Court test is that in making intention the crucial fact in criminality it exposes all who discuss heated questions to an inquiry before a jury as to their purposes. That inquiry necessarily is of the widest scope and if the general attitude of the person is singular and intransigent, there is an insufficient protection."[199] The reflection of Hand's ideas and language in Chafee's book shows that it was Hand who had convinced Chafee of the administrative problem that arose for any test that focused on the speaker's intent. Consequently, at the time that Chafee wrote *Freedom of Speech*, he had no choice but to reconsider Hand's and Holmes's standards of free speech.

In the main, Chafee's solution was to understand Hand's incitement test as the proper interpretation of the Espionage Act, one that was sufficiently sensitive to the nation's policy of free speech. Holmes's clear-and-present-danger doctrine, in contrast, was to function as the outermost limit of Congressional power. By this time, however, Chafee was sensitive to certain criticisms of Hand's incitement test. According to it, a speaker who literally incited illegality was outside of the amendment regardless if there was no chance of harm.[200] This was unacceptable. Incitement also required a set of circumstances in which the speaker would "directly cause" harm. By adding this condition, Chafee may have distorted Hand's standard of free speech, but he nevertheless insisted that it was this policy of free speech that Hand had applied in *Masses*.[201]

With this understanding of the *Masses* test, Chafee once again equated it with traditional common-law criteria of solicitation and incitement.[202] A "correct" interpretation of the Espionage Act, an interpretation sensitive to the nation's policy of free speech, imposed liability only if the speaker's language literally incited unlawful acts, only if there was a strong probability that the speech would "directly cause" harm, and only if the speaker was guilty of solicitation or incitement; that is, "only if he would have been indictable for the crime itself, had it been committed, either as accessory or principal."[203] By appealing to the authority of Hand's opinion in *Masses* in this manner, Chafee narrowed the statutory provisions of the Espionage Act to a greater degree than Hand had done. He interpreted the Espionage Act in this manner because he believed that the policy of free speech required that all statutes that affected speech be interpreted as narrowly as possible. It was in this fashion that he, though strongly influenced by Hand, adopted an independent speech-protective course.

It bears emphasis that Chafee was not able to put the pieces of his theoretical perspective together until the end of 1920, well after Holmes wrote his dissent in *Abrams*. And since the constitutional issue was now relatively unimportant to Chafee, it should cause no surprise that his exact opinion of the limit of free speech was vague even after his views had finally hardened. He still rejected the bad-tendency doctrine and the idea that free speech only prevented prior restraints. Since much of the book was reprinted from his early articles, he even repeated the idea that he had solved the problem by defining the boundary line of free speech "close to the point where words will give rise to unlawful acts."[204] Later in the book, however, he announced his new view that Holmes's clear-and-present-danger doctrine substantially coincided "with the conclusion reached by our investigation of the history and political setting of the First Amendment."[205] Though Chafee may have preferred his version of Hand's interpretation of the Espionage Act, he thought that Holmes had a better sense of the constitutional limits of the right of free speech.

It is possible that Chafee endorsed Holmes's clear-and-present-danger test as the constitutional limit because it had the virtue of being law. He, we are told, would have preferred Hand's incitement test as the constitutional test, but took what was available to him—Holmes's test—and got as much protection for speech out of it as he could.[206] But since the underlying assumption of Chafee's mature outlook was that the constitutional issue was not the most important matter, it is puzzling why he would have endorsed Holmes's test as the constitutional standard unless he in fact approved of it. It is especially mysterious since Chafee lived long enough to deny the clear-and-present-danger doctrine, if he wanted to deny it, without causing any harm to free speech. His preference for Hand's objective test was always in the context of what the policy of free speech required. It is therefore unclear why Chafee remained quiet about his secret preference for Hand's standard as a constitutional test.

It is possible that he remained committed to Holmes's standard as the limit of free speech for the simple reason that he preferred it. It should be recalled that Chafee was generally unwilling to find any statute unconstitutional, and he more than once explicitly stated that Congress could go further than the Espionage Act.[207] In regard to state sedition laws, he said that it was "probable that the open advocacy of sabotage and the doctrines of revolutionary syndicalism . . . does present a sufficient danger to bring such speech within the range of legislative discretion."[208] Advocacy of sabotage and syndicalism was punishable even if there was little likelihood of harm in the particular case. In a similar discussion of a hypothetical federal sedition statute, he said, contra John Stuart Mill, that abstract advocacy of tyrannicide was punishable because "assassination is so easily carried out that there is always a sufficiently clear and present danger of its occurrence to bring such discussions within the range of legislative discretion."[209] These comments support the conclusion that Chafee had a very relaxed notion of Holmes's clear-and-present-danger doctrine. He thought that certain types of speech were so dangerous that their advocacy alone was sufficient to create a clear and present danger. While Holmes would have insisted that the likelihood of assassination had to be assessed on a case-by-case basis, Chafee excluded a whole category of speech from constitutional protection.

The argument that Chafee endorsed Holmes's standard as a constitutional test only because it was law, that he secretly preferred some sort of direct incitement test, does not fit well with his statements that Congress could go beyond the Espionage Act and that sedition laws and laws punishing abstract advocacy of tyrannicide were constitutional. He certainly believed fervently in free speech and generally thought that the best policy was not to punish speech. But his occasional judgments of constitutionality suggest that he had a wide sense of Congress's power over speech. His evaluation of *Herndon v. Lowry*,[210] in the second edition of his book, is especially troublesome. The case concerned a black communist convicted of attempting to cause an insurrection in Georgia. Chafee agreed with the Supreme Court's decision that the defendant's activities were outside of the statute. Herndon may have demanded equal rights and more relief for blacks, but he had not attempted an insurrection. He did have in his possession a booklet that advocated the creation of a new southern state with a black majority, but he had not distributed it. On this set of facts, it was impossible to say that Herndon had attempted to cause an insurrection.

Nonetheless, of all the free-speech cases that Chafee considered in his book, he thought only Herndon had created a clear and present danger.

The one exception is Herndon. Not that there was clear and present danger of the insurrection for which he was indicted. Not that the Black Belt Free State could have suddenly emerged into being. But, given the unrest of Negroes, share croppers, mill-workers, his demands for equal racial rights, lavish relief, and the virtual abolition of debts might have produced some sort of disorder in the near future. Smoking is all right, but not in a powder magazine.[211]

This means that Chafee would have supported the constitutionality of Herndon's conviction if a properly drafted statute had been in place. There is thus no way that he favored some kind of direct incitement test, at least not in 1946. Long after Chafee could have publicly abandoned Holmes's test without causing any harm to free speech, he was in favor of the constitutionality of imposing liability on black communist agitators in the South, even though he rejected this option on policy grounds. Again, the point is not only that he used the idea of a clear and present danger to ascertain the limits of Congress's power, but he applied the notion in a very loose way. Just as the advocacy of tyrannicide was placed completely outside the Constitution, so also was communist agitation by blacks in southern states.

Chafee's reputation as a defender of free speech should not be unduly tarnished because he had a wide sense of Congress's ultimate power over speech. His mature perspective concentrated on free speech as a matter of policy, and he generally found it unwise to suppress speech in any way. It just seems that he was sensitive, perhaps overly sensitive, to how dangerous speech could be in emergencies. Even though he encouraged the greatest protection for speech as a matter of policy, he did not want to deprive Congress of its constitutional authority to act if the situation warranted it.[212] Accordingly, it is possible that Chafee adhered to his own interpretation of Holmes's doctrine of the limit of free speech for substantive reasons. He may well have thought that in times of crisis, Congress could punish speech even if it was not literally incitement, even if the speech was not directly causing harm and the speaker could not be punished as an accessory or principal.

The standard account of the relationship between Holmes and Chafee must thus be reversed. Chafee did not convince Holmes to use his doctrine in a more speech-protective fashion; this was not possible because his ideas were tentative and incoherent prior to 1920. But once Hand had explained the differences between his and Holmes's theories of free speech, it is possible that Chafee endorsed Holmes's test as the limit of free speech because he realized that no matter how valuable free speech was, and no matter how our nation was based on the policy of free speech, Congress had to have authority, in reserve so to speak, to go beyond a direct incitement test.

Ernst Freund

The last of Holmes's peers who, it has been claimed, persuaded Holmes to a more pro-speech position is Ernst Freund. Douglas H. Ginsburg has made this suggestion,[213] but there is little evidence to support it. Freund did have definite views on the subject of free speech. Indeed, in comparison to the other theorists that we have discussed, his doctrine was clear, and his commitment to free speech unwavering. What is hard to believe is that he, during that crucial period between *Debs* and *Abrams,* could have induced Holmes to undergo an intellectual transformation. First, there is little reason to believe that a transformation occurred; second, the contact between Freund and Holmes was minimal—in 1919 Freund only published one article critical of Holmes's opinion in *Debs;* and third (the issue that I concentrate on), Freund's constitutional standard was so different from Holmes's, so radically pro-speech, that the most commonsense conclusion is that Holmes entirely rejected Freund's approach.

In a major work entitled *The Police Power,*[214] Freund made it clear that he preferred a "direct provocation" or direct incitement test of free speech. In this work, though he admitted that the purpose of the free-speech clause was only to prevent prior restraints,[215] he argued that "the long continued practice of toleration" was "sufficient warrant" to give constitutional protection to the "most ample freedom of discussion of public affairs."[216] With this assumption, he admitted that it would not be easy "to draw the line between discussion or agitation that must or should be tolerated and methods that are or may be criminal,"[217] but it had to be drawn. Freund's direct provocation test was his attempt to fulfill this need.

The first, and least controversial, condition of this test is implicit in Freund's conclusion that a statute "may validly forbid all speaking and writing *the object of which* is to incite directly to the commission of violence and crime." (emphasis mine).[218] Before liability could be imposed, the speaker's intent had to be unlawful. But that was not all. The language of the speaker had to constitute direct incitement. As long as the speaker couched his or her language in conditional terms, the speaker was free of liability If an anarchist argued "that the overthrow of government cannot be accomplished otherwise than by force," the anarchist was not punishable, since he or she was only making an empirical hypothetical claim: "if you want to overthrow the government, you must use force." The speaker, no matter what the intent, was protected since that speaker had not explicitly told the audience to use force to overthrow the government. On the same principle, an anarchist can teach that a person is justified in committing some illegal act *if* the state does not dissolve itself, or that the masses will realize that they have the right to smash the state *if* some illegal act is committed.[219]

Freund's early constitutional standard was therefore quite protective of speech. It was more protective than Learned Hand's incitement test because it did not recognize the possibility of indirect incitement. The speaker had to intend illegality *and* directly incite violence in a categorical fashion. From this perspective, Freund criticized Holmes's opinion in *Debs*. He objected that it permitted the punishment of "indirect provocation, i.e. implied or inferential incitement."[220] Debs had not used the language of direct incitement. He had only expressed his disapproval of "the war, its motives and objects" and his warm admiration "of the conduct and attitude of persons who had been convicted of obstructing recruitment."[221] Since there was no direct incitement, Debs should have been exonerated even if his intent was to obstruct the draft and cause insubordination in the military.

Also, in regard to the requirement of unlawful intent, Freund argued that Debs could not have satisfied it because "he could hardly have intended what he could not hope to achieve." Since Debs's "power to create actual obstruction to a compulsory draft was practically nil,"[222] he was free of liability. He was free not only because he did not engage in direct incitement, but because his intent could not conceivably have been illegal. What Freund seems to have been suggesting was a rule that liability could be imposed on speech only if the speaker's unlawful goal was within his power. Even if Debs was trying to induce individuals to avoid the draft, he was to go free because there was no way for him either to destroy the draft or to obstruct it in a serious way.

Freund also hinted in his 1919 article that Debs was not punishable because he had not in fact caused any obstruction of the draft. He commended "present French law" because it punished "even direct provocation not resulting in actual crime only in connection with specified aggravated offenses."[223] The implication was that Debs should have escaped liability. He had not in fact caused either obstruction of the draft or insubordination. Liability was proper only if speech caused harm. Freund had already come close to this conclusion in 1904. Not "even the fact that an adherent of a doctrine commits a crime is conclusive that the teaching of the doctrine amounts to incitement; for the crime may as well have been induced by a morbid brooding over the conditions which are the cause of social discontent."[224] Accordingly, even if Debs's speech had been followed by draft obstruction, that in itself would not have justified liability. The obstruction may have been the result of general "social discontent." To substantiate liability, the state had to show that but for Debs's speech the obstruction of the draft would not have occurred.

The severity of the last requirement of Freund's direct provocation test is obvious. It reveals how his test was much more speech-protective than Holmes's. According to it, liability could be imposed on speech only if the speaker's intent was unlawful and within the speaker's power, only if the words constituted direct incitement, and only if the state could show that the speech activity, rather than general socioeconomic circumstances, actually caused an illegal harm. Though Holmes agreed with Freund that unlawful intent was necessary before liability could be imposed on seditious speech, that was as far as he would go. He did not accept any of Freund's other conditions.

Not only does Holmes's correspondence with Learned Hand (discussed above) show that he never favored any kind of a direct incitement test, but his vote to affirm the defendant's conviction in *Gilbert v. Minnesota*[225] is strong evidence that he never made either direct incitement or an "efficacious illegal intent" a necessary condition of liability for speech. In this case, which occurred well after his dissent in *Abrams* and therefore well after Freund's criticisms had had their effect, Holmes imposed liability even though Gilbert never directly incited disobedience of the draft laws and even though Gilbert had absolutely no chance of destroying the draft system. All that he had done was to hint that *if* the members of his audience (a small rural crowd) disobeyed the law *en masse* (as others had done in St. Paul), the state would not bother to prosecute.[226] His action fell within Freund's sense of the limits of free speech, but Holmes voted to affirm the conviction. It is therefore hard to believe how Holmes could have been influenced by Freund.

In addition, he never accepted Freund's position that liability for speech was appropriate only if the speech activity in fact caused the harm. Such a conclusion conflicted with his entire theory of criminal attempts. It was one of Holmes's settled convictions that an innocent act could be punished if done with unlawful intent and if it was sufficiently proximate to a serious harm. In his reaction to Hand's criticism of his reasoning in *Debs,* Holmes explicitly insisted "that words may constitute an obstruction within the statute, even without proof that the obstruction was successful to the point of preventing recruitment. *That I at least think plain.*" (emphasis mine).[227] Such strong and unambiguous language makes it improbable that Holmes ever limited liability to cases of speech that in fact caused harm. Thus Freund definitely favored a theory of free speech that was more speech-protective than Holmes's, but there is no evidence that the former in any way influenced the latter's outlook.

Adherents of the Bad-Tendency Doctrine

In this chapter, I have tried to show that Holmes's theory was relatively coherent and stable when compared to those of his peers. Now, by turning to judges and constitutional commentators who suppressed speech to a greater degree than Holmes did, I wish to establish that his theory was moderately protective. After all, no matter how arguable the case may be in regard to the speech protective character of Hand's and Chafee's theories, it is quite clear that Freund from the beginning and Brandeis in time adopted positions that were, in varying degrees, more protective of speech than Holmes's. Moreover, David Rabban has described in some detail the scholars of the pre-World War I era who sought to expand the right of free speech: Thomas Cooley, Roscoe Pound, Henry Schofield, and Theodore Schroeder.[228] Though it may well be doubted whether all of these constitutional commentators protected speech more than Holmes did, it is indisputable that some did. He was therefore far from being the most extreme defender of free speech.

The writings of Theodore Schroeder help to show the moderate character of Holmes's theory. His general principle was that citizens had

the right to say with impunity anything and every thing which anyone chooses to say, and to speak it with impunity so long as no actual material injury results to anyone, and when it results then to punish only for the contribution to that material injury and not for the mere speech as such.[229]

This criterion of liability, of course, is nearly identical to the one that Ernst Freund endorsed: speech was punishable only if its purpose was unlawful and if it actually caused harm.[230] No matter what the speaker's intent was, speech alone was not a sufficient basis for an attempt. An actual harm had to result. But Schroeder had difficulty maintaining this extreme position. At another place, he admitted that a person's free-speech rights were violated unless liability rested "on the basis of an ascertained, actual and material injury or the imminent danger thereof."[231] To the degree that he approved of liability for a speaker who intended harm and produced an imminent danger of it, his test approached Holmes's. But since Freund also required actual harm, the safe conclusion is that Holmes's constitutional test was not the most speech-protective standard of his era.

Conversely, Holmes's theory of free speech, properly understood, was clearly more protective of speech than the bad-tendency doctrine endorsed by many of his colleagues on the bench and by eminent scholars of his day. The adherents of the bad-tendency test denied two of the requirements of Holmes's theory: a clear and a present danger. In his opinion in *Gitlow v. New York*, Justice Sanford implied that a clear harm was not needed. The Constitution did not protect speech that tended "to subvert or imperil the government, or to impede or hinder it in the performance of its governmental duties."[232] These were not clear harms; they were vague and amorphous in character. In contrast, Holmes imposed liability on speech that was likely to cause "obstruction of the draft" or "causing insubordination in the military," harms that were far more clear than the elusive ones of "subverting," "imperilling," or "hindering" the government.

In the same case, Sanford argued that it was "unreasonable" to require the state to wait until speech posed a present danger. On the contrary, the state could "suppress the threatened danger in its incipiency."[233] All that was necessary was that the speech have a tendency to cause harm, no matter how far removed the harm was from the speech itself. The adherents of the bad-tendency doctrine also made it perfectly clear that the tendency of speech did not have to be decided by the circumstances of the particular case. As Chief Justice White put it, "the wrong depends upon the tendency of the act to accomplish this [harmful] result without reference to the consideration of how far they may have been without influence in a particular case."[234] Speech harmless in the circumstances was still punishable if in other hypothetical circumstances the speech would have a tendency to cause some vague harm, whether immediately or in the distant future.

In my judgment, Holmes disagreed with this entire line of reasoning. Before liability could be imposed, the harm had to be present, which meant that *in the particular case* the speaker was creating the *immediate likelihood* of a *specific* illegal act. But since all legal distinctions were ultimately matters of degree, it was a matter of judgment whether a harm was clear and present enough to impose liability on a speaker. Judges had to draw the line on a case-by-case basis. But even so, his denial that speech could be punished merely because it was a type of a speech-act that had a tendency to cause some vague harm in the distant future does much to establish the conclusion that he was, when compared to his peers, a moderate defender of free speech.

Another tenet of the bad-tendency doctrine required judicial deference to a legislature's assessment of harmfulness. If a legislature decided that the advocacy of a certain doctrine—for example, criminal anarchy—was harmful in itself and therefore prohibited the advocacy of it, judges were not to step in. *Gitlow v. New York*, with Holmes and Brandeis dissenting, upheld the idea that judges should defer to the legislature[235] as long as the policy was not completely irrational.[236] But since the harm could be both vague and in the distant future, the requirement of a rational policy was not a serious restriction of legislative discretion. If a legislature wanted to suppress an unpopular doctrine, it could find some vague distant harm that would justify imposing liability on the advocacy of it. Therefore, the bad-tendency doctrine provided the individual speaker with no constitutional protection.

Holmes once again refused to go along with the majority of his colleagues. His dissent in *Gitlow* can only be understood as an affirmation of the judiciary's role in monitoring legislative determinations of harmful speech. Of course the legislature was free to punish speech that was traditionally understood as harmful—libel, contempt of court, deceit—and Holmes hinted that state legislatures may have some discretion in redefining the boundaries of harmful speech.[237] But if free speech was to be preserved, no legislature could punish innocent advocacy of doctrine on the basis of vague distant harms. Holmes argued that if "the beliefs expressed in proletarian dictatorship are destined to be accepted by the dominant forces of the community, the only meaning of free speech is that they should be given their chance and have their way."[238] Judges had the responsibility of defending free speech against legislative attempts to punish unpopular doctrines, even if the attempts were disguised as efforts to punish harmful speech.

The bad-tendency doctrine also addressed the issue of the speaker's intent. Was it necessary for the speaker to intend some harm, no matter how vague and distant it may be, or was it sufficient if the speaker should have foreseen the possible harmful consequences of his or her speech activity? In *Schaefer* and *Gilbert*,[239] Justice McKenna did refer to the purpose of the speaker, but the adherents of the bad-tendency doctrine were generally willing to presume illegal intent from the likelihood of harm. In *Abrams*, in which the defendants advocated strikes in the munitions industry for the purpose of ending American interference with the Russian revolution, Justice Clarke argued:

It will not do to say, as is now argued, that the only intent of these defendants was to prevent injury to the Russian cause. Men must be held to have intended, and to be accountable for, the effects which their acts were likely to produce. Even if their primary purpose and intent was to aid the cause of the Russian Revolution, the plan of action which they adopted necessarily involved ... defeat of the war program of the United States.[240]

Accordingly, intent was not equal to the actual purpose or foresight of the speaker. In the Court's opinion, if Abrams should have foreseen the harm, he was "to be held accountable," whether he in fact intended or foresaw the harm or not.

Because the test of intent was the harmful tendency of the act that the speaker should have foreseen, there was in fact no requirement of intent in the bad-tendency doctrine. If the likelihood of some harm—whether vague or distant—was increased by some speech, then the speaker intended it. This was exactly the reasoning that Justice Pitney used in *Pierce v. United States*.

It was shown without dispute that defendants distributed the pamphlet—"The Price We Pay"—with full understanding of its contents; *and this of itself furnished a ground for attributing to them an intent* to bring about, and for finding that they attempted to bring about, any and all such consequences as reasonably might be anticipated from its distribution. (Emphasis mine)[241]

Hence the only real requirement of the bad-tendency doctrine was that the speech have a tendency to produce some vague distant harm. If it did, the speaker intended the harm and was outside constitutional protection.

My contention is that Holmes understood a speaker's unlawful intent as an independent and crucial requirement. As long as the speaker was not engaged in speech activity harmful per se, the only time a speaker lost constitutional protection was when he or she actually intended— not merely foresaw—a specific unlawful act. Creating a clear and present danger was not enough to lose protection: the speaker had also to intend the harm. It is true that the line between creating a clear and present danger and engaging in harmful speech activity was one of degree. Circumstances could be so awful that even expressions of opinion or exhortations could constitute a harmful speech act. It was in this spirit that Holmes advised Americans to be "eternally vigilant against attempts to check the expressions of opinions that we loathe . . . *unless they so imminently threaten immediate interference with the lawful and pressing purposes of the law that an immediate check is required to save the country."* (emphasis mine).[242] That he was referring to mere expressions of opinion, not to ill-intentioned advocacies of illegal acts, is shown by what he said next: "Only the emergency that makes it immediately dangerous to leave the correction of evil counsels to time warrants making any exception" to free speech. "Of course I am speaking only of expressions of opinion and exhortations, which were all that were uttered here."[243] The implication was that in certain circumstances mere expressions of opinion could constitute harmful speech activity, and the speaker could then be punished if an average person would have foreseen the danger. But these situations were the exceptions. The more likely situation would involve a speaker who produced a clear and present danger that a specific illegal act would result. In this kind of case, Holmes never inferred the unlawful intent from the possibility or likelihood of harm. He always required actual unlawful intent.

Any impression that the bad-tendency doctrine received universal acclaim from academia and the legal profession would of course be inaccurate.[244] It would be just as fallacious, however, to think that its support was limited to a few reactionary federal judges. For example, Edward S. Corwin summarized and endorsed several of the doctrine's crucial tenets:

first, Congress is not limited to forbidding words which are of a nature "to create a clear and present danger" to national interests, but it may forbid words which are intended to endanger those interests if in the exercise of a fair legislative discretion it finds it "necessary and proper" to do so; second, the intent of the accused in uttering the alleged forbidden words may be presumed from the reasonable consequences of such words, though the presumption is a rebuttable one; third, the court will not scrutinize on appeal the findings of juries in this class of cases more strictly than in other penal cases.[245]

John H. Wigmore not only endorsed the suspension of civil liberties during war time,[246] but also gave his support to the Supreme Court's claim that the tendency of speech was not to be assessed in accordance with the facts of a particular case. His position was that the "relative amount of harm that one criminal act can effect is no measure of its criminality, and no measure of the danger of its criminality."[247] The harmful tendency of any speech activity was to be measured in the abstract. Considering the defendant's act as a type of speech activity, would it have a tendency to produce harm, whether now or in the distant future? Others endorsed the view that Congress was the best judge of what types of speech activity were harmful. Day Kimball claimed that

the First Amendment . . . does not inhibit the suppression, whenever reasonably necessary, of utterances whose aims render them a menace to the existence of the state. In the case of such utterances it is for Congress to judge, in the light of existing conditions, whether of war or peace, as to the kind and amount of repression necessary.[248]

Thus the bad-tendency doctrine was not without its defenders throughout Holmes's era on the Court. It received the support of prominent legal scholars in prestigious law journals.[249] Therefore, though Holmes was not the most extreme defender of the faith, the only possible conclusion is that he, when compared to his peers, must at a minimum be described as a moderate defender of free speech.

Notes

1. See especially Fred D. Ragan, "Justice Oliver Wendell Holmes, Jr., Zechariah Chafee, Jr., and the Clear and Present Danger Test for Free Speech: The First Year, 1919," *Journal of American History* 58 (1971–72): 24–45; Gunther, "Learned Hand and the Origins of Modern First Amendment Doctrine: Some Fragments of History," *Stanford Law Review* 27 (February

1975): 719–55; David M. Rabban, "The First Amendment in Its Forgotten Years," *Yale Law Journal* 90 (1981): 514–95; idem, "The Emergence of Modern First Amendment Doctrine," *University of Chicago Law Review* 50 (Fall 1983): 1205–1355.

2. See Gunther, "Learned Hand," 720.

3. See generally Gunther, "Learned Hand." Also see Marvin Schick, *Learned Hand's Court* (Baltimore: Johns Hopkins University Press, 1970), 177; Kathryn Griffith, *Judge Learned Hand and the Role of the Federal Judiciary* (Norman, Okla.: University of Oklahoma Press, 1973), 144. But Griffith's understanding of Hand's test is unclear. On the same page that she describes the test as "word-oriented," she also says that it "provided the jury with a concrete problem to consider—the nature of the words themselves and the threat they imposed of interference with the armed forces" (ibid). Earlier she had argued that Hand's test was "not the justice of its [the language used] substance or the decency and propriety of its temper but the strong danger that it will cause injurious acts." It seems clear that the ambiguities of Hand's free speech doctrine have crept into the commentary.

4. Learned Hand, *Bill of Rights* (New York: Atheneum, 1979), 56.

5. Ibid., 66.

6. Ibid., 58–60.

7. Ibid., 60–61.

8. Ibid., 59.

9. Ibid.

10. 183 F.2d 201, 207 (1950).

11. Id.

12. Id.

13. Id.

14. Id.

15. Id.

16. Id.

17. 295 U.S. 441 (1935).

18. *Dennis v. United States*, 183 F.2d 201, 209 (1950).

19. Hand thought that *Dennis* involved "indirect" calls for revolution. Even though the Communist party intended to capture political power by unlawful means, it "covered" this fact "by an innocent terminology, designed to prevent its disclosure" (id. at 212). In Hand's opinion, the jury had enough evidence to find that the defendants were acting in concert for the purpose of advocating unlawful activity. This was true even though the defendants did not directly instigate unlawful action (see id. at 206–7).

20. Id. at 212.

21. Kathryn Griffith suggests that Hand would have applied the bad-tendency test in *Dennis* if intervening precedents had left him that option (see her *Judge Learned Hand and the Role of the Federal Judiciary*, 147). She also argues that Hand's opinion in *Dennis* was consistent with the statutory rule that he announced in *Masses Publishing Company v. Patten* (see ibid., 143).

If so, then the speech-protective character of Hand's early incitement test is clearly open to question. Also see Martin Shapiro, *Freedom of Speech* (Englewood Cliffs, N.J.: Prentice-Hall, 1966), 65. Shapiro claims that Hand's test in *Dennis* was indistinguishable from the bad-tendency doctrine.

22. Since there was evidence that the defendants intended a revolution and since the defendants associated together, it is arguable that Holmes would have also found them liable on the ground that they were part of a conspiracy. Though it is true that a harm need not be clear or present to impose liability on conspirators, in all likelihood Holmes would not have found a conspiracy in *Dennis* because there was no evidence linking the defendants to any specific criminal act, only to a distant ill-defined revolution.

23. *Dennis v. United States*, 183 F. 2d 201, 212 (1950).

24. Id.

25. Id.

26. Id.

27. Gunther ignores Hand's later opinions (see "Learned Hand," 752).

28. Gerald Gunther has been instrumental in establishing this interpretation of Hand (see ibid., 722–29). Other studies have argued that Hand's doctrine of judicial deference to the legislative will was the defining thread that united his early and late opinions. On this interpretation, the early Hand may have been a philosophical supporter of free speech, but he never formulated a constitutional test that restricted the scope of permissible legislative action. See Marvin Schick, *Learned Hand's Court*, 176–84; Kathryn Griffith, *Judge Learned Hand*, 132–33, 143–44. As the text makes clear, I think this alternative account is quite convincing.

29. 244 F. 535 (S.D.N.Y.), rev'd. 246 F. 24 (2nd Cir. 1917).

30. Id. at 538. See also Griffith, *Judge Learned Hand*, 132–33; Schick, *Learned Hand's Court*, pp. 176–77.

31. *Masses Publishing Company v. Patten*, 244 F. 535, 538 (S.D.N.Y. 1917).

32. Gunther argues that Hand was providing a constitutional standard by way of statutory construction (see his "Learned Hand," 725–26).

33. *Masses Publishing Co. v. Patten* 244 F. 535, 539 (S.D.N.Y. 1917).

34. Id.

35. Id.

36. Id. at 540.

37. Id.

38. Gunther, "Learned Hand," 724–29.

39. *Masses Publishing Co. v. Patten*, 244 F. 535, 542 (S.D.N.Y. 1917).

40. Letters from Learned Hand to Zechariah Chafee, Jr., 3 December 1919 and 8 January 1920, appended to Gunther, "Learned Hand," 763, 765, documents 9 and 11 respectively.

41. Letter from Learned Hand to Holmes, March 1919, appended to Gunther, "Learned Hand," 759, document 4. For Gunther's discussion of Hand's rationale of his "word-oriented" test, see his "Learned Hand," 738–41.

42. *Masses Publishing Co. v. Patten*, 244 F. 535, 540 (S.D.N.Y. 1917).

43. *United States v. Nearing*, 252 F. 223, 228 (S.D.N.Y. 1918).

44. *Masses Publishing Co. v. Patten*, 244 F. 535, 542 (S.D.N.Y. 1917).

45. But see Gunther, "Learned Hand," 729. Some passages from Hand's correspondence do suggest, as Gunther argues, that Hand adopted a word-oriented test. See Letter from Learned Hand to Zechariah Chafee, Jr., 8 January 1920, appended to Gunther, "Learned Hand," 766, document 11: "I own I cannot see any escape from construing the privilege as absolute, so long as the utterance objectively regarded, can by any fair construction be held to fall short of counselling violence." But Hand may have believed that cases of indirect advocacy could be "objectively regarded" as cases of counseling violence. Marc Antony was liable because his utterance, if "objectively regarded," counseled violence.

46. Letter from learned Hand to Zechariah Chafee, Jr., 3 December 1919, appended to Gerald Gunther, "Learned Hand," 763, document 9.

47. Letter from Learned Hand to Zechariah Chafee, Jr., 2 January 1921, appended to Gunther, "Learned Hand," 770, document 15.

48. Ibid., 771.

49. 252 F. 223 (S.D.N.Y. 1918).

50. Hand's decision in *Masses* was reversed by the Second Circuit in *Masses Publishing Co. v. Patten*, 246 F. 24 (2d Cir. 1917).

51. *United States v. Nearing*, 252 F. 223, 227 (S.D.N.Y. 1918).

52. Id. at 228. Also see id. at 227: "Yet the terms, 'counsel' or 'advise' have a content which can be determined objectively, and do not depend upon the subjective intent of their author." In *Nearing*, Hand nonetheless imposed liability, even though what the defendants had done failed to satisfy the common-law test. The Espionage Act (at least as interpreted by the Court of Appeals) laid down "an added measure of liability" (id. at 228).

53. Letter from Learned Hand to Zechariah Chafee, Jr., 8 January 1920, appended to Gunther, "Learned Hand," 765, document 11. It is fair to ignore Hand's requirement that the "only" effect of the speech was to counsel illegality. He could not have meant what he said because even cases of direct advocacy of unlawful action have effects over and above the one of counseling illegality. Such speeches also provide information, entertain the crowd, as well as produce insight and revulsion. Hence, I understand Hand to be saying that a speaker is liable if one of the main effects of the speech is to give the audience the impression that they ought to disobey the law.

54. For an opposing view, see Gunther, "Learned Hand."

55. It seems to many that it is obviously true that a jury could all too easily repress speech, if they used Holmes's clear-and-present-danger standard, while Hand's incitement test would function as an admirable restraint. See generally Gunther, "Learned Hand," and Rabban, "The Emergence of Modern First Amendment Doctrine." But I do not quite see the obviousness of this conclusion. The records of many free-speech cases show that there was often more than a little dispute about the speaker's exact words. Therefore, even if it used Hand's test, an overly "patriotic" jury could repress speech

in a cavalier fashion. Hand's test might be more protective in the way that it would be administered in the case of written circulars. However, I doubt whether any legal standard would prevent a determined jury, assuming that they got the case, from reaching its objective. And I doubt whether theories of free speech should be evaluated on this basis because there is no empirical data to decide the question either way.

56. Robert K. Murray, *Red Scare* (Minneapolis: University of Minnesota, 1955), 53, citing *Annual Report of the Attorney General, 1920* (Washington, D.C., 1920), 179.

57. See Gunther, "Learned Hand," 732–35. Gunther has appended the letters to his article, documents 1–7.

58. Ibid., 732.

59. Letter from Learned Hand to Holmes, 22 June 1918, appended to Gunther, "Learned Hand," 756, document 1.

60. Ibid.

61. Letter from Holmes to Learned Hand, 24 June 1918, appended to Gunther, "Learned Hand," 757, document 2.

62. See generally Letter from Learned Hand to Holmes, 22 June 1918, appended to Gunther, "Learned Hand," 756, document 1.

63. Letter from Holmes to Learned Hand, 24 June 1918, appended to Gunther, "Learned Hand," 757, document 2.

64. Ibid.

65. Ibid.

66. Letter from Learned Hand to Holmes, 22 June 1918, appended to Gunther, "Learned Hand," 756, document 1.

67. Gunther, "Learned Hand," 734.

68. *Holmes-Laski Letters*, ed. M. D. Howe, 2 vols. (Cambridge: Harvard University Press, 1953), 2:948. Also see 1:8, 762, 2:1183.

69. Letter from Holmes to Learned Hand, 25 February 1919, appended to Gunther, "Learned Hand," 758, document 3.

70. Letter from Learned Hand to Holmes, March 1919, appended to Gunther, "Learned Hand," 758, document 4.

71. Gunther, "Learned Hand," 739.

72. Letter from Learned Hand to Holmes, March 1919, appended to Gunther, "Learned Hand," 758, document 4.

73. Gunther, "Learned Hand," 739–40. Gunther also suggests that Hand's endorsement of Deb's conviction conflicts with "the tenor of his remarks to others" (ibid). More likely than not Gunther is referring to Hand's letter to Ernst Freund, which expressed admiration for the latter's article published in *The New Republic* that criticized Holmes's opinion in *Debs*. But Hand may well have only been endorsing Freund's view that a test of likelihood of harm allowed juries to suppress hostile speech. Accordingly, Hand's letter to Freund is consistent with his letter to Holmes. He supported Debs's conviction, but he believed that Holmes's test gave juries too much latitude. See Ernst Freund, "The *Debs* Case and Freedom of Speech," *The New*

Republic, 3 May 1919, 13, in *University of Chicago Law Review* 40 (Winter 1973): 239–42. Part of Hand's letter to Freund is quoted in an "Afterword" by Douglas H. Ginsburg (see *University of Chicago Law Review* 40 [Winter 1973]: 244).

74. Gunther, "Learned Hand," 739.
75. Letter from Learned Hand to Holmes, March 1919, appended to Gunther, "Learned Hand," 758, document 4.
76. Letter from Holmes to Learned Hand, 3 April 1919, appended to Gunther, "Learned Hand," 759, document 5.
77. Gunther, "Learned Hand," 741.
78. Letter from Holmes to Learned Hand, 3 April 1919, appended to Gunther, "Learned Hand," 760, document 5. For Hand's view that liability could be imposed even though the obstruction was unsuccessful, see *Masses Publishing Co. v. Patten,* 244 F. 535, 541 (S.D.N.Y. 1917): "One may obstruct without preventing, and the mere obstruction is an injury to the service; for it throws impediments in its way."
79. Ibid., 760.
80. Letter from Learned Hand to Holmes, 25 November 1919, appended to Gunther, "Learned Hand," 760, document 6.
81. Ibid.
82. Ibid.
83. Letter from Learned Hand to Zechariah Chafee, Jr., 3 December 1919, appended to Gunther, "Learned Hand," 763, document 9.
84. Letter from Learned Hand to Zechariah Chafee, Jr., 2 January 1919, appended to Gunther, "Learned Hand," 770, document 15.
85. Ibid.
86. Ibid.
87. See *Lopez v. Howe,* 259 F. 401 (2d Cir. 1919).
88. Letter from Learned Hand to Zechariah Chafee, Jr., 2 January 1921, appended to Gunther, "Learned Hand," 772, document 15.
89. Ibid., 771.
90. Samuel J. Konefsky, *The Legacy of Holmes and Brandeis: A Study in the Influence of Ideas* (New York: MacMillan, 1956), 182, 202; John Raeburn Green, "The Supreme Court, the Bill of Rights and the States," *University of Pennsylvania Law Review* 97 (1949): 630.
91. See David Rabban, "The Emergence of Modern First Amendment Doctrine," *University of Chicago Law Review* 50 (Fall 1983): 1283–1345.
92. 254 U.S. 325 (1920).
93. See Rabban, "The Emergence of Modern First Amendment Doctrine," 1330–32.
94. 251 U.S. 466 (1920). Brandeis did write the opinion in *Sugarman v. United States,* 249 U.S. 182 (1919), but the opinion denied jurisdiction without getting to the merits of the free-speech claim.
95. 252 U.S. 239 (1920).
96. Transcript of conversations between Louis D. Brandeis and Felix Frank-

furter (manuscript in Brandeis Papers, Harvard Law School, Box 114, Folder 14), 23, cited by Rabban, "The Emergence of Modern First Amendment Doctrine," 1329.

97. *Schaefer v. United States,* 251 U.S. 466, 482 (1920).

98. Id. at 486.

99. See Rabban, "The Emergence of Modern First Amendment Doctrine," 1336 n. 808.

100. Chafee's article, "Freedom of Speech in War Time," appeared in the June issue of the *Harvard Law Review* 32: 932–73.

101. Rabban, "The Emergence of Modern First Amendment Doctrine," 1336 n. 808.

102. Earlier in his dissent, Brandeis had emphasized that a unanimous court had endorsed the clear-and-present-danger doctrine and then quoted Holmes's formulation of the rule from his *Schenck* opinion (see *Schaefer v. United States,* 251 U.S. 466, 482 [1920]). It is therefore somewhat surprising to read Rabban's claim that "Brandeis cited Chafee's 'Freedom of Speech in War Time' rather than any of Holmes's prior opinions" (Rabban, "The Emergence of Modern First Amendment Doctrine," 1336).

103. Rabban, "The Emergence of Modern First Amendment Doctrine," 1337.

104. *Schaefer v. United States,* 251 U.S. 466, 483–84 (1920).

105. Id. at 484.

106. 252 U.S. 239 (1920).

107. See *Schaefer v. United States,* 251 U.S. 466, 492–93 (1920): "The act punishes the wilful making and conveying of 'false reports and false statements with intent to interfere with the operation or success of the military or naval forces of the United States or to promote the success of its enemies.' Congress sought thereby to protect the American people from being wilfully misled to the detriment of their cause by one actuated by the intention to further the cause of the enemy. Wilfully untrue statements which might mislead the people as to the financial condition of the government and thereby embarrass it; as to the adequacy of the preparations for war or the support of the forces; as to the sufficiency of the food supply; or wilfully untrue statements or reports of military operations which might mislead public opinion as to the competency of the Army or Navy or its leaders (see 'The Relation between the Army and the Press in War Times,' War College Publication, 1916); or wilfully untrue statements or reports which might mislead officials in the execution of the law, or military authorities in the disposition of the forces. Such is the kind of false statement, and the only kind which, under any rational construction, is made criminal by the act."

108. *Pierce v. United States,* 252 U.S. 239, 255 (1920).

109. Id.

110. 254 U.S. 325 (1920). Rabban argues that Brandeis's war theory of free speech was inspired by Zechariah Chafee, Jr. (see Rabban, "The Emergence of Modern First Amendment Doctrine," 1343).

111. Id. at 343.
112. Id.
113. Id. at 336.
114. Id. at 340.
115. The term *political* speech is necessarily vague. I use it because there is no reason to think that Brandeis ever denied to states the right to limit certain types of private speech: libel, invasion of privacy, obscenity, etc. I think Brandeis at a minimum would have placed all speech concerned with the war effort within what I have called political speech. Also, Congress would have had a great deal of latitude in determining what speech was thereby within its power.
116. Brandeis-Frankfurter Conversations, Box 114, Folder 14, 23, cited by Rabban, "The Emergence of Modern First Amendment Doctrine," 1331.
117. *Gilbert v. Minnesota*, 254 U.S. 325, 336 (1920).
118. In reference to this case, it is reported that Holmes wrote to Brandeis, "I think you go too far." See Note from Holmes to Brandeis (Louis D. Brandeis Papers, Box 5, Folder 13, Harvard Law School Library), cited by Rabban, "The Emergence of Modern First Amendment Doctrine," 1319.
119. See *Gilbert v. Minnesota*, 254 U.S. 325, 341 (1920).
120. 254 U.S. 51 (1920).
121. Id. at 55–56.
122. *Abrams v. United States*, 250 U.S. 616, 627–28 (1919).
123. Id. at 628.
124. See Brandeis's dissent in *Schaefer v. United States*, 251 U.S. 466, 495 (1920): "The constitutional right of free speech has been declared to be the same in peace and in war." At this point, Brandeis was still in Holmes's camp.
125. *Hamilton v. Kentucky Distilleries & W. Co.*, 251 U.S. 146 (1919).
126. Id. at 163.
127. *Gilbert v. Minnesota*, 254 U.S. 325, 338 (1920).
128. For Brandeis's view of the Espionage Act, see *Gilbert* at 340.
129. See Id. at 339: "Congress, being charged with responsibility for those functions of government, must determine whether a paramount interest of the nation demands that free discussions in relation to them should be curtailed."
130. *United States ex rel. M.S.D. Pub. Co. v. Burleson*, 255 U.S. 407 (1921).
131. Id. at 436.
132. Id. at 437.
133. 268 U.S. 652 (1925).
134. 274 U.S. 359 (1927).
135. Id. at 373.
136. Id. at 374.
137. See Rabban, "The Emergence of Modern First Amendment Doctrine," 1336–38.
138. See ibid., 1338.

139. Ibid.
140. *Whitney v. California,* 274 U.S. 357, 376 (1927).
141. Id.
142. Id.
143. Rabban, "The Emergence of Modern First Amendment Doctrine," 1336–37.
144. *Whitney v. California,* 274 U.S. 357, 377 (1927).
145. *Abrams v. United States,* 250 U.S. 616, 630–31 (1919).
146. Rabban, "The Emergence of Modern First Amendment Doctrine," 1337.
147. *Whitney v. California,* 274 U.S. 357, 377 (1927).
148. See Rabban, "The Emergence of Modern First Amendment Doctrine," 1337.
149. *Whitney v. California,* 274 U.S. 359, 378 (1927).
150. Id. at 378.
151. Id.
152. Robert Cover, "The Left, The Right and the First Amendment: 1918–1928," *Maryland Law Review* 40 (1981): 381. Once Cover established to his satisfaction that Holmes's justification of free speech was nonpolitical, he then showed how Brandeis's theory of free speech—whose "chief refrain" was that free speech was "necessary to deliberative politics"—filled the vacuum (see ibid., 377). But in my judgment there was no vacuum.
153. Abrams v. United States, 250 U.S. 616, 630 (1919).
154. *Gitlow v. New York,* 268 U.S. 652, 673 (1925).
155. *Whitney v. California,* 274 U.S. 359, 375 (1927). For a recent discussion of Brandeis's philosophy of free speech, see Pnina Lahou, "Holmes and Brandeis: Libertarian and Republican Justification for Free Speech," *Journal of Law and Politics* 4 (Winter 1988): 451–82.
156. John S. Mill, *On Liberty* (New York: Library of Liberal Arts, 1956), chap. 3; Wilhelm von Humboldt, *The Sphere and Duties of Government* (London: J. Chapman, 1854).
157. (Cambridge: Harvard University Press, 1920). The second edition of this book was entitled *Free Speech in the United States* (Cambridge: Harvard University Press, 1941).
158. In regard to this book, Mark DeWolfe Howe wrote, "No single piece of writing did more than Chafee's *Freedom of Speech* to define the nature of personal liberty and to measure the scope of governmental power to restrict its exercise" (see his "Zechariah Chafee, Jr.: 1885–1957," *Nation* 184 (2 March 1957): 183. Jerold S. Auerbach has described this work as the "seminal twentieth-century treatise" on the subject of free speech and claimed that a generation of civil liberties lawyers were guided by it (see his "The Patrician as Libertarian: Zechariah Chafee, Jr., and Freedom of Speech," *New England Quarterly* 42 (March–December 1969): 531. Arthur Garfield Hayes described the book as a "bible on civil-liberties questions," and a later commentator, Jonathan Prude, has endorsed this characterization. See Letter from Hayes to Chafee, 22 January 1942, 74/4,

Chafee Papers, Harvard Law School, cited by Auerbach, "The Patrician as Libertarian," 531, and Prude, "Portrait of a Civil Libertarian: The Faith and Fear of Zechariah Chafee, Jr.," *Journal of American History* 60 (June–March 1973–74): 639.

159. See generally Fred D. Ragan, "Justice Oliver Wendell Holmes, Jr., Zechariah Chafee, Jr., and the Clear and Present Danger Test for Free Speech: The First Year, 1919," *Journal of American History* 58 (1971); Rabban, "The First Amendment in Its Forgotten Years"; idem, "The Emergence of Modern First Amendment Doctrine."

160. 17 (16 November 1918), 66–69.

161. Ibid., 67.

162. Ibid., 67–68.

163. Ibid., 68.

164. "Freedom of Speech in Wartime," *Harvard Law Review* 32 (1919): 932–73.

165. Ibid., 933.

166. Ibid., 941–43.

167. Ibid., 945–54.

168. Ibid., 960.

169. Ibid., 969.

170. Ibid., 943–44.

171. Ibid., 944.

172. See Letter from Zechariah Chafee, Jr., to Judge Charles F. Amidon, 30 September 1919, Box 4, Folder 1, Chafee Papers, cited in part by Donald Smith, *Zechariah Chafee, Jr., Defender of Liberty and Law* (Cambridge: Harvard University Press, 1986), 30.

173. Chafee, "Free Speech in War Time," 957.

174. Ibid. Chafee inherited this interest-oriented approach to law from Roscoe Pound (see ibid., 958 n. 85). It is ironic that Chafee also recognized Holmes as the judge who had "done [the] most to bring social interests into legal thinking" (see ibid., 959). Also, later in his article, Chafee cited with approval Holmes's opinion that liability was always a question of degree (see ibid., 963). But if so, why was Chafee searching for "the major premise" that judges could then use in cases involving speech to deduce correct answers?

175. Ibid., 945.

176. Ibid., 935.

177. Ibid., 934.

178. Ibid., 934–35.

179. Ibid., 960.

180. Ibid., 967. Chafee believed that Holmes's free-speech opinions were derived from his doctrine of attempt (see ibid., 963, 967).

181. David Rabban has argued that Chafee *deliberately* mischaracterized history and theory for the purpose of expanding the protection of free speech (see his "The Emergence of Modern First Amendment Doctrine," 1289–

90). Whether Rabban is right or not in regard to whether Chafee was deliberately misleading, he is not sensitive to how the distortions, whether deliberate or not, must have seriously undermined Chafee's credibility in the eyes of his contemporaries. At some point, his mistakes would have had to catch up with him.

182. Letters from Alfred Bettman to Zechariah Chafee, Jr., 20 September 1919 and 27 October 1919, Box 14, Folder 3, Chafee Papers. Even though Bettman thought that Chafee was confused, the latter did not abandon his position (see Letter from Zechariah Chafee, Jr. to Alfred Bettman, 16 October 1919, Box 14, Folder 3, Chafee Papers). For a discussion of these letters and an argument that Chafee's article was nonetheless influential in regard to Holmes's theory of free speech, see Rabban, "The Emergence of Modern First Amendment Doctrine," 1290–93.

183. Chafee, "Free Speech in War Time," 963.

184. For example, Chafee in 1920 described the limit of free speech as "problematical" (see *Freedom of Speech*, 1st ed., 8; ibid., 2d ed., 8.

185. Letter from Zechariah Chafee, Jr., to Charles F. Amidon, 30 September 1919, Box 4, Folder 1, cited in part by Donald Smith, *Zechariah Chafee, Jr.*, 30.

186. Chafee, *Freedom of Speech*, 1st ed., 4–6; ibid., 2d ed., 6–7.

187. Of course Chafee's emphasis on the policy of free speech was related to his educational goals. Jonathan Prude has shown that the purpose of all of Chafee's books was "educational." It reflected his common-sense belief that the future of civil liberties, including free speech, depended more on public opinion than on a particular test (see Jonathan Prude, "Portrait of a Civil Libertarian," 641–42). Later in his life, Chafee wrote, "In endeavoring to oppose suppressive measures, I have found it best to keep on the level of wisdom and policy as much as possible. . . . The First Amendment comes into the discussion chiefly as a powerful means of persuasion. If persuasion fails, then the First Amendment will be invoked in the courts, but that is a last resort" (Zechariah Chafee, Jr., book review, *Harvard Law Review* 62 [1949]: 894).

188. See Chafee, *Freedom of Speech*, 1st ed., 56–66, 80–87; ibid., 2d ed., 74–89.

189. See ibid., 1st ed., 94–106, 120–160; ibid., 2d ed., 86–140. Chafee also said that the appellate process took too long for the Supreme Court to fulfill any important checking function. "The nine Justices in the Supreme Court can only lock the doors after the Liberty Bell is stolen" (see *Free Speech in the United States*, 80). He was also critical of juries (see ibid., 1st ed., 76–80; ibid., 2d ed., 70–73). Paradoxically, Chafee had the most praise for executive officials at the Justice Department (see ibid., 73; ibid., 2d ed., 67, 354).

190. Chafee, "A Contemporary State Trial—The United States versus Jacob Abrams, et al.," *Harvard Law Review* 33 (April 1920): 773, in *Freedom of Speech*, 1st ed., chap. 3; ibid., 2d ed., chap 3.

191. Chafee, *Freedom of Speech in the United States,* 84. It is probably true that Chafee became more convinced during the 1920s and 1930s that the wisdom of laws hostile to free speech was more important than their constitutionality. But this attitude was already present in the 1920 edition of his book. His opinion of how sedition laws ought to be considered is especially revealing: "But I do not think we ought to let the discussion of sedition laws turn on the controversy whether they are unconstitutional" (*Freedom of Speech,* 1st ed., 193; ibid., 2d ed., 167; also see 1st ed., 194–228; ibid., 2d ed., 170–195).

192. See *Freedom of Speech,* 1st ed., 8; ibid., 2d ed., 8.

193. By 1941, Chafee was of the following opinion: "Our interest, however, is in wisdom rather than constitutionality, not in what the government *cannot* do but in what it *ought not* to do" (see *Freedom of Speech in the United States,* 232). For Chafee's later opinion that a constitutional definition was not as important as the legal machinery that defined the scope of the right, see ibid., 519.

194. Chafee, *Freedom of Speech,* 1st ed., 49; ibid., 2d cd., 45.

195. Ibid., 1st ed., 89; ibid., 2d ed., 82.

196. See ibid., 1st ed., 46–56, 87–92; ibid., 2d ed., 42–51, 80–86.

197. Letter from Zechariah Chafee, Jr., to Learned Hand, 6 January 1920, Hand Papers, Box 15, Folder 26, Harvard Law Library, appended to Gunther, "Learned Hand," 764, document 10.

198. Letter from Learned Hand to Zechariah Chafee, 8 January 1920, Chafee Papers, Box 4, Folder 20, Harvard Law Library, appended to Gunther, "Learned Hand," 766, document 11.

199. Chafee, *Freedom of Speech,* 1st ed., 67; ibid., 2d ed., 61.

200. For Gunther's discussion of Hand and the "harmless inciter," see Gunther, "Learned Hand," 729.

201. "Somewhere in such a range of circumstances is the point where direct causation begins and speech becomes punishable as incitement under the ordinary standards of statutory construction and the ordinary policy of free speech, *which Judge Hand applied"* (emphasis mine). See Chafee, *Freedom of Speech,* 1st ed., 53–54; ibid., 2d ed., 48.

202. Ibid., 1st ed., 51; ibid., 2d ed., 46.

203. Ibid., 1st ed., 52; ibid., 2d ed., 47. Chafee cited Joseph H. Beale, "Criminal Attempts," *Harvard Law Review* 16 (1903): 491–507, to support his idea of the common-law criteria of incitement and solicitation.

204. Ibid., 1st ed., 38; ibid., 2d ed., 35.

205. Ibid., 1st ed., 89; ibid., 2d ed., 82.

206. Hand understood that Chafee supported Holmes's clear-and-present-danger doctrine only because it was law. See letter from Learned Hand to Zechariah Chafee, Jr., 2 January 1921, Hand Papers, Box 15, Folder 26, Harvard Law Library, appended to Gunther, "Learned Hand," 770, document 15.

207. Chafee, *Freedom of Speech,* 1st ed., 49–50; ibid., 2d ed., 45. In 1919,

however, Chafee did say that certain of the "clauses of the Espionage Act of 1918 punishing attacks on the Constitution and our form of government seem clearly unconstitutional" (see his "A Contemporary State Trial—The United States versus Jacob Abrams et al.," *Harvard Law Review* 33 (April 1920): 752; idem, *Freedom of Speech*, 128. This language does not appear in the second edition, though Chafee does criticize the 1918 amendments on 103–4, 114–15, and 129–40.

208. Chafee, *Freedom of Speech*, 1st ed., 192. Similar language appears in the second edition on 166–67.

209. Ibid., 205; ibid., 2d ed., 175.

210. 301 U.S. 242 (1937).

211. Chafee, *Freedom of Speech in the United States*, 397.

212. Writings which do not actually urge illegal acts should never be made criminal except perhaps in great emergencies like war or revolt when the mere statement of the author's views creates a clear and present danger of injurious acts" (Chafee, *Freedom of Speech*, 1st ed., 176; ibid., 2d ed., 155). Note that Chafee, in circumstances of war and revolt, endorsed liability for speech even if there was no literal illegal incitement and even though the speaker intended no specific illegal acts. The harmful context alone was enough. This of course pushed liability beyond what Holmes would have permitted. According to him, in emergencies a person was punishable on the external standard of liability only if he or she engaged in speech harmful in itself.

213. Douglas H. Ginsburg, "Afterword," *University of Chicago Law Review* 40 (Winter 1973): 243.

214. (Chicago: Callaghan, 1904).

215. Ibid., 502–9.

216. Ibid., 509.

217. Ibid., 511.

218. Ibid., 510.

219. For these two examples, see ibid., 510–11.

220. Freund, "The *Debs* Case and Freedom of Speech," *The New Republic*, 3 May 1919, 13, in *University of Chicago Law Review* 40 (Winter 1973): 239. All references hereafter are to the reprint of the original article.

221. Ibid., 240.

222. Ibid., 241.

223. Ibid., 240.

224. Freund, *The Police Power*, 511.

225. 254 U.S. 325 (1920).

226. For a more extended discussion of the facts of the *Gilbert* case, see chap. 3 above.

227. Letter from Holmes to Learned Hand, 3 April 1919, Hand Papers, Box 103, Folder 24, Harvard Law Library, appended to Gunther, "Learned Hand," 760, document 5.

228. Rabban, "The First Amendment in Its Forgotten Years" *Yale Law Journal*

90 (1981): 559–79. See Thomas Cooley, *Constitutional Limitations*, (1868; New York: De Capo Press, 1972); Roscoe Pound, "Equitable Relief Against Defamation and Injuries to Personality," *Harvard Law Review* 29 (1916): 640–82; "Interests of Personality," *Harvard Law Review* 28 (1915): 343–65; Henry Schofield, "Freedom of the Press in the United States," in *Essays on Constitutional Law and Equity*, 2 vols. (1921; New York: De Capo Press, 1972), 2:510–71; Theodore Schroeder, *Free Speech for Radicals* (New York: Free Speech League, 1916); *"Obscene" Literature and Constitutional Law* (1911; New York: De Capo, 1972).

229. Schroeder, *Free Speech for Radicals*, 20.

230. Schroeder granted protection unless "a criminal act follows, as a direct and designed result of his utterance." "In that event," however, the speaker was "to be punished for the subsequent crime and his intentional participation in it, and not merely for his utterances, as such" (see ibid., 33).

231. Ibid., 88. Also see his *"Obscene" Literature and Constitutional Law*, 207. For a similar discussion, see Rabban, "The First Amendment In Its Forgotten Years," 577. But Rabban argues, incorrectly in my view, that even if Schroeder permitted a speaker to be punished if his intent was bad, and if he posed an imminent danger, Schroeder's test was very different from Holmes's clear-and-present-danger doctrine.

232. *Gitlow v. New York*, 268 U.S. 652, 667 (1925).

233. Id. at 669.

234. *Toledo Newspaper Co. v. United States*, 247 U.S. 402, 421 (1921), Holmes dissenting.

235. *Gitlow v. New York*, 268 U.S. 652, 670 (1924): "In other words, when the legislative body has determined generally, in the constitutional exercise of its discretion, that utterances of a certain kind involve such danger of substantive evil that they may be punished, the question whether any specific utterance coming within the prohibited class is likely, in and of itself, to bring about the substantive evil, is not open to consideration." If the legislature has prohibited a class of utterances, the judge's only function was to determine if the utterance was one of the class, not to assess its proximity to harm. Justice Sanford reconciled this position with the Court's previous endorsements of the clear-and-present-danger doctrine by denying its relevance to convictions under statutes that prohibited language (see id. at 670–71). It is paradoxical to note that some commentators accept Sanford's delineation of the scope of Holmes's theory and then criticize it as clearly deficient on this ground (see Yosal Rogat, "The Judge as Spectator," *University of Chicago Law Review* 31 [Winter 1964]: 217; Yosal Rogat and James M. O'Fallon, "Mr. Justice Holmes: A Dissenting Opinion —The Free Speech Cases," *Stanford Law Review* 36 [1984]: 1399–1404). But the fact that he dissented in *Gitlow* and the nature of the dissent that he wrote clearly establish that Holmes did believe that his theory of speech was applicable to statutes that prohibited the advocacy of doctrine. He clearly thought that the judicial role included preserving free speech against

such hostile legislative actions. The judge had to assess the legislative decision that certain forms of speech activity were harmful in themselves.

236. Id. at 668–69.

237. Id. at 672: "The general principle of free speech, it would seem to me, must be taken to be included in the 14th Amendment, in view of the scope that has been given to the word liberty as there used, although perhaps it may be accepted with a somewhat larger latitude of interpretation than is allowed to Congress by the sweeping language that governs, or ought to govern, the laws of the United States." In *Abrams v. United States,* the Court also made it clear that it would defer to Congress's judgment that certain utterances were punishable if made with a certain intent, even if no likelihood of harm was present in the case. Here again the Court's only perceived responsibility was to determine if Abram's intent placed his speech activity within the statute, not to assess the constitutionality of the statute by way of evaluating the likelihood or the existence of harm (see *Abrams v. United States,* 250 U. S. 616, 618–24 [1919]). Early commentators understood judicial deference to Congress's determination of the harmfulness of speech to be the essential point of *Abrams* (see James P. Hall, "Comment on Recent Cases," *Illinois Law Review,* 20 [1926]: 810; Day Kimball, "The Espionage Act and the Limits of Toleration," *Harvard Law Review* 33 (1920): 443–44).

238. Gitlow v. New York, 268 U.S. 652, 673 (1925).

239. *Schaefer v. United States,* 251 U.S. 466, 478–79 (1919): If the defendants "had not that purpose, what purpose had they? Were they the mere expression of peevish discontent—aimless, vapid, and innocuous? We cannot so conclude. We must take them at their word, as the jury did, and ascribe to them a more active and sinister purpose." See also *Gilbert v. Minnesota,* 254 U.S. 325, 333 (1920).

240. *Abrams v. United States,* 250 U.S. 616, 621 (1919).

241. *Pierce v. United States,* 252 U.S. 239, 249 (1920).

242. *Abrams v. United States,* 250 U.S. 616, 630 (1919).

243. Id. at 630–31.

244. Besides the writings of those critics of the bad-tendency doctrine discussed in the text, see Sir Frederick Pollock, "Abrams v. United States," *Law Quarterly Review* 36 (1920): 334–38; M. G. Wallace, "Constitutionality of Sedition Laws," *Virginia Law Review* 6 (1920): 385–99; Fred B. Hart, "Power of Government over Speech and Press," *Yale Law Journal* 29 (1920): 410–28; Karl L. Llewellyn, "Free Speech in Time of Peace," *Yale Law Journal* 29 (1920): 337–44; comments by C. E. Clark, *Yale Law Journal* 30 (1920): 68–71 and by L. G. C., *Illinois Law Review* 14 (1920): 601–7 and in *Harvard Law Review* 41 (1928): 525–28; Herbert F. Goodrich, "Does the Constitution Protect Free Speech," *Michigan Law Review* 19 (1921): 487–501; and finally Hugh E. Willis, "Freedom of Speech and the Press," *Indiana Law Journal* 4 (1929): 445–55.

245. Edward S. Corwin, "Freedom of Speech and Press under the First Amend-

ment: A Resume," *Yale Law Journal* 30 (1920): 55. Also see his "Constitutional Law in 1919–1920," *American Political Science Review* 14 (1920): 655–58.

246. John H. Wigmore, "Abrams v. United States: Freedom of Speech and Freedom of Thuggery in Wartime and Peacetime," *Illinois Law Review* 14 (1920): 552–53.

247. Ibid., 550.

248. Day Kimball, "The Espionage Act and the Limits of Legal Toleration," 447. Kimball argued that his approach did not reduce the First Amendment to a "nullity" (see ibid., 448). But if judges were always to defer to Congress's assessment of the tendency of speech, then clearly free speech, understood as a judicially enforceable right of the individual, was completely undermined.

249. Other articles in support of the bad-tendency doctrine were James P. Hall, "Free Speech in Wartime," *Columbia Law Review* 21 (1921): 526–37; W. R. Vance, "Freedom of Speech and of the Press," *Minnesota Law Review* 2 (1918): 239–60; G. P. Garrett, "Free Speech and the Espionage Act," *Journal of Criminal Law and Criminology* 10 (1919): 71–75; Thomas F. Carroll, "Freedom of Speech and of the Press in Wartime: The Espionage Act," *Michigan Law Review* 17 (1919): 621–65; "Freedom of Speech during the Civil War," *Virginia Law Review* 9 (1923): 516–51; Abraham Pinsky, "Freedom of Speech under Our Constitution," *West Virginia Law Review* 31 (1925): 273–79.

6. Holmes's Constitutionalism

THERE IS LITTLE consensus about Holmes's jurisprudence or his understanding of American constitutionalism. More specific discussions of how his theory of free speech fits into the wider context of his thought reflect this controversy. The underlying assumption that there must be some kind of relationship between his theory of speech and his constitutionalism is quite plausible. Or, to put the issue in a different way, an interpretation gains credibility the more it integrates the various aspects of a jurist's thought. Yet there is no assurance of success. Mistakes about Holmes's theory of free speech can lead to misunderstandings of his more basic doctrines and vice versa. There are, quite simply, several conceivable pictures of Holmes as a coherent thinker, some less accurate than others. In this chapter, I enter the debate about his constitutionalism by sketching my understanding of the theoretical background of his theory of free speech. My hope is that the result will be a better appreciation for the substance and coherence of his legal and constitutional philosophy.

In earlier chapters, I have tried to defend my interpretation of Holmes as a coherent and moderately protective theorist of free speech. He would impose liability on harmful speech according to an external standard: if the speaker knew facts that would have warned an average person of danger, the speaker was outside the guarantee. A speaker who said or wrote nothing harmful in itself was liable only if that speaker actually intended harm and either created a clear and present danger or conspired with others to obtain an unlawful objective. This particular interpretation is relatively novel, even though others have linked Holmes's views on speech to his doctrine of attempts.[1] Accordingly, by functioning as a window into Holmes's constitutionalism, this interpretation will enable us to see more clearly what heretofore has been either overlooked or misunderstood.

Free Speech and Historical Intent

A good place to begin is the claim that Holmes limited free speech, at least early in his career, to protection from prior restraints.[2] He had this relatively narrow view of the scope of this guarantee because he thought that the framers of the Constitution had understood free speech in this restrictive way. David S. Bogen has provided the most extensive and persuasive presentation of this thesis. His argument is that Holmes from an early age may well have been personally impressed with the value of free speech, but that throughout his life he was unwilling to inject his own personal prejudices into the law. The judge's job was to enforce the law as it was, not as it ought to have been. He therefore reduced free speech to a mere protection from prior restraint because he had every reason to believe, up until 1919, that the law demanded no less. His legal education at Harvard Law School introduced him to important cases of the Massachusetts Supreme Judicial Court that upheld this restrictive idea of free speech and to important legal commentators— Chancellor Kent, Joseph Story, and Timothy Walker—who all, it is argued, concurred that free speech only prohibited prior restraints, not the subsequent punishment of speech.[3] Holmes brought this notion of free speech along with him to the bench, first to the Massachusetts Supreme Judicial Court and then to the United States Supreme Court. Only in 1919 did he change his mind. In all likelihood, it was, Bogen concludes, either Zechariah Chafee, Jr., or the briefs filed in the 1919 espionage cases that convinced Holmes to make free speech something more than a protection from prior restraints.[4]

Bogen's argument that Holmes reduced free speech to protection from prior restraints does not rely exclusively on the repressive character of the legal tradition that he inherited. Two crucial pieces of evidence are much more specific. First, there is language from Holmes's opinion in *Patterson v. Colorado*,[5] a case in which he upheld a conviction for contempt of court against the defendant's objection that all that he said was true. In part quoting from an earlier Massachusetts opinion written by Chief Justice Isaac Parker, Holmes wrote

In the first place, the main purpose of such constitutional provisions is "to prevent all such *previous restraints* upon publications as had been practiced by other governments," and they do not prevent the subsequent punishment of such as may be deemed contrary to the public welfare.[6]

This language suggests that the primary reason why Holmes affirmed Patterson's conviction was that free speech did not protect any speech from subsequent punishment. The limit of free speech was drawn at the line of prior restraints, and if drawn there, the legislature could impose liability on speech as it saw fit.

Second, in a letter in which Holmes provided Zechariah Chafee, Jr., with an explanation of the origin of the phrase "clear and present danger," he left the impression that he was at one time a follower of William Blackstone and Judge Parker.

My Dear Professor Chafee
Your letter arrives here just after myself—and I must make a hurried answer. The expression that you refer to was not helped by any book that I know—I think it came without doubt after the later cases (and probably you—I do not remember exactly) had taught me that in the earlier Paterson [sic] case, if that was the name of it, I had taken Blackstone and Parker of Massachusetts as well founded, wrongly. I surely was ignorant. But I did think hard on the matter of attempts in my Common Law and a Mass. case, later in the Swift case (U.S.). And I thought it out unhelped.[7]

This letter, in conjunction with the passage from *Patterson*, constitutes a strong argument that Holmes at one point reduced freedom of speech to freedom from prior restraints. And if nineteenth-century law was as hostile to speech as Bogen claims, these two pieces of evidence make a persuasive case that Holmes was a part of this repressive tradition, at least up to 1919.

But there are a few soft spots in this argument. Though Holmes did say in his opinion in *Patterson* that the "main purpose" of the free speech clause was "to prevent previous restraints," he did not say that the prevention of previous restraint was the *only* purpose of free speech or that the scope of protection provided by the First Amendment was limited for all time to what the framers intended. Rather, the specific point of the passage from *Patterson* seems to have been that free speech did not prevent the subsequent punishment of speech "deemed contrary to the public welfare." He was not saying that free speech permitted the subsequent punishment of all types of speech, but only of types incompatible with the public welfare. The main purpose of the clause was the reason Holmes gave for his judgment that free speech did not prevent the subsequent punishment of harmful speech activity—in this case a contempt of court. But he did not mean to imply that the legislature could punish any type of speech, that free speech was reducible to freedom from prior restraints. All that he meant was that harmful speech could be punished notwithstanding the guarantee.

The briefs filed in *Patterson* support this interpretation of Holmes's reference to the main purpose of free speech. He was not offering previous restraints as the limit of free speech, but rather using the main purpose of the clause as a reason to exclude harmful speech from protection from subsequent punishment. This is the more reasonable view because neither the state of Colorado nor the defendant Patterson was arguing that free speech should be limited to protection from previous restraints. Both of these parties agreed that the clause protected nonabusive speech activity from subsequent punishment.[8] The issue before the Supreme Court therefore had nothing to do with prior restraints, which bears on how the passage from Holmes's opinion in *Patterson* should be understood.

The real dispute of the case was whether Colorado, whose constitution required that truth be admitted as a defense in any "suits or prosecutions for libel,"[9] could punish someone for contempt of court if what was said was true. Patterson claimed that the right to publish truth was one of the rights "retained by the people" by way of the Ninth Amendment, and that Colorado could not therefore constitutionally punish him for contempt of court without giving him the opportunity to prove the truth of what he had said.[10] The state argued that there was no such federal right, that the Supreme Court therefore had no jurisdiction, and that it had the power to punish contempts that harmed the judicial system regardless if what was said or published was true.[11] On this specific issue, Holmes sided with Colorado's position that there was no federal right to publish truth in every context. In accordance with the common law, a state could punish contempts of court regardless of truth and violate no federal right. His reference to the main purpose of the free-speech clause was a reason that he gave for his conclusion, but he did not use the idea of previous restraints to define the limit of free speech.

Other language from Holmes's opinion supports the conclusion that he drew the line at harmful speech, "speech contrary to the public welfare," not at previous restraints. He said that "when a case is finished courts are subject to the same criticism as other people,"[12] implying that criticism of the Colorado Supreme Court would have been constitutionally protected if the case that Patterson ridiculed had no longer been pending according to local law. A statute that prohibited all criticism of judges would therefore have been invalid, which indicates that Holmes did not reduce freedom of speech to a mere protection from prior restraints. He was unwilling to reduce free speech to that extent, even if he thought that the main purpose of the framers was to protect speech from prior restraint.

Holmes also hinted that if Patterson's activity was of a completely innocent character, the state could not have punished it even if the case was still pending according to local law. But after he had examined the evidence, he concluded that it was "far from showing that innocent conduct had been laid hold of as an arbitrary pretense for an arbitrary punishment."[13] There was evidence sufficient for a jury to find that Patterson had engaged in speech "detrimental to the public welfare." Here too Holmes implied that if the defendant's speech had not been harmful, had not been detrimental to the system of justice, it would have been constitutionally protected. He was, in short, using the concept of harmful speech, rather than previous restraints, to draw the line of liability. The main purpose of the framers was a reason to deny constitutional protection to harmful speech, but it itself was not the limit of free speech.

The authorities that Holmes acknowledged in the opinion[14] complement my explanation of his reference to the main purpose of free speech. Judge Parker is now thought to have strictly confined free speech to freedom from prior restraints, which tends to establish that Holmes's citation of him meant that he too reduced free speech to a protection from prior restraint. A full reading of Parker's opinion in *Commonwealth v. Blanding*,[15] however, suggests an alternative view. Even if Parker did describe the main purpose of free speech as "the prevention of previous restraints," he also said that the "wisdom of those who formed it" requires that "the *liberty* of the press" be protected, not its *"licentiousness."* Free speech that stayed within the confines of liberty and avoided licentiousness was therefore protected.

Nor does our constitution or declaration of rights abrogate the common law in this respect, as some have insisted. The 16th article declares, that "the liberty of the press is essential to the security of freedom in a state; it ought not, therefore, to be restrained in this commonwealth." The *liberty* of the press, not its licentiousness; this is the construction which a just regard to the other parts of that instrument, and to the wisdom of those who formed it, requires. In the 11th article it is declared, that every "subject of the commonwealth ought to find a certain remedy, by having recourse to the laws, for all injuries or wrongs which he may receive in his person, property or *character.*" And thus the general declaration in the 16th article is qualified. Besides, it is well understood, and received as a commentary on this provision for the liberty of the press, that it was intended to prevent all such *previous restraints* upon publications as had been practiced by other governments, and in early times here, to stifle the efforts of patriots towards enlightening their fellow subjects upon their rights and the duties of rulers. The liberty of the press was to be unrestrained, but he who used it was to be responsible in case of its abuse; like the right to keep fire arms, which does not protect him who uses them for annoyance or destruction.[16]

Parker's substantive criterion of protected versus unprotected speech was therefore not the idea of previous restraints, but the idea of an abuse of speech—quite similar to Holmes's notion of harmful speech. Accordingly, Holmes cited Parker's *Blanding* opinion in *Patterson,* not to establish prior restraints as the limit of free speech, but to buttress the argument that the intent of the framers was a reason to deny constitutional protection to harmful speech.

Blanding was also analogous to *Patterson* on a more specific ground. In *Blanding,* Parker believed that the defendant (who publicly charged an innkeeper with poisoning a guest and advised others to avoid the inn) had abused the liberty of speech even if he could have proven the truth of what he had said.

The general principle decided is, that it is immaterial to the character of a [criminal] libel as a public offense, whether the matter of it be true or false; not, as some have affirmed, because the law makes no distinction between truth and falsehood, but because the interest of the public requires that men not invested with authority by the laws shall not usurp the power of public accusation, and arraign before the public, with malicious motives, their neighbors and fellow citizens, exposing them to partial trials in forms not warranted by the constitution or laws, and condemning them to a species of ignominy which is often a heavier punishment than the law would inflict for the offenses or misconduct of which they are thus officiously accused.[17]

Like Patterson, the defendant was liable even if what he said was true; just as truthful speech could constitute a contempt of court, so also it could be a criminal libel. Holmes therefore cited this case, not to limit free speech to protection from prior restraints, but to establish the proposition that truth was not always a defense. If it was sufficiently harmful in character, truthful speech was outside the guarantee.

Elsewhere in his opinion, Parker enumerated some of the exceptions to the general rule that any "propagator of written or printed tales to the essential prejudice of any one in his estate or reputation" was "a public offender."[18] The common law protected from subsequent punishment all publications of any proceedings of legislative assemblies and courts of justice, any complaint made to a "public constituted body," and even an honestly made though mistaken character reference.[19] Parker also cited approvingly *Commonwealth v. Clap*,[20] a case which extended free speech beyond what the common law allowed.

An attack upon public men, even in regard to their private characters, has been viewed as a right growing out of our free institutions and essential to the support of them. And so far forth as this notion is correct and salutary, it has been incorporated into our law, and serves to form an exception to the general rule, not distinctly admitted by the common law, though not at all inconsistent with its general character. The case of *Commonwealth v. Clap* was the first, since the adoption of the constitution, which called for a discussion of these principles, and in that case it is very clearly and distinctly settled, that if the *truth only* is told of public elective officers, or of acknowledged candidates for offices, in a decent manner and with a view properly to influence an election, it is justifiable.[21]

Even if the intent of the framers had mainly been to prevent prior restraints, the free-speech clause protected from subsequent punishment true characterizations of public officers or candidates if they were made with good motives. The right to publish such opinions "grew out of our free institutions," "were incorporated into our law," had developed "since the adoption of the constitution," and were "essential to the support of free institutions." These passages show that Parker did not confine the scope of free speech to what the framers intended. He may not have, according to our standards, protected a great deal of speech from subsequent punishment, but the common view that he understood free speech *merely* as freedom from prior restraint is not true.

Holmes's citations in *Patterson* of *Respublica v. Oswald*[22] and William Blackstone can be explained in a similar fashion. In *Respublica*, the Pennsylvania Supreme Court upheld a contempt of court conviction against a claim of free speech and added:

The true liberty of the press is amply secured by permitting every man to publish his opinion; but it is due to the peace and dignity of society to inquire into the motives of such publications, and to distinguish between those which are meant for use and reformation, and with an eye solely to the public good, and those which are intended merely to delude and defame. To the latter description, it is impossible that any good government should afford protection and impunity.[23]

The state court's goal was therefore not to confine freedom of the press to freedom from previous restraints. Rather it thought that only speech meant "to delude and defame" was punished by a "good government." And though Blackstone understood free speech to be only a protection from previous restraint, Holmes did not cite his definition of free speech, but his definition of criminal libel. According to Blackstone, truth was not a defense in this type of case because criminal libels were "challenges to fight." "The provocation, and not the falsity, is the thing to be punished criminally."[24] The point of Holmes's citation of this definition was therefore not to exclude all speech from constitutional protection from subsequent punishment. His objective was the more narrow one, that certain types of harmful speech activity—contempts of court and criminal libels—were "detrimental to public welfare" and were therefore punishable even if what was said was true.

Bogen and others may have misunderstood the passage from Holmes's opinion in *Patterson,* because they overestimated the degree to which nineteenth-century law upheld Blackstone's definition of free speech.[25] For example, Chancellor Kent, we are told, limited free speech to a protection from prior restraints, though he wanted as a matter of policy to protect truth offered with good motives from any subsequent punishment.[26] But this conclusion, in my opinion, is too strong. Kent did realize that his position, announced in *People v. Coswell,*[27] was not completely in accord with the common law, especially the common-law treatment of criminal libel. Justice Parker's general position in *Blanding* was the predominant one.[28] Truth was not ordinarily a defense. But that does not mean that either Kent or Parker reduced free speech to freedom from prior restraints. The alternatives were not that stark.

In the case of criminal libel, for example, Kent insisted that the defendant "may repel the criminal charge, by proving that the publication was for a justifiable purpose, and not malicious; and if the purpose be justifiable, the defendant may give in evidence the truth of the words when such evidence will tend to negative the malicious intent to defame."[29] He noted, without disapproval, Parker's ruling in *Blanding* that the judge was to decide if a case was one in which the defendant was entitled to present evidence of good motives and of the truth of what was published. In his opinion, this procedure was not adverse to his rule that speech was protected from subsequent punishment if the defendant acted for justifiable ends, with good motives, and only published the truth. This is why he concluded that *Blanding* "went only to control the malicious abuse or licentiousness of the press," commending this approach as "the most effectual way to preserve its [the press's] freedom in the genuine sense of the constitutional declarations on the subject."[30]

Thus the limit of free speech that Kent recognized as law in the nineteenth century was not mere protection from previous restraints. Protection from such restraints may have been the primary or even the only purpose of the framers, but public opinion, according to Kent, had gradually required the expansion of the right. The "current of opinion seems to have been setting strongly, not only in favor of erecting barriers against any previous restraints upon publications, (and which were all that the earlier sages of the Revolution had in view,) but in favor of the policy that would diminish or destroy altogether every obstacle or responsibility in the way of the publication of the truth."[31] Indeed, he was a little worried. The "tendency of measures in this country has been to relax *too far* the vigilance with which the common law surrounded and guarded character." In his judgment, Americans were too "animated with a *generous* anxiety to maintain freedom of discussion" (emphasis mine).[32] Accordingly, the rule he announced in *Croswell*, that truth published with good motives and for justifiable ends was protected from subsequent punishment, was meant to some degree to be a bar to the further expansion of free speech. As with Parker, truth in some contexts was still punishable, and the judge was to decide if the speaker's motives or ends placed his or her truthful speech beyond the guarantee of free speech. But neither Parker nor Kent reduced free speech to protection from previous restraints.

Thomas Cooley, of course, had a different view of the purpose of free speech. Writing in the 1860s, he argued

that the mere exemption from previous restraints can not be all that is secured by the constitutional provisions. . . . [T]he liberty of the press might be rendered a mockery and a delusion, and the phrase itself a byword if, while every man was at liberty to publish what he pleased, the public authorities might nevertheless punish him for *harmless* publications. (Emphasis mine)[33]

But the contrast in tone should not hide the similarities between Cooley's opinion and those opinions that had preceded him. He did not mean that all forms of speech were immune from liability. A publisher had complete immunity for any publication, "so long as it is not harmful in its character, when tested by such standards as the law affords."[34] The exceptions were blasphemy, obscenity, scandalous writing, public offensiveness, and libel. The test of harm was to be decided in particular cases by "the common-law rules which were in force when the constitutional guarantees were established."[35] The same common-law rules applied by his predecessors thereby constituted, in a rough way, Cooley's own sense of the limits of free speech. Even if he believed that the framers intended by the free-speech clause to do more than prohibit previous restraints, he agreed with Kent and Parker that harmful or abusive speech was still punishable.

The significance of the new understanding of the intent of the framers that Cooley endorsed should not, of course, be underestimated. He was convinced that the "evils" the framers "guarded against were not the censorship of the press merely, but any action of the government by means of which it might prevent such free and general discussion of public matters as seems absolutely essential to prepare the people for an intelligent exercise of their rights as citizens."[36] The clause's primary purpose was therefore to limit the subsequent punishment of public speech, especially the punishment of seditious libel. Once in place, this new view of the purpose of free speech permitted the scope of the right to expand more readily against the common-law exceptions: libel, obscenity, and blasphemy. The older view, that the purpose of the clause was only to prevent previous restraint, could no longer function as an obstacle to the expansion of the right.

It is fairly clear from Holmes's opinion in *Patterson* and his letter to Chafee that he understood the main purpose of free speech in the more traditional manner of Parker and Kent, at least up until 1919. It is also likely that this understanding of the framers' intent restrained Holmes from expanding the right in any radical way. Yet it would be a serious error to think that Holmes reduced free speech to a protection from prior restraints because he accepted Parker's and Kent's view of the purpose of the amendment. In *Gandia v. Pettingill,*[37] he held that a newspaper was privileged to publish truth in the absence of express malice.[38] This decision was not too far removed from Kent's rule that truth published with good motives and justifiable ends was protected. Accordingly, Holmes may have had the more traditional understanding of the purpose of free speech, but, like Kent, he extended protection to speech beyond freedom from previous restraints.

In *Toledo Newspaper Company v. United States,*[39] a case decided a few months prior to *Schenck,* Holmes tried to draw a line between harmful contempts of court and reasonable comments about a federal judge. The case was similar in many respects to *Patterson.* The issue was whether a federal judge could find a newspaper in contempt if it published news, comment, and cartoons that questioned the impartiality of a judge who was considering an injunction against the enforcement of a popular municipal ordinance establishing a three-cent maximum railroad fare. Without abandoning his conviction that harmful speech was punishable, Holmes judged that the published material contained only adverse comment and criticism that the federal judge could have endured without any harm to the judicial system. "A judge of the United States is expected to be a man of ordinary firmness of character," and the newspaper had printed nothing that could have prevented the judge from "performing his sworn duty."[40] In contrast, Patterson was subject to liability because his remarks did not just question the impartiality of a judge but claimed that the judges on the Colorado Supreme Court had conspired with others to commit electoral fraud. His speech activity was not so innocent that Holmes could justifiably overturn a state's judgment that he was guilty of contempt.[41]

Hence *Patterson* and *Toledo Newspaper Company* were consistent with one another. Neither endorsed previous restraints as the limit of free speech, but both favored liability for harmful speech. And Holmes's dissent in the latter case shows that he was willing to interpret narrowly an exception to free speech at a time when he still believed that the main purpose of free speech had been to prevent previous restraints. Accordingly, the letter he later sent to Chafee, in which he said that Blackstone and Parker were wrong, does not mean that he abandoned the notion of previous restraints as the limit of free speech. It only shows that he gave up the more traditional understanding of the purpose of the free speech clause.[42] By this time, Chafee had published his article that attacked the idea that the framers intended only to prevent prior restraints,[43] and

Holmes had confronted similar arguments in the briefs filed in the espionage cases.[44] It is not hard to believe that Holmes was persuaded at this point that Cooley was right and Parker and Kent were wrong about the main purpose of the free-speech clause.

What is hard to believe is that this letter to Chafee shows that Holmes's understanding of the limits of free speech underwent some kind of fundamental change. It is difficult to reconcile this thesis with his expression of puzzlement as to who had inspired this major transformation of his thinking. How could he not have remembered who persuaded him to change his mind if the change concerned his basic sense of the limits of free speech? It is extremely doubtful that he would have been so forgetful if he had undergone such a significant intellectual conversion. It is much more believable that Holmes was puzzled because the "metamorphosis" that he underwent only concerned his understanding of the framers' intent. It is plausible that he had forgotten who inspired this transformation in his thinking because for him the framers' intent never defined the limit of free speech. He protected speech from subsequent punishment prior to the 1919 espionage cases, when he still believed that the main purpose of the First amendment was to prevent prior restraints, and he punished harmful speech after 1919 notwithstanding his new view of the framers' intent.

If, however, the letter to Chafee is interpreted as an admission that Holmes's understanding of the limits of free speech had undergone a metamorphosis, it implies that he had committed a grievous constitutional error in *Patterson*. This view of the letter, though, does not ring true. Holmes described himself as "ignorant," not "mistaken." His language is more compatible with the interpretation that in late 1918 and early 1919 he was reconsidering his understanding of the purpose of free speech, but that this reorientation had no *direct* bearing on his sense of the limits of free speech.

In *Schenck*, Holmes implied that the intent of the framers did not establish forever the limits of free speech. "It may well be," he began, "that the prohibition of laws abridging the freedom of speech is not confined to previous restraints, although to prevent them may have been the main purpose, as intimated in *Patterson v. Colorado*."[45] This language endorsed the same view of the framers' intent that Holmes had enunciated in *Patterson*, though he qualified it by changing the verb from the indicative to the subjunctive mood. While in *Patterson* he had said that the main purpose "is" to prevent previous restraints, in *Schenck* he was only willing to say that it "may have been" the main purpose.

Commentators have argued that this switch in mood shows that Holmes underwent a radical change in his understanding of the limits of free speech.[46] A more reasonable conclusion is that Holmes was still undecided about the major purpose of free speech in early 1919, but that he had never reduced it to a mere protection from previous restraints. Later that year, there is reason to believe that he made up his mind about the framers' intent. In his dissent in *Abrams,* Holmes announced that he "wholly disagree[d] with the argument of the government that the 1st amendment left the common law as to seditious libel in force. History seems to me against the notion."[47] At this point, Holmes was convinced that one of the main purposes of the free-speech clause, if not the main one, was to prevent the subsequent punishment of seditious libel.

The significance of this new understanding of the purpose of free speech should not be minimized. It may well have, in particular cases, inclined Holmes to a more protective attitude toward free speech. My view, however, is that there was not a radical change in his basic theoretical understanding of the limits of free speech. Harmful speech had always been outside of constitutional protection, and his wider sense of the purpose of free speech did not induce him in 1919 to protect such speech from subsequent punishment. Also, advocacy of illegal action, if proximate to a harm, had also been excluded from constitutional protection long before he was persuaded that one of the purposes of free speech had been to prevent the punishment of seditious libel. Since Holmes linked the phrase "clear and present danger" to the question of liability for illegal advocacy, his letter to Chafee, in which he explained the origin of this phrase, is especially relevant. He responded that the phrase came from no book and after the "later cases," presumably after the early 1919 espionage cases.

But Holmes did not mean that prior to 1919 illegal advocacy could have been punished even if there was no proximity to a harm. He was merely referring to the origin of a rhetorical phrase—"clear and present danger." As he said in the letter, "I did think hard on the matter of attempts in my Common Law and a Mass. case, later in the Swift case (U.S.). And I thought it out unhelped." Not only does this sentence link

Holmes's theory of speech to his theory of legal liability, but it also shows that his sense of the substantive limits of free speech in cases of illegal advocacy had developed prior to the appearance of the rhetorical phrase "clear and present danger." Long before Holmes changed his mind about the purpose of free speech, when he still believed that its main purpose had been to prevent prior restraints, he protected illegal advocacy from subsequent punishment unless there was an illegal intent and some proximity to harm. Free speech was not reduced to a mere protection from prior restraints.

The conclusion is that Holmes never confined the scope of free speech to what the framers intended. This is so whether he thought that the clause's main purpose was to prevent prior restraints or the punishment of seditious libel. Instead he perceived the limits of free speech according to the basic structure of his theory of legal liability. Since Holmes did not reduce the free-speech clause to what the framers' intended, one would expect that he had a similar approach to other constitutional clauses, whether the clauses defined governmental powers or established individual rights. He did not think that historical intent was irrelevant or that it should be completely ignored. It was an important factor in constitutional adjudication but it was not the whole story—the judge's job was not over when it was discovered. Several famous passages from Holmes's opinions show that he had a more evolutionary understanding of the American Constitution. It had an "organic" character. It was a "living" entity:

when we are dealing with words that also are a constituent act, like the Constitution of the United States, we must realize that they have *called into life a being* the development of which could not have been foreseen completely by the most gifted of its begetters. It was enough for them to realize or to hope that they had *created an organism;* it has taken a century and has cost their successors much sweat and blood to prove that they created a nation. The case before us must be considered *in the light of our whole experience, and not merely in that of what was said a hundred years ago.*[48] (Emphasis mine.)

The provisions of the Constitution are not mathematical formulas having their essence in their form; *they are organic living institutions* transplanted from English soil. (Emphasis mine.)[49]

Though these quotes are taken from context, they show that Holmes did not invariably assume that the limits of a constitutional provision were settled conclusively by ascertaining its main purpose. His comments about the main purpose of free speech also provide little reason to believe that he ever reduced free speech to protection from prior restraints. Judge Parker and Chancellor Kent had the same understanding of the framers' intent, and they did not reduce free speech to such a narrow role. My belief is that Holmes did not either.[50] Throughout his career on the bench, he used his theory of legal liability to adapt free speech and thereby the Constitution to the emerging needs and interests of twentieth-century American society.

Formalism and Constitutional Adjudication

The previous section used Holmes's theory of free speech to elucidate the role that historical intent played in his constitutional jurisprudence. The conclusion was that the intent of the framers was not the sole basis for constitutional adjudication. Once the mistaken view of his theory of free speech was set aside, the coherence of his constitutional thought readily became apparent. A similar result is possible in regard to the view that Holmes decided cases in a deductive manner. The charge is that he used the clear-and-present-danger standard as a formula and that his general theory was of a formalist or conceptualist character. In my opinion, both of these propositions are untrue. A mistaken interpretation of Holmes's theory of free speech has led to a deeper misunderstanding of his constitutional jurisprudence.

The contention that Holmes applied his clear-and-present-danger standard as a formula has been around for a long time. In 1952, Edward S. Corwin claimed that the doctrine operated as "a kind of slide rule whereby all cases involving the issue of free speech simply decide[d] themselves automatically."[51] Paul Freund agreed: "No matter how rapidly we utter the phrase 'clear and present danger,' or how closely we hyphenate the words, they are not a substitute for the weighing of values." The test is a disservice for judges since it "convey[s] a delusion of certitude when what is most certain is the complexity of the strands in the web of freedom which the judge must disentangle."[52] Herbert Wechsler has argued that the clear-and-present-danger standard functioned as a "disguise for the essentially legislative nature of constitutional adjudication."[53] A preferable test was one that revealed the legislative nature of the judge's activity. Perhaps then judicial review would be "limited by what is in effect a presumption of validity, or a deference to legislative judgment, at least where the legislation condemns specific doctrine or specifically described types of meetings."[54] In all of these criticisms, there is the implication that Holmes decided free-speech cases in a deductive or mechanical sort of way: in the judgment of one critic, an "absurd 'heads-off' automatism."[55] He was not sufficiently sensitive to the legislative role that judges played in cases involving free speech.

Yosal Rogat has provided the most persuasive argument that Holmes's entire jurisprudence was formalist or conceptualist in character. Rogat argued that Holmes "wrote his opinions in the forceful and succinct style for which he was known precisely because he did in a sense decide 'concrete' cases by 'general propositions,' although these 'general propositions' were more often direct consequences of his political attitudes than they were of legal doctrines."[56] After he wrote this, however, Rogat seems to have implicitly withdrawn the claim that Holmes decided cases according to his own "political attitudes." In an article entitled "The Judge as Spectator," he concluded that Holmes was "detached" from the judicial function and from life in general.[57] He may thus have decided cases deductively, but it is hard to understand how he could have been applying, in the cases that came before him, his own "attitudes." Indeed, it seems relevant that many of his judicial opinions indicate that he considered any judicial infusion of personal values into constitutional law to be an abuse of power.[58]

Rogat's characterization of Holmes as a formalist or conceptualist has in varying degrees and ways been endorsed by Grant Gilmore, Robert W. Gordon, Saul Touster, and G. Edward White.[59] Hence, a widespread, if not predominant, view of Holmes is that he decided cases deductively, relying heavily on general principles. Once again a particular interpretation of Holmes's theory of free speech finds its home in a compatible interpretation of his constitutional jurisprudence. A picture of him as a coherent jurist is presented, but it is one that in my opinion distorts more than it reveals. The claim that Holmes treated the clear-and-present-danger standard as a formula to decide *all* cases involving free speech is not true. The phrase had nothing to do with harmful speech or conspiracies. In cases of harmful speech, the key issue was whether the speaker knew facts that would have warned an average person of the harmful character of his or her speech activity—a subtle question that in no way could be decided in any mechanical or deductive way. Conspiracies, in contrast, required a finding that the parties were acting "in concert" to achieve an unlawful result through speech—an inductive empirical matter. The reduction of Holmes's theory of free speech to the formula of a clear and present danger therefore mistakes a part of his theory for the whole.

The clear-and-present-danger standard was used by Holmes to determine liability in only one type of speech activity: illegal advocacy. In such cases, he required unlawful intent and a proximity (measured by the harm's nearness, seriousness, and the degree of apprehension felt by the community) to an illegal harm. Neither of these questions could be answered according to a formula. The matter of intent was empirical: did the speaker actually have an illegal purpose? And the decision as to the proximity of harm was a judgment of value about which rational people could disagree. Hence, besides mistaking a part of the theory for the whole of it, commentators who have charged Holmes with treating free speech according to a formula have not been sensitive to the underlying criteria that he used in cases of illegal advocacy.

The phrase "clear and present danger" was itself nothing more than a rhetorical embellishment that Holmes added to his theory in 1919. The actual substantive criteria had already been in place for many years. It may be true that his successors placed too much emphasis on the rhetorical phrase and not enough on the surrounding theory. He himself would not have been surprised at this development. "It is one of the misfortunes of law," he recorded, "that ideas become encysted in phrases and thereafter for a long time cease to provoke further analysis."[60] But even if the phrase "clear and present danger" in time suffered this fate, becoming an obstacle to "further analysis," it is incorrect to say that Holmes either understood the phrase as a formula or decided free-speech cases deductively in accordance with it.

At one point, Zechariah Chafee, Jr., did want to decide cases of free speech in a deductive fashion. Though he eventually gave up the search, he spent some time hunting for a suitable "major premise." In conversation, he explained his position to Holmes, but Chafee later reported in a letter to Judge Amidon that Holmes responded that no clear line could be drawn beforehand. Cases could be put on either side of the spectrum, both those that clearly incurred liability and those that clearly did not. The relevant factors were those derived from his theory of liability: harm, its likelihood, imminence, and seriousness; the apprehensions of the community; intent; and conspiracy. Falsely shouting fire in a crowded theater was clearly on the shaded side of the line.[61] It could certainly be punished. Political propaganda was on the sunny side. Congress could not "forbid all effort to change the mind of the country."[62] But as cases approached the middle of the spectrum, the constitutionality of liability for speech became more controversial. All that was possible was to indicate on a case-by-case basis which statutes were beyond the line of constitutionality and which ones were not. The line beyond which Congress could not go was a gray one somewhere in the middle of this spectrum.

Holmes's idea that judges slowly over time drew the hazy gray line separating the individual's right of free speech from the community's power to impose liability was not some new idea that he came up with in 1919. It was one of his old insights into the nature of common law development that he applied to constitutional adjudication.

Two widely different cases suggest a general distinction, which is a clear one when stated broadly. But as new cases cluster around the opposite poles, and begin to approach each other, the distinction becomes more difficult to trace; the determinations are made one way or the other on a very slight preponderance of feeling, rather than articulate reason; and at last a mathematical line is arrived at by the contact of contrary decisions, which is so far arbitrary that it might equally well have been drawn a little further to the one side or to the other.[63]

All distinctions of law, as Holmes never tired of saying, were therefore "matters of degree." Even in the case of constitutional adjudication, in which the issue was whether a particular exercise of power was within or without the legislature's authority, the judge's decision "will depend on a judgment or intuition more subtle than any articulate major premise."[64] As the particular exertion of legislative power approached the hazy gray line separating individual rights from legislative powers, the judge's assessment of constitutionality became a subtle value judgment. The judge's decision was therefore not deductive, formal, or conceptual in any sense.

A brief description of a few of Holmes's opinions can help to elucidate and substantiate my view of his theory of constitutional adjudication. In *Pennsylvania Coal Company v. Mahon,* [65] Holmes invalidated a state statute that regulated mining. The question was, could a state prohibit the mining of coal if it endangered human habitations and apply the law against a coal company that had explicitly reserved the right to mine the coal when it had sold the land to the city? Holmes said no. The state had to compensate the coal company because the regulation constituted a taking of property. The state's power to regulate land use was in tension with the individual's right to be compensated if the state took the property. But the case could not be decided on general propositions. The issue was "a question of degree—and therefore cannot be disposed of by general propositions."[66] Deducing logical implications of constitutional principles was not the way a judge assessed the validity of a statute. Even in a case in which Holmes exercised judicial review and cut down the legislature's power, he did not seek security in logic. In his mind, a common-law understanding of constitutional adjudication was compatible with judicial review.

A good example of Holmes's approach in a case in which he validated the exertion of legislative power is his opinion in *Interstate Consolidated Railway Company v. Massachusetts.*[67] In this case, he considered a state statute that required a street railway company to carry children to and from school at half fare. Though he believed that the law came close to the line of unconstitutionality, he upheld the law as a form of taxation for education: an exercise of legislative power whose constitutionality was indisputable. However, "It does not follow that it would be equally in accord with the conceptions at the base of our constitutional law to confer equal favors upon doctors, or working men, or people who could afford to buy 1000-mile tickets. Structural habits count for as much as logic in drawing the line."[68] Once again Holmes envisioned a constitutional spectrum. Taxation for education was on one side of the spectrum; it was clearly constitutional. A regulation that forced a street company to carry doctors at half-fare was on the other side; it was clearly not constitutional. A regulation that required the same company to carry children to and from school at half-fare was somewhere in between. By deciding whether the case was more analogous to those exertions of legislative power that had been condemned by previous judges or to those that had been upheld, the judge was making the line of constitutionality a little clearer than it was before. In this way, the constitutional line of authority was "pricked out by the gradual approach and contact of decisions from the opposing sides."[69] Holmes judged that the half-fare law was closer to exertions of power that had been upheld, and he therefore denied that the company's rights were violated.

The basic approach was therefore the same whether Holmes affirmed or denied the validity of the law in question. In either type of case, precedent deserved respect. When judges, because of the kinds of cases that came before them, had to confront a constitutional question, when they had to darken and deepen the line of constitutionality, they were to take into account how earlier judges had received analogous exertions of legislative power. They did not work on a blank slate. Judges had to decide "whether this case lies on one side or the other of a line which has to be worked out between cases differing only in degree."[70] As intimated in *Interstate Consolidated Railway Company,* precedents deserved respect because they reflected the "structural habits" and history of the community. And "upon a question of constitutional law," Holmes insisted, "the long-settled habits of the community play a part as well as grammar and logic."[71] A precedent, the specific holding itself, should be overruled only for a good reason.

If Holmes understood constitutional adjudication in this fashion, and if he believed that judges made the line of constitutionality more definite by a slow incremental process of comparing the relevant statute to how earlier judges received analogous ones, then it is fairly clear that his approach to constitutional adjudication was not formalistic or conceptualistic. The rhetorical style of Holmes's opinions may have misled some commentators to this conclusion. But the underlying substance of his approach was inductive, empirical, and comparative. His attention was focused on the particular facts of the case and (as they were reflected in precedent) the history and structural habits of his community. He paid little or no attention to general propositions or logical deductions therefrom.

A more specific reason why Rogat, in particular, came to his mistaken interpretation of Holmes's theory of constitutional adjudication may be that he misconceived the nature of the "greater-includes-the-lesser" test.[72] It was used when there was not a sufficient number of previous analogous exertions of legislative power for the judge to decide if the law was constitutional or not. When he found himself in this situation, Holmes would imagine a more radical exertion of legislative power, reasoning that if the more radical exertion of power was constitutional, then the less radical exertion was also. But this variation of his basic methodology hardly shows that he was deciding cases deductively. Indeed, it seems to show the exact opposite.

Holmes's dissent in *Bailey v. Alabama,*[73] which Rogat criticized as formalistic in character, is a good example of the greater-includes-the-lesser test. Holmes's conclusion was that a state could constitutionally presume, until the defendant had shown otherwise, that a person who violated a contract of labor had made the contract with an intent to commit fraud. He came to this admittedly harsh decision by first imagining the two sides of the constitutional spectrum: peonage violated the Thirteenth Amendment, but a state could impose civil liability on persons who breached their contracts. If civil liability was constitutional, then criminal liability, with punishments of imprisonment and hard labor, could be imposed without any constitutional violation. Bailey's conviction was thus constitutional, since Alabama had not gone so far as to impose criminal liability on a person who violated a contract. The law that Bailey violated did not punish a mere breach of a contract to labor; rather, it punished fraud, which required actual unlawful intent. The statute did consider the failure to return the money advanced prima facie evidence of fraudulent intent. But that did not alter, in Holmes's judgment, the law's position on the constitutional spectrum. The law often used such presumptions, and in this case it was only prima facie, not conclusive. The jury was permitted to find that the presumption was insufficient to establish guilt.

Thus Holmes's reasoning in *Bailey,* was not deductive. He decided the case by placing Alabama's exertion of legislative power on a constitutional spectrum; he compared the Alabama law with other possible exertions of legislative power, some of which were clearly constitutional and others which were clearly not; and he held that the Alabama law was closer to those laws that would be upheld by hypothetical courts rather than to those that would be invalidated. This was how he decided *Bailey v. Alabama,* even if he came to the wrong result. Disagreements with the results of Holmes's decisions should not tempt us to mischaracterize his approach.

Holmes's focus on a country's history and habits, as they were reflected in previous legal precedents, rather than on legal principles, complemented his general understanding of the Constitution. It was a "living" entity that had to be "considered in the light of our whole experience, and not merely in that of what was said a hundred years ago." It evolved as judges drew and redrew the continually hazy line separating the power of government from the rights of the individual. As the law became definite in one area, different cases with new questions arose elsewhere and judges had to begin anew their struggle to adapt the law inherited from the past to the exigencies of the present.

Judges therefore played, just as they played in other areas of law, an active role in constitutional development. The doctrine of separation of powers did not prevent Holmes from coming to this conclusion. Judges, he recorded, had been making law for a thousand years.[74] The difference between judicial and legislative action was not a distinction between what the two branches were doing, but how they were doing it.

A judicial inquiry investigates, declares, and enforces liabilities as they stand on present or past facts and under laws *supposed* already to exist. . . . Legislation, on the other hand, looks to the future and changes existing conditions by making a new rule, to be applied thereafter to all or some part of those subject to its power. (Emphasis mine)[75]

But the distinctiveness of their method did not effect the legislative character of the judge's activity. "To make a rule of conduct applicable to an individual who but for such action would be free from it is to legislate—yet it is what the judges do whenever they determine which of two competing principles of policy shall prevail."[76] Hence judges made law in a distinctive way, but they made law nonetheless.

With constitutional law, the same kind of development took place as judges compared an exertion of legislative power to relevant precedents. Was the new law more like those that have been invalidated or those that have been upheld? Two bundles of precedents, one supporting the legitimacy of legislative action and the other the right of the individual, compete to control the case. The decision as to which bundle was more analogous, at least in a difficult case, was essentially a policy question. Decisions "follow earlier decisions that are not identical on the ground that the policy implied [in the earlier set of decisions] covers the present case."[77] As the next section will show, the policy implied need not be the one a judge personally favored. The judge may be obliged to apply an understanding of legislative power and individual rights that is abhorrent to him or her. Nevertheless, judges had their own distinctive way of making constitutional law. They made law "interstitially," as Holmes referred to it, on a case-by-case basis.

Holmes therefore did not decide the free speech cases that came before him in a deductive or conceptualist manner. He understood that the right of free speech and the power that government had over it were not set in stone. All aspects of the American Constitution had to evolve. Change was inherent to law as it was to life. Judges had an active role to play in this process of constitutional development. The form of constitutional law might appear to be logic, but its substance was inherited from the past, and it had to be adapted in an incremental way to society's changing needs, beliefs, and values. Deductive logic had little to do with the matter. Much more important were the judge's understanding of the community—its past, present, and future.

Positivism and Judicial Review

Any interpretation of Holmes's theory of free speech must come to terms with his legal positivism. This is so not only because the two facets of his thought must be compatible with one another, at least if he was a coherent jurist, but because commentators have rested a negative characterization of his theory of free speech on this basis. Their argument is that Holmes had to have been, until his dissent in *Abrams v. United States,* an adherent of the bad-tendency doctrine because he was a legal positivist. David M. Rabban has provided the most sophisticated form of this argument,[78] though it can be found in other studies as well.[79]

According to Rabban, Holmes was hostile to free speech in the period prior to *Abrams,* because he believed that "legal development necessarily replaces internal and moral standards with external and objective ones and that the law must enforce the community's will against individual claims."[80] These two different reasons for his hostility were intimately associated with one another; his external and objective theory of legal liability was an outgrowth of his reduction of law to power. Yosal Rogat first made the argument that Holmes's theory of legal liability grew out of his positivism,[81] and Rabban seems to rely heavily on it. Holmes's own account of why he endorsed the external theory of legal liability is set aside in favor of this deeper explanation. He had argued that persons, no matter with what intent or foresight, who acted dangerously according to community standards should be punished to prevent as much harm as was humanly possible. But Rogat and Rabban do not believe that the prevention of harm can sufficiently explain Holmes's commitment to the objective standard of liability. He "believed that a preventive theory led to externality," but he "obviously liked the external standard apart from preventive purposes." Holmes's "stress on 'acts' rather than 'thoughts' can be understood when seen as one part of his general attempt to separate law and morals."[82] It was a product of his perception of a legal system as "a mechanism to enforce, by whatever means, the desires of the dominant group."[83] If law was confused with morals, a judge might attribute "to moral ideas a legal relevance independent of the sovereign's desires" and thereby "arrive at a distorted interpretation of those desires."[84] Since Holmes reduced law to power, he sharply separated law from morality by adopting an external theory of legal liability.

Rabban carries these arguments into the debate concerning the meaning and scope of Holmes's theory of free speech. The theory of legal liability permitted the punishment of conduct that the community found blameworthy in the average person.[85] Accordingly, it would justify the punishment of all speech having a tendency to cause harm. It did not matter whether the judgment of bad tendency was made by a legislature or a jury.[86] Both of these institutions, according to Rabban, were authoritative mouthpieces of the community's will. If either of them favored the imposition of liability on a particular instance or type of speech, the judge's job was to defer. He himself exercised no independent judgment of the community's beliefs or desires. Holmes's theory of legal liability was therefore a license for legislatures and juries to do what they willed with individual rights, including the right of free speech.

There is much that is correct with Rabban's and Rogat's description of Holmes's theory of law, but in my judgment the pieces have to be rearranged if an accurate representation of his outlook is to be achieved. First, Holmes did believe in legal absolutism. Law was "not a brooding omnipresence in the sky but the articulate voice of some sovereign."[87] And furthermore, it

is admitted by every one that who is the sovereign is a question of fact equivalent to the question who has the sum of the political powers of a state in his hands. That is to say, sovereignty is a form of power, and the will of the sovereign is law, because he has power to compel obedience or punish disobedience, and for no other reason.[88]

Law therefore had its origin, not in the dictates of nature, but in human will, the will of those powerful enough to compel obedience. Even constitutional rights were based on human will, and it followed that they could be withdrawn by the power that established them. There was "no such thing as a right created by law, as against the sovereign who

224 JUSTICE OLIVER WENDELL HOLMES

makes the law by which the right is to be created."[89] All rights were ultimately subject to the sovereign's discretion.

Though the sovereign was legally absolute, it was subject to all types of de facto limits. Though "the lawmaker cannot admit that any thing it enacts is not law, there is a large margin of de facto limit in the common consciousness that various imaginable enactments would provoke a general uprising. But that is an extra legal fact of uncertain boundaries. The only limit that I can see to the power of the law-maker is the limit of power as a question of fact."[90] Accordingly, the coercive power that ultimately was the source of all law had no legal limits. The existence of de facto limits in no way effected the validity of legal absolutism.

But who was the sovereign in the American constitutional order? Holmes rarely discussed this question in an explicit fashion, but his position was fairly straightforward. In his reaction to the Gas Stokers' strike, after chiding Herbert Spencer for trying to reconcile social evolution with absolute limits on political authority, he said that if "the welfare of the living majority is paramount, it can only be on the ground that the majority have the power in their hands."[91] Popular sovereignty was a fact of the contemporary world. Accordingly, in the United States, the states were not sovereign. Neither was any branch of the federal government nor the federal government itself.[92] All were limited by law, whether in regard to their powers or functions. Only the American people were beyond legal control. They were the source of all law in the United States.

As a state judge, Holmes used the doctrine of popular sovereignty in an advisory opinion to evaluate the constitutionality of the referendum. The objection to it was that it violated the principle of representative government. Massachusetts was not a direct democracy; legislative power had been delegated to the legislature, and there it remained. Though the state supreme court accepted this argument and advised the legislature that the referendum was unconstitutional, Holmes dissented. The question was not, he wrote, "whether the people of their own motion could pass a law without any act of the Legislature. That no doubt, *whether valid or not,* would be outside the Constitution" (emphasis mine). The question was rather "whether an act of the Legislature is made unconstitutional by a proviso that, if rejected by the people, it shall not go into effect."[93] The case would be different, Holmes argued, if the law was subject to the approval of one person. "The difference is plain between that case and one where the approval required is that *of the sovereign body.* The contrary view seems to me an echo of Hobbes's theory that the surrender of sovereignty by the people was final" (emphasis mine).[94] The people were sovereign; they delegated legislative power to the legislature. But the referendum was constitutional since the people retained their ultimate sovereignty.

The people of Massachusetts were sovereign within the borders of Massachusetts, but they were subject to the federal Constitution and to the wider sovereignty of the American people. It is, however, arguable that Holmes's opinion that the American people were sovereign had little significance. After all, the Constitution itself began with the phrase, "We the people" and established an amendment process that empowered the American people to alter it. There is nothing necessarily incompatible between the doctrine of popular sovereignty and the existence of a written constitution specifying the powers delegated to government and the rights retained by individuals.

But by placing the idea of a written constitution within the context of a theory of popular sovereignty and by boldly stating and restating the doctrine of legal absolutism, Holmes changed the emphasis. The Constitution was not the source of legal authority because it contained "natural rights" or "natural principles of government." It was not a "brooding omnipresence in the sky" or a "mystic overlaw." It was the charter of government established by the sovereign American people and subject to its control. The focus was no longer on an eighteenth-century document, but rather on the needs and desires of a historically changing people.

An implication of Holmes's idea of popular absolutism reveals the significance of this new form of American constitutionalism. If the people were sovereign, if they were legally illimitable, they could alter the Constitution in ways not specified by the Constitution itself. Holmes hinted at this conclusion in his advisory opinion on the constitutionality of the referendum. A direct legislative act was outside the Constitution, he conceded, but it might still be *legally valid* because the people were sovereign.

It seems that Holmes came to this conclusion about the extraconstitutional authority of the popular sovereign in 1871, long before he became a judge. At that time the constitution of North Carolina required, before an amendment could go to the people, the approval of three-fifths of the legislature. A certain proposed amendment had no chance of obtaining the requisite number of votes in the legislature, though the measure was widely supported by the people at large. A public discussion ensued as to whether the people could lawfully change the state constitution in an un- or extraconstitutional manner. John Norton Pomeroy argued that "sovereignty cannot exist under limitations, nor can its free exercise be controlled."[95] Hermann von Holst objected that Pomeroy had abandoned a basic principle of American constitutionalism. The people must respect the constitutional restrictions that they have imposed on themselves. Holmes entered the debate and sided with Pomeroy. "It is true that if the will of the majority is unmistakable, and the majority is strong enough to have a clear power to enforce its will, and intends to do so, the courts must yield, as must everybody else, because the foundation of sovereignty is power, real or supposed."[96] The people of North Carolina, if they had the power and were intent on having their way, could "unconstitutionally" alter their state Constitution.

The only limitation was the federal Constitution and the wishes of the American people. North Carolina was part of a larger political entity, and the American Civil War had drawn out the implications of that connection. Holmes knew that the constitutional issues of the Civil War could not be settled by a legal analysis of the Constitution.[97] They had to be decided on the battlefield. The question was which side was stronger and more determined to have its way, not which side was legally right. The North won and the postwar amendments were ratified accordingly, with gun and saber at hand.[98]

Later generations, with the complacency that historical distance provides, drifted to the opinion that the North had the right interpretation of the Constitution all along. Holmes, conversely, fought in the war, and this experience shaped his outlook in many ways. For one thing, it convinced him that law, including constitutional law, rested on power. The North's interpretation was right because it had the power to enforce its will and for no other reason. Accordingly, the Civil War may have been in Holmes's eyes an extraconstitutional alteration of the Constitution by the American sovereign. Here, as in the North Carolina crisis, Judges were to defer to the new order.

I can't understand how anyone should think that an instrumentality established by the United States to carry out its will, and that it can depose upon a failure to do so, should undertake to enforce something that *ex hypothesi* is against its will. It seems to me like shaking one's fist at the sky, when the sky furnishes the energy that enables one to raise the fist. There is a tendency to think of judges as if they were independent mouthpieces of the infinite, and not simply directors of a force that comes from the source that gives them their authority.[99]

Judges were therefore ultimately subject to the sovereign. The written Constitution could not insulate them from the source of their power. In the context of the American constitutional order, they were to acquiesce to the abiding wishes of the American people.

Rabban therefore has not mischaracterized Holmes's belief in legal absolutism. He has, however, in my opinion, mistaken the respective roles that judges, legislatures, and juries had in relationship to the sovereign will, and he misapplied Holmes's theory of liability to speech. His argument that Holmes must have been an adherent of the bad-tendency doctrine, because he adhered to an external standard of liability, is not convincing.[100] The central thrust of Holmes's theory was to rest liability on harm or (in the case of attempts) its proximity.[101] Rogat, himself, who was critical of Holmes's theory of free speech, said that it was "precisely the exaggerated emphasis on actions and potential harm (as opposed to purposes) that can be desirable and liberal when applied to problems involving the freedoms of expression."[102] Hence Rabban is working at cross purposes: to the degree to which Holmes's theory of speech is explicable by reference to his theory of legal liability, it is difficult to substantiate any claim that he did not require, at a minimum, a real proximity to harm before imposing liability on speech. Holmes never imposed liability without a proximity to harm or harm itself. It was for this very reason that Chafee understood and admired Holmes's test as an attractive alternative to the bad-tendency doctrine.[103]

The claim that Holmes's external standard of liability explains his early hostility to free speech because it induced him to ignore the speaker's intent is partially true.[104] He did impose liability on harmful speech even if the speaker's intent was innocent. He, however demanded *actual* unlawful intent in attempts and conspiracies. In attempts, unlawful intent functioned as "an index to the probability of certain future acts which the law seeks to prevent."[105] Its purpose was "not to show that the act was wicked, but to show that it was likely to be followed by hurtful consequences."[106] Since this explanation for requiring intent ultimately rested on the idea of external harm, commentators have ignored the condition, assumed that Holmes resorted to legal presumptions to establish the actor's unlawful intent, or reduced the requirement to one of several factors used to measure the proximity of harm.[107] According to these interpretations, the state did not necessarily have to establish the actual unlawful intent of the speaker before imposing liability.

In my judgment, these accounts confuse Holmes's rationale for requiring unlawful intent with the nature of the requirement itself. Just because intent was an "index to the probability of harm" does not mean that probability of harm, much less a mere tendency, sufficed to establish unlawful intent. If he said that actual unlawful intent had to be shown in certain crimes, then the common-sense conclusion is that it had to be shown no matter what his rationale for the condition was or whether the rationale was convincing or not. Thus Holmes's theory of legal liability does not show that he, by the use of legal presumptions, inferred intent from bad tendency. Actual unlawful intent had to be established in attempts and conspiracies. It could be inferred when the external standard was applied, but then the speech itself had to be harmful. In either case, a bad tendency was not enough.

Holmes's theory of legal liability is therefore compatible with the conclusion that he, for his time and place, had a moderately protective doctrine of free speech. But what of his doctrine of legal absolutism? Did it place individual rights, including the right of free speech, at the whim of legislatures and juries? In 1919 Holmes himself responded to the charge that he was overly deferential to juries. Ernst Freund, in an article in the *New Republic*,[108] had made this claim, and Holmes answered that the objection to the jury was "an objection to pretty much the whole body of law, which for thirty years I have made my brethren smile by insisting to be everywhere a matter of degree." He continued, quoting from one of his own opinions,[109] "the law is full of instances where a man's fate depends on his estimating rightly, that is, as the jury subsequently estimates it, from matters of degree."[110] This passage leaves the impression that juries had a role in defining the right of free speech for the puzzling reason that all questions of law were ultimately matters of degree. To understand why this characteristic of law explained why juries had a role in defining free speech, one must be sensitive to the legislative role that Holmes assigned juries.

When a case arises in which the standard of conduct, pure and simple, is submitted to the jury, the explanation is plain. It is that the court, not entertaining any clear views of public policy applicable to the matter, derives the rule to be applied from daily experience, as it has been agreed that the great body of the law of tort has been derived. But the court further feels that it is not itself possessed of sufficient practical experience to lay down the rule intelligently. It conceives that twelve men taken from the practical part of the community can aid its judgment. Therefore it aids its conscience by taking the opinion of the jury.[111]

Hence the jury played a legislative role whenever the judge left "the standard of conduct" up to the jury.[112] Since a judge would rely on the jury only when the law was unclear, the imposition of liability would revolve around a matter of degree. A person's fate would depend on how well he or she could guess what a jury would decide.

But what is often overlooked is that Holmes was leery of giving the jury too much latitude in its legislative role. He described it as a "temporary surrender of the judicial function," claimed that it all too often left "all our rights and duties throughout a great part of the law to the necessarily more or less accidental feelings of a jury," and insisted that it "may be resumed at any moment in any case when the court feels competent to do so."[113] The major saving grace of the legislative role of the jury was that it enabled popular prejudice to shape the law and thereby kept "the administration of the law in accord with the wishes and feelings of the community."[114] Nonetheless, Holmes believed that judges should monitor closely the legislative role that juries performed. It should be withdrawn if and when the judge thought it appropriate.

In constitutional adjudication, the jury could play the same function. Clear cases, those on either side of the spectrum, would be decided by the judge without the jury. The judge would uphold the legislature's exertion of power or the individual right. In controversial cases, when the case was close to that hazy gray line separating governmental power from individual right, the judge could ask the jury for its help. If requested, the jury would be participating in the kind of judicial development of the Constitution that was described earlier in this chapter. The jurors would play an active but incremental role in adapting the organic Constitution to an everchanging society.

Even in cases involving constitutional adjudication, however, the jury's role was still a "temporary surrender of the judicial function": one which the judge could revoke "at any moment in any case when the court feels competent to do so." And it is fairly obvious that Holmes believed that an experienced judge would rarely need a jury. A "judge who has sat long at *nisi prius* ought gradually to acquire a fund of experience which enables him *to represent* the common sense of the community in ordinary instances far better than the average jury" (emphasis mine).[115] A trial judge had a representative role that was superior to the jury's. And if Holmes believed an ordinary trial judge could represent the community better than a jury, it is likely that he would have also thought that an experienced appellate judge would be able to do so to an even greater degree.

Alongside of its legislative role, the jury continued its important function of finding the facts. Holmes was not suggesting, when he referred to the "temporary surrender of the judicial function," that an appellate judge could or should second-guess a jury's findings of simple facts. Not only would it have been presumptuous of someone who was not at the trial to overturn the jury's factual findings, but the jurisdiction of federal appellate courts was defined by statutes that sharply limited their authority to look into the facts. In *Cedar Rapids Gas Light Co. v. Cedar Rapids,* Holmes explained why the Supreme Court could not review a state court's findings of fact because the writ of error, established by the Judiciary Act of 1789, confined its jurisdiction to errors of federal law.[116] In contrast, he expressed a willingness to get into the facts in *German Savings and Loan Society v. Dormitzer,* because section 5 of the Judiciary Act of 3 March 1891 had extended the Court's jurisdiction in certain cases coming from the lower federal courts.[117] These statutory rules that defined the Supreme Court's jurisdiction had an impact on free-speech cases. Liability could depend on the presence or absence of simple facts: Did the speaker intend an unlawful result? Did these individuals conspire to obtain an illegal result through speech? If these questions were answered affirmatively by a jury in a state case, Holmes would have had great difficulty overturning them. This did not mean that he was overly timid or deferential to juries, only that he had a sense of his proper role as an appellate judge within a large and complicated system.

But once a jury made any kind of a finding or judgment that *came close* to an issue of federal law—since the distinction between fact and law was also one of degree—Holmes was not shy about taking jurisdiction.

But of course, findings, either at law or in equity, may depend upon questions that are re-examinable here. The admissibility of evidence or its sufficiency to warrant the conclusion reached may be denied; or the conclusion may be a composite of fact and law, such as ownership or contract; or in some way the record may disclose that the finding necessarily involved a ruling within the appellate jurisdiction of this court. Such questions, properly saved, must be answered, and, so far as it is necessary to examine the evidence in order to answer them or to prevent an evasion of real issues, the evidence will be examined.[118]

The suggestion is that Holmes had less reluctance to overturn a jury's finding that a certain form of speech was harmful in character or that a certain instance of speech posed a clear and present danger. Since such findings were not of simple fact, he could overturn them because they were "a composite of fact and law," or because the "admissibility of evidence or its sufficiency to warrant the conclusion reached may be denied," or because "the finding necessarily involved a ruling within the appellate jurisdiction of this court." He was not timid if the jury was performing a legislative function in regard to a federally protected right, including the right of free speech.

Holmes's refusal to overturn convictions under the Espionage Act is therefore not evidence that he was overly deferential to juries. He did believe that law reflected power, that juries were in charge of finding the facts, and that juries could play a constitutional role. They were to adapt constitutional law to the common sense of the community. But their legislative work was done in subordination to and within the immediate control of the judge. And in the same way, when the judge performed his or her duties, when either deciding cases that helped to draw the hazy line of constitutionality or, more rarely, when monitoring juries as they drew the line, the judge too was to represent the beliefs, values, and interests of the American people.

Legislatures, of course, were more explicitly representative of the sovereign than either juries or judges. For this reason, Holmes described them as having "paramount" power.[119] He did not mean that they were sovereign or legally absolute, only that they deserved the benefit of the doubt rather than the burden of proof. Whenever they exerted their power, courts were generally to defer for two reasons. As discussed earlier, the line of constitutionality was a matter of degree. Since there was no "mathematical" or "scientific" way to draw this line, a law close to it should be accepted by courts. "But when it is seen that a line or point there must be, and that there is no mathematical or logical way of fixing it precisely, the decision of the legislature must be accepted unless we can say that it is very wide of any reasonable mark."[120] And if legislatures had the benefit of the doubt, it followed that "constitutional provisions must be administered with caution."[121] The "interpretation of constitutional principles must not be too literal,"[122] because "delusive exactness is a source of fallacy throughout the law."[123] Judges were not to limit the moderate use of legislative power by any kind of logical exegesis from the written provisions of the Constitution.

A related reason for Holmes's general deference to legislative will relied more heavily on the legislature's more immediate relationship to the sovereign's will. If the law rested on pervasive and predominant opinion, the judge should defer not because constitutional adjudication consisted of drawing subtle lines, but because the sovereign had spoken. Holmes's understanding of the police power reveals this particular quality of his constitutionalism. It was an apology "for the general power of the legislature to make a part of the community uncomfortable by a change."[124] He himself did not believe that the apology was necessary since the issue was ultimately a policy question. The question as to whether the legislature had the power or whether the individual had the right was reducible to what the community wanted.

All rights tend to declare themselves absolute to their logical extreme. Yet all in fact are limited by the *neighborhood of principles of policy* which are other than those on which the particular right is founded, and which become strong enough to hold their own when a certain point is reached. *The limits set to property by other public interests* present themselves as a branch of what is called the police power of the state. (Emphasis mine)[125]

But if the right of property and the police power were reducible to the community's policies and interests, courts should allow the legislature to do what the community wanted it to do. "It may be said in a general way that the police power *extends to all the great public needs.* It may be put forth in aid of what is sanctioned by *usage,* or *held by the prevailing morality or strong and preponderant opinion to be greatly and immediately necessary to the public welfare*" (emphasis mine).[126]

Though these passages specifically addressed the police power, they reflect Holmes's general understanding of all legislative powers and individual rights. Ultimately the legislature had as much power as the community wanted it to have. Constitutional adjudication was therefore fundamentally reducible to giving the community what it wanted.

A number of Holmes's famous aphorisms point in the direction that judges should defer when the legislature reflected the pervasive and predominant values and interests of the community. He had, for example, no "practical" criterion to go on except "what the crowd wanted."[127] He suggested, in a humorous vein that his epitaph "out to say, 'Here lies the supple tool of power.' "[128] No judge ought to interpret a provision of the Constitution in a way that would prevent the American people from doing what it *really* wanted to do. If the general consensus was that a certain condition was an "evil" that ought to be corrected by certain means, then the government had the power to do it: "Legislation may begin where an evil begins"[129]; "Constitutional law like other mortal contrivances has to take some chances."[130] "Some play must be allowed to the joints if the machine is to work."[131] All of these rhetorical flourishes suggest that Holmes deferred to the legislature if and when he thought it accurately mirrored the abiding beliefs, interests, and values of the American public.

Constitutional law's corresponding evolutionary character did not trouble Holmes. "Historic continuity with the past is not a duty, it is only a necessity." The "present has a right to govern itself so far as it can."[132] Judicial deference to the sovereign will of the community, however, did not mean a slavish submission to the legislature. Holmes believed in the doctrine of judicial review.[133] While legislatures were "ultimate guardians of the liberties and welfare of the people in quite as great a degree as the courts,"[134] he insisted that courts "must exercise a judgment of their own."[135] They too represented the sovereign.

Judicial review might seem to us to be at odds with Holmes's doctrine of popular legal absolutism because it is often thought to imply legal limitations of sovereign power. But Holmes criticized Leon Duguit for making just this kind of argument.[136] "As to Duguit whom you don't speak of, but whom I dispraised, perhaps I might sum up my impression by saying that he seemed to assume that if a court upset a statute, that indicated a decay of sovereignty—as if a court means anything but a voice of the sovereign power—the dominant voice in the case supposed."[137] When a court invalidated a statute, it spoke in the name and on the behalf of the sovereign. A statute was unconstitutional because it conflicted with the long-term interests and values of the sovereign. It followed that a court should exercise the power of judicial review only when it could honestly say that it represented the interests and values of a predominant part of the community.

The representative role that the judge played in the exercise of judicial review was neither new or abnormal. Holmes was of the opinion that judges had a similar function in common-law development. "Sometimes courts are induced to lay down rules by facts of a more specific nature; as that the legislature passed a certain statute, and that the case at bar is within the fair meaning of its words; or that *the practice of a specially interested class, or of the public at large, has generated a rule of conduct outside the law which it is desirable that the courts should recognize and enforce*" (emphasis mine).[138] Common-law judges were to pay attention to the evolving habits and expectations of "specially interested" classes and "the public at large." That was their job; they were "to represent" the community. Holmes transferred this basic idea from common law to constitutional adjudication. When judges confronted constitutional questions, they were not to pay exclusive attention to the words of a document or the intent of its framers. They had a more statesmanlike role to play: they were to act as special representatives of the sovereign American people.

At times, of course, there would be no general consensus on the constitutionality of a particular exertion of legislative power. The community would have no firm conviction as to whether it constituted a violation of a constitutional right. The sovereign would be divided into two camps: those insisting on the law's constitutionality and those who denied it. In this situation, Holmes recommended that the judge look on the matter as a question of which "desire is stronger at the point of conflict."

But I think it most important to remember whenever a doubtful case arises, with certain analogies on one side and other analogies on the other, that what really is before us is a conflict between two social desires, each of which seeks to extend its dominion over the case, and which cannot both have their way. The social question is which desire is stronger at the point of conflict. The judicial one *may* be narrower, because one or the other desire may have been expressed in previous decisions to such an extent that logic requires us to assume it to preponderate in the one before us. But if that be clearly so, the case is not a doubtful one. *Where there is doubt the simple tool of logic does not suffice,* and even if it is disguised and unconscious, *the judges are called on to exercise the sovereign prerogative of choice.* (Emphasis mine)[139]

When there was a doubtful case, with analogies on both sides, the community was divided into hostile groups. Logic could not decide the issue. No longer was the judicial question narrower than the social one. The judge had to take into account the strength of the social desires involved.

An interesting case to see Holmes's method at work was *Laurel Hill Cemetery v. San Francisco.*[140] The city had enacted an ordinance prohibiting cemeteries within the municipal limits. A cemetery owner sued, arguing that the ordinance was an unconstitutional taking of property because the best scientific evidence substantiated the harmlessness of urban cemeteries. Holmes upheld the ordinance, arguing that the owner "must wait until there is a change of practice, or at least an established consensus of civilized opinion, before it can expect this court to overthrow the rules that the lawmakers and the court of his own state uphold."[141] The implication was that individual rights evolved according to the consensus of public opinion. Judges should not act "prematurely." It was "a misfortune if a judge reads his conscious or unconscious sympathy with one side or the other prematurely into the law."[142] But when the time came, when the judge could discern an emerging consensus, the judge was entitled to cut down legislative acts that conflicted with the sovereign's sentiments.

Even if sovereign public opinion was divided, it should be noted that Holmes assumed that the legislature could exercise its power in a way that was not wide of the mark. Holmes always deferred to the legislature if the law was not too far from the hazy line of constitutionality. But if the law was a radical exertion of power, and if it did not square with any predominant public opinion then existing or emerging, the judge could act as a spokesperson for the sovereign and invalidate the law. His discussion of a series of rate cases that the Court decided in 1926 are quite revealing in this regard.[143]

At our conference yesterday p.m. (for now it is Sunday) we had some rate cases, the question being whether the rate fixed by the N.Y. legislature for gas companies in New York was confiscatory and so, unconstitutional. We solemnly weigh the valuation of the property and all the tests and decide pro or con—but really it is determining a line between grabber and grabbee *that turns on the feeling of the community.* You say the pubic is entitled to this and the owners to that. I see no a priori reason for the propositions except that that is *the way the crowd feels.* (Emphasis mine) [144]

Community sentiment was ultimately to decide if the rates were confiscatory or not. But in each of these rate cases, Holmes joined the Court in overturning the New York legislature. He believed that the legislature was out of step with the predominant feeling of the American community. When the legislature acted radically and in opposition to public opinion, judges were empowered by the community to invalidate the law.

The constitutional crisis in North Carolina, discussed earlier, was another clear example of a legislature that was out of step with predominant public opinion. The legislature would not pass a proposed amendment by the required three-fifths majority. It therefore could not be ratified by the people notwithstanding its popularity. Holmes had argued that popular opinion must prevail over the specific provisions of North Carolina's written Constitution because "the foundation of sovereignty is power." If there was any doubt about the sovereign's power or intent, however, a judge should adhere to the traditional understanding of governmental power and individual rights.

But so long as there is a reasonable doubt of that power and intent . . . the question is in substance the question of recognition, which so often perplexes foreign governments. Where sovereign power resides at any time, and what is the sovereign will, are questions of fact. But the old constitution is an admitted expression of the sovereign will, and that assures us that no other is authentic which does not come through certain channels. The courts may properly abide by that until they see that the new manifestation is not only unmistakable, but irresistible. [145]

When the popular sovereign demands something that clearly conflicts with the existing constitution, judges have every right to be cautious. They can stick with the old Constitution until the sovereign's will is "irresistible." Only then must a judge acquiesce.

Constitutional law, like all other forms of law, was therefore inherently conservative. It inevitably had to evolve, but it ought to do so slowly. The example of North Carolina was unusual because it involved an abandonment of a specific constitutional provision by general consensus. The more usual situation would involve a radical exertion of legislative power when the community is torn into divisive groups: one group in political and social decline claiming that the law is of course unconstitutional; the other group, one that is slowly growing in numbers and power, claiming the exact opposite. Nonetheless, even here, the conservative character of constitutional law is still present. The judge need not abandon traditional understandings of legislative power and individual right until the demands of the new group become irresistible.

Holmes's famous address "Law and the Court" had as its primary theme the inherently conservative character of constitutional law. In this speech, he began by noting that the Court had been charged by the socialists with corruption. The Justices were depicted as "the representatives of a class—a tool of the money power." This condemnation made his "heart ache," but he insisted that judges "must take such things philosophically and try to see what we can learn from hatred and distrust and whether behind them there may not be *some germ of inarticulate truth*" (emphasis mine).[146] After condemning the socialist agenda and praying that the general public could be educated to a few obvious economic truths, he returned to the "truth embodied" in the criticism levelled against the Court by the socialists. He said

It cannot be helped, it is as it should be, that the law is behind the times. I told a labor leader once that what they asked was favor, and if a decision was against them they called it wicked. The same might be said of their opponents. It means that the law is growing. As law embodies beliefs that have triumphed in the battle of ideas and then have translated themselves into action, while there still is doubt, while opposite convictions still keep a battle front against each other, the time for law has not come; the notion destined to prevail is not yet entitled to the field.[147]

The law to which Holmes was referring, the one that was "destined to prevail yet not entitled to the field," was some conception of the respective powers of the legislature and the rights of individuals. If socialism decisively won the "battle of ideas," a distinctive outlook governing the relationship of the individual to the state would be "translated" into "action." If an extreme form of capitalism or social Darwinism won, then another orientation would be embodied into law. But in the existing circumstances, with neither of the extremes victorious, a judge "cannot help" but stick with the existing understanding of legislative powers and individual rights. Law, including constitutional law, is inherently conservative. It reflects yesterday's balance of political forces. The judge should readjust the hazy line of constitutionality in a radical way only when the new balance of power proves irresistible.

Constitutional law is therefore slowly to adapt—"but not too slowly" —to the changing relationships of political power that exist in the community. It has a corresponding moderate character, and the judge's duty is to avoid the extremes. The judge should be slow to overrule constitutional precedent. The past contains much that is valuable and yesterday's political relationships should be set aside only when there is a clear reason to do so. A transitory whim of the public is not enough. Constitutional law must bend to the predominant and enduring will of the majority, but it does not have to dance to every popular tune. Since the organic Constitution is meant to satisfy the needs of people across generations, the majority vote that counts is the one "in the long run." And in regard to that vote, Holmes once said, "we have to rely for consolation upon a few, at times."[148] A judge could therefore invalidate a statute notwithstanding the popular sovereign's support if the judge sincerely believes that the public will have second thoughts about what the legislature has done.

A judge who stands alone against the legislature and the immediate beliefs and wishes of the community is standing on the weakest of foundations. The judge cannot oppose the source of his or her power for very long. Deference to the wishes of the public is necessary if they are not only pervasive and strong but abiding. This is so because power will have its way. If the change cannot be accomplished peacefully, then violence is the only alternative, and it is an important part of a judge's job to see that violence is ultimately unnecessary. The judge must transcend his or her own personal convictions and permit a lot of what he or she personally holds dear "to be done away with short of revolution by the orderly change of law."[149] The Constitution therefore balances on the horns of a dilemma: it retains from the past those fundamentals that unite several generations into a people and at the same time bends to the pervasive and fundamental changes that occur in any human society. A judge, when practicing the art of constitutional adjudication, tries to make this dilemma a workable reality.

The judge's personal intellectual and moral commitments should therefore have no conscious effect whatsoever on the development of constitutional law. The judge should affirm laws that are stupid or even harmful to the public. If a silly law is close to the hazy line of constitutionality, a judge has to defer to the legislature's policy decision. Even a radical exertion of power has to be upheld if the predominant groups of the community have irresistible power and are intent on having their way. Such a law has to be affirmed even if the judge personally considered it abhorrent or even if the law clearly violates constitutional rights as they were understood by previous generations.

Holmes himself expressed deep regret about certain laws that he upheld, which reveals the selfless character of his sense of the judicial role. "The whole collectivist tendency seems to be toward underrating or forgetting the safeguards in bills of rights that had to be fought for in their day and that still are worth fighting for. I have had to deal with cases that made my blood boil and yet seemed *to create no feeling in the public* or even in most of my brethren" (emphasis mine).[150] In a tragic sort of way, a judge's personal values were not relevant to the job. They were more of a temptation to abuse the judicial office by ignoring the community's sentiments than a justification for overturning a statute. Of course, a judges's personal philosophy may have an impact on how he or she measures the radicalness of legislative action and evaluates the content and character of the beliefs and wishes of the popular sovereign. This kind of unconscious effect is unavoidable and certainly excusable if the judge conscientiously tries to represent the community's long-term wishes. Conversely, a judge who self righteously imports personal values into law, when the values are at odds with the community's, has violated Holmes's basic conception of the judicial function. Only if a judge is selfless could constitutional law achieve the single ideal of which it was capable—"to embody the preference of a given body in a given time and place."[151] With law there is no "higher formula than organic fitness at the given moment."[152] "Correspondence to the actual equilibrium of force in the community" is the "proximate test of excellence" of all law, including constitutional law.[153]

This slow, but not too slow, development of constitutional law is what occurred in the history of free speech. Whether free speech was intended only to prohibit prior restraints, as Holmes first thought, or whether it was meant to prevent the punishment of seditious libel, as he later came to believe, the guarantee had slowly evolved according to the community's beliefs and values throughout the nineteenth and twentieth centuries. As a judge in Massachusetts, Holmes participated in the evolution of this constitutional right by applying his theory of legal liability. He thought that this theory captured the drift in the law because it reflected the beliefs and values of modern civilization. According to this theory, harmful speech was punished according to the external standard; advocacy of illegal acts was punished if there was unlawful intent and a proximity to harm; and conspiracies were punished even if speech was the means by which the unlawful result was to be achieved.

On the Supreme Court, Holmes continued to use his theory of legal liability to decide cases involving speech. He understood the guarantee according to a theory that reflected, in his mind, the general wishes of the American sovereign. The Espionage Act of 1917 was not considered by Holmes to be a radical departure from the existing legal background. It only punished obstructions, attempts, and conspiracies. Holmes thought it was not only a constitutional law, clearly within the line that marked the edge of the legislature's power, but also a wise one.[154] After the 1918 amendments to the Espionage Act were enacted, when the federal government started to prosecute cases that did not qualify as attempts or conspiracies under Holmes's theory of legal liability, he stepped back. He would not punish Abrams because there was no evidence of harmful speech or illegal intent. Nor later would he punish Gitlow for an attempt when there was no evidence of any proximity to a harm.

Holmes's actions in these early free-speech cases may seem to be in tension with the theory of constitutional adjudication presented in this chapter. The American people widely supported Abram's and Gitlow's convictions, as well as thousands of others across the country. They were applauding the punishment of people whose speech activity did not satisfy the criteria of Holmes's theory of legal liability. Why did Holmes not defer to popular will and affirm all convictions of unpopular political agitation? The answer is that Holmes was protecting an important American value from a transitory whim of the popular sovereign. He knew that free speech was not permanently linked to the Constitution. It "was an experiment." It very well might be abandoned. Certainly if the enduring consensus of the American public is that politically offensive or shocking speech should be punished, in time that is exactly what will happen. But Holmes was not willing to cave in to popular opinion immediately. Constitutional law has to evolve, but it must do so slowly to insure that important values of the past are not lost in periods of hysteria. His moderate defense of free speech can therefore be fitted into his general theory of constitutional adjudication. He was not applying the historical intent of the framers or deducing his preference from general legal principles. In his capacity as a special representative of the American sovereign, he was protecting a traditional constitutional value for future generations. He acted because he hoped and believed that free speech would once again regain the support of the sovereign American people.

Notes

1. See above, chap. 2, n. 1.
2. See Samuel Konefsky, *The Legacy of Holmes and Brandeis: A Study of the Influence of Ideas* (New York: MacMillan, 1956), 187; Fred D. Ragan, "Justice Oliver Wendell Holmes, Jr., Zechariah Chafee, Jr., and the Clear and Present Danger Test for Free Speech: The First Year, 1919," *Journal of American History* 58 (June-March 1971–72): 27; David M. Rabban, "The First Amendment in Its Forgotten Years," *Yale Law Journal* 90 (1981): 535–34, 570: "The Emergence of Modern First Amendment Doctrine," *University of Chicago Law Review* 40 (Fall 1983): 1265–66; Michael T. Gibson, "The Supreme Court and Freedom of Expression from 1791– 1917," *Fordham Law Review* 55 (1986): 283–90. The most thorough account of this interpretation of Holmes's theory of free speech, however, is to be found in David S. Bogen, "The Free Speech Metamorphosis of Mr. Justice Holmes," *Hofstra Law Review* 11 (1982): 97–189.
3. See Bogen, "The Free Speech Metamorphosis of Mr. Justice Holmes," 107– 15.
4. Ibid., 141–44, 147–49. Note that Bogen's interpretation is distinctive because he understands *Schenck v. United States* as the pivotal case in which Holmes was converted to a more pro-speech position. The more common view (see sources cited in n. 2 above) is that one must wait until his dissent in *Abrams v. United States* for any sign that Holmes appreciated the value of free speech. Bogen believes that the more eloquent passages in *Abrams* were simply a "product of Holmes's frustration at what he considered the misreading by critics and the pubic of his position in *Schenck*" (ibid., 99). Also, he argues that the conversion was not a deep change in personal values because Holmes was throughout his life sympathetic to free speech. It was only a change in his understanding of the law. I think this account is more accurate than the more popular one, but see Rabban, who characterizes Bogen's argument as "unpersuasive" ("The Emergence of Modern First Amendment Doctrine," 1209–10 n. 14).
5. 205 U.S. 454 (1907).

6. Id. at 462.
7. Letter from Holmes to Zechariah Chafee, Jr., 12 June 1922, Box 14, Folder 121, Zechariah Chafee Papers (Manuscript Division, Harvard Law School Library), cited by Bogen, "The Free Speech Metamorphosis of Mr. Justice Holmes," 100.
8. See Brief of Plaintiff in Error at 88, *Patterson:* "The right of criticism does not, of course, exempt a person from the responsibilities for his utterances, nor does it mean a license to indulge in 'wanton defamation', abuse or vilification, and to escape therefrom without punishment. . . . but it must be kept clearly in mind that one is punished solely for an abuse of the liberty of speech, or the abuse of the liberty of the press." Also see Brief of Defendant in Error at 62–63, *Patterson:* "But liberty of speech may be abused. For abuse thereof every citizen of Colorado is, by the Constitution of that State, made responsible. . . . It is the use, not the abuse of the right, that is protected."
9. For the relevant provision of Colorado's Constitution, see Brief of Defendant in Error at 59, *Patterson.*
10. See Brief of the Plaintiff in Error at 88–103, *Patterson* and Reply Brief of Plaintiff in Error at 31–42, *Patterson.*
11. See especially Brief of Defendant in Error in Support of Motion to Dismiss or Affirm at 37–39, *Patterson.* On the jurisdictional issue, see Brief of Defendant in Error at 39–67, *Patterson.*
12. *Patterson v. Colorado,* 205 U.S. 454, 463 (1907).
13. Id. at 461.
14. Id. at 462.
15. 20 Mass. 304 (1825).
16. Id. at 313.
17. Id. at 312.
18. Id. at 314.
19. Id. at 313–14.
20. 4. Mass. 163 (1808).
21. *Commonwealth v. Blanding,* 20 Mass. 304, 315 (1825). Parker went on to say that a public allegation of illegality on the part of some private person may also be protected if "great mischief" could thereby be avoided. For example, a correct charge made with good intentions that a certain apothecary was selling poison in the form of medicine or that a certain individual was engaged in "gross swindling" was protected (see id. at 319).
22. 1 Dall. 319 (1788).
23. Id. at 325.
24. William Blackstone, *Commentaries on the Laws of England,* 4 vols. (1765–69; Chicago: University of Chicago Press, 1979), 4:150. Blackstone's discussion of freedom of speech immediately follows on 151–52.
25. The brief discussion of Chancellor Kent and Thomas Cooley that follows is not meant, of course, to be a full discussion of the nineteenth-century American tradition of free speech. My main point is only to show that

certain prominent commentators believed that the purpose of the First Amendment was to prohibit prior restraints and yet extended protection from subsequent punishment to certain types of speech. If the argument has any merit, it is quite plausible that Holmes was a part of this tradition.

26. Bogen, "The Metamorphosis of Mr. Justice Holmes," 111–12: "Thus, although Kent personally believed that truth offered with good motives should not be punishable, his *Commentaries* did not explicitly repudiate the validity of Blackstone's formulation as the prevailing definition of freedom of the press."

27. 3 Johns. Cas. 336 (N.Y. 1804).

28. See James Kent, *Commentaries on the American Law,* 11th ed., ed. George F. Comstock, 3 vols. (Boston: Little, Brown, 1867), 1:612: "The same rule, that the truth cannot be admitted in evidence on indictment for a libel, though it may be in a civil suit for damages, has been adjudged in Louisiana; and the weight of judicial authority undoubtedly is that the English common-law doctrine of libel is the common-law doctrine in this country, in all cases in which it has not been expressly controlled by constitutional or legislative provisions."

29. Ibid., 611–12.

30. Ibid., 612–13. In his *Commentaries on the Constitution of the United States,* 3 vols. (Boston: Hilliard, Gray, 1833), 3:742, Joseph Story came to the same conclusion. He cited *Blanding* and endorsed Kent's discussion of free speech. And though he emphasized that state governments had the authority to punish abuses of free speech and that originally free speech meant only protection from prior restraints, he too seems to have extended the scope of free speech beyond the framers' intent. The guarantee protected from subsequent punishment certain types of speech See ibid., 732: "It is plain, then, that the language of this amendment imports no more, than that every man shall have a right to speak, write, and print his opinions upon any subject whatsoever without any prior restraint, so always that he does not injure any other person in his rights, person, property, or reputation; and so always, that he does not thereby disturb the public peace, or attempt to subvert the government. It is neither more nor less, than an expansion of the great doctrine, recently brought into operation in the law of libel, that every man shall be at liberty to publish what is true, with good motives and for justifiable ends." Since Story understood free speech to include the right to publish truth with good motives and for justifiable ends, he had to have believed that free speech prevented, not only prior restraints, but the subsequent punishment of nonabusive speech. For a similar interpretation of Story, see Roscoe Pound, "Equitable Relief against Defamation," *Harvard Law Review,* 29 (April 1916): 651.

31. Kent, *Commentaries,* 1:615.

32. Ibid.

33. Thomas Cooley, *A Treatise on the Constitutional Limitations* (Boston: Little, Brown, 1868), 421.

34. Ibid., 422.
35. Ibid. Cooley meant the common-law of late-eighteenth-century America, not early English law. See ibid., 420: "liberty of the press, as now exercised, is of modern origin."
36. Ibid., 422.
37. 222 U.S. 452 (1912).
38. Id. at 458.
39. 247 U.S. 402 (1918).
40. Id. at 424.
41. It should be noted, however, that Holmes hinted that if a jury had found in a regular proceeding that the Toledo Newspaper Company had obstructed justice, he might have deferred to the lower court's finding of fact (see id. at 425). But in the actual case, the same judge that issued the injunction tried the contempt case summarily. Holmes thought that the judge had gone completely beyond his authority by acting in this fashion. And so, if a more impartial tribunal or jury had come to the conclusion that the newspaper had obstructed justice, Holmes would have been more inclined to uphold the conviction. Nonetheless, it is still true that adverse comment on judicial activities was constitutionally protected unless it obstructed the administration of justice.
42. Because of Holmes's difficult handwriting, there has been some confusion as to what cases he was referring to in this letter. Ragan misread "Paterson" as a reference to "The Patriotic case," which he took to mean *Schenck v. United States.* Accordingly, he concludes that Holmes underwent a major transformation in his understanding of the limits of free speech during 1919, after *Schenck* and the "later cases" of *Frohwerk v. United States* and *Debs v. United States* (see Ragan, "Holmes, Chafee, and Free Speech," 26 and n. 12). Both Bogen and Rabban have pointed out difficulties with this interpretation. If he meant *Schenck,* how could Holmes have any doubt about the name of the case since Chafee explicitly referred to it in his letter to Holmes. See Bogen, "The Free Speech Metamorphosis of Mr. Justice Holmes," 99–100. Rabban finds it unlikely that Holmes would have referred to *Frohwerk* and *Debs* as the "later cases" since all of the early 1919 espionage cases came down within a few weeks of each other (see Rabban, "The Emergence of Modern First Amendment Doctrine," 1226 n. 366). A major step forward was the realization that Holmes meant *Patterson,* not "the Patriotic case." Now the only dispute is what did Holmes mean by the "later cases." Rabban speculates that Holmes was referring to *Toledo Newspaper Company v. United States,* the implication being that Holmes changed his basic understanding of the limits of free speech during the middle of 1918. (see ibid., 1266). My own view, if only because *Toledo Newspaper Company* is a single case, is that Rabban's suggestion is unlikely. A better view is Bogen's account that Holmes meant the espionage cases decided in early 1919. If so, he changed his mind in late 1918 or early 1919 after he read Chafee's article and the briefs that were filed in these cases. In contrast to Bogen's interpre-

tation, however, I think that Holmes's metamorphosis (if that is an appropriate term) only involved his understanding of the purpose of the free speech clause, not his sense of the theoretical limits of free speech.

43. See Chafee, "Freedom of Speech," *The New Republic* 17 (16 November 1918): 66–69.

44. See especially the amicus curiae brief filed by Gilbert E. Roe in *Debs v. United States*. Roe explicitly denied that the main purpose of the free speech clause was to prevent prior restraints, and his argument was composed primarily of quotes from historical sources (see Brief of Gilbert E. Roe, as Amicus Curiae at 22–49, *Debs*). It should be noted that if Holmes reduced in 1919 free speech to a mere protection from previous restraints, he had a significantly more narrow notion of what free speech protected than the officials then at the Justice Department. In the 1919 cases, the government had argued that preventing licensing was the main purpose of the amendment, but it conceded that it now also protected certain types of speech from subsequent punishment (see Brief for the United States at 81, *Debs;* also see the government's brief in response to Gilbert Roe's brief, Brief for the United States at 1–17, *Debs*). For another argument denying Blackstone's notion of free speech, see Brief for Plaintiffs in Error at 5–7, *Schenck.*

45. *Schenck v. United States,* 249 U.S. 47, 51–52 (1919).

46. Bogen, "The Metamorphosis of Mr. Justice Holmes," 149; Rabban, "The Emergence of Modern First Amendment Doctrine," 1260 n. 24. Also see Ragan, "Holmes, Chafee, and Free Speech," 34. Ragan has to treat this passage from *Schenck* very carefully because it is his thesis that Holmes had no change of heart until the summer of 1919, after he had a conversation with Zechariah Chafee, Jr.

47. *Abrams v. United States,* 250 U.S. 616, 630 (1919).

48. *Missouri v. Holland* 252 U.S. 416, 433 (1920).

49. *Gompers v. United States,* 233 U.S. 604, 610 (1914).

50. Even today a prominent historian believes that the main purpose of the amendment was to prevent prior restraints, but also concedes that the guarantee quickly developed as a protection from subsequent punishment. I think Holmes shared this outlook (see Leonard Levy, *Legacy of Suppression: Freedom of Speech and Press in Early American History* [1960]; *Emergence of a Free Press* [New York: Oxford University Press, 1985]).

51. Corwin, "Bowing Out 'Clear and Present Danger,' " *Notre Dame Lawyer* 27 (1952): 358.

52. Freund, *On Understanding the Supreme Court* (Boston: Little, Brown, 1949; Westport, Conn.: Greenwood Press, 1977), 27–28.

53. Wechsler, "Symposium on Civil Liberties," *The American Law School Review* 9 (1941): 889.

54. Ibid., 887.

55. Corwin, "Bowing Out 'Clear and Present Danger,' " 358.

56. Rogat, "Mr. Justice Holmes: A Dissenting Opinion," *Stanford Law Review* 15 (December 1962): 6–7. Robert W. Gordon suggests that Karl Llewellyn

was the first to recognize the "formalistic" character of Holmes's theory of judicial decision-making and identifies other commentators who share this judgment (see his "Holmes' *Common Law* as Legal and Social Science," *Hofstra Law Review* 10 (1982): 727 n. 60.

57. Rogat, "The Judge as Spectator," *University of Chicago Law Review* 31 (Winter 1964): 213–56. For a warmer description of Holmes's personality, see Sheldon Novick, *The Honorable Justice: The Life of Oliver Wendell Holmes* (Boston: Little, Brown, 1989).

58. For example, see Holmes's dissents in *Lochner v. New York*, 198 U.S. 45, 76 (1904); *Adkins v. Childrens' Hospital*, 261 U.S. 525, 567–68 (1922); *Coppage v. Kansas*, 236 U.S. 1, 27 (1914).

59. Grant Gilmore, *The Ages of American Law* (New Haven: Yale University Press, 1977), chap. 3; Saul Touster, "Holmes a Hundred Years Ago: *The Common Law* and Legal Theory," *Hofstra Law Review* 10 (1982): 685, 691; Robert Gordon, "Holmes' *Common Law* as Legal and Social Science," 729; G. Edward White, "The Integrity of Holmes' Jurisprudence," *Hofstra Law Review* 10 (1982): 633–53; "Looking at Holmes in the Mirror," *Law and History Review* 4 (Fall 1986): 439–49. White argues, however, that Holmes abandoned conceptualism because his experience as a Massachusetts Supreme Court judge convinced him that logic had no significant role to play in judicial decision making. Accordingly, White realizes that it is very difficult to describe the later Holmes as a conceptualist. But in my view, White overestimates the early conceptualist tendencies because he equates Holmes's inclination to theorize in the law with some belief in the objective reality of general principles. But one can be a skeptical empirical legal philosopher: one who believes that general legal principles have no validity beyond the particulars they contain. A general proposition, in Holmes's view, was not "worth a damn" because it was only a barrel for the facts. But even if he evaluated the validity of general principles in this way, he could still think that the intellectual enterprise was one of the most valuable activities that humans could pursue. "Anything that will discourage men from believing general propositions I welcome only less than anything that will encourage them to make them" (Letter from Holmes to H. Laski, 7 January 1924, in *Holmes-Laski Letters*, 1:579. In the spirit of this quotation, Holmes theorized throughout his life but remained skeptical of the validity of all theories. His intellectual inclinations are therefore no ground to charge him with formalism or conceptualism.

Thomas Grey has also claimed that Holmes can usefully be described as a conceptualist and a formalist (see his "Holmes and Legal Pragmatism," 816–26). But Grey only means that Holmes "viewed legal systematization as a practical aid in teaching and understanding law" (816). Unlike Christopher Langdell, he did not understand legal categories "as ideal realities which the legal scientist could discover and describe and which a judge could simply follow" (822). Accordingly, Grey's sense of conceptualism is not the same as the one used by Gilmore and others. And since according to

Grey "all the leading Anglo-American legal thinkers of the period from about 1870 to 1920 were conceptualists" (824) in this sense, one can see that he has a wide conception of the term, which suggests that the term cannot be a useful means by which to understand the distinctive feature of Holmes's theory of judicial decision making.

60. *Hyde v. United States*, 225 U.S. 347, 390 (1912).

61. See *Schenck v. United States*, 249 U.S. 47, 52 (1919).

62. *Abrams v. United States*, 249 U.S. 204, 628 (1919). Also see *Gitlow v. New York*, 268 U.S. 652, 673 (1925), and *Frohwerk v. United States*, 249 U.S. 204, 208 (1919).

63. Holmes, "Theory of Torts," *American Law Review. 7 (1873), in Harvard Law Review* 44 (March 1931): 775. Also See Holmes, *The Common Law* (Cambridge: Harvard University Press, Belknap Press, 1963), 101. Frederic R. Kellogg has insightfully examined the common-law origins of Holmes's theory of constitutional adjudication ("Common Law and Constitutional Theory: The Common Law Origins of Holmes's Constitutional Restraint," *George Mason University Law Review* 7 [Fall 1984]: 177–234). Kellogg, however, argues that Holmes abandoned the common-law insight—that law develops on a case-by-case basis as judges decide cases that approach each other from opposite poles—during the 1890s before his dissent in *Lochner v. New York*. Holmes came to see law as "a medium for the working out of urgent conflicts," and so law had to develop "in a far less leisurely manner than the gradual growth of common law rules out of particular jury determinations" (199). The time for law only came after the socio-economic battles were won or lost in the legislature (200, 234). Judges were to let the winners have their way. In Kellogg's opinion, deference to the legislature was therefore the gist of Holmes's mature theory of constitutional adjudication.

There are a number of problems with Kellogg's thesis that Holmes abandoned a common-law approach to constitutional adjudication. First, there is no necessary incompatibility between the common-law model of constitutional development, which emphasized the judicial role of drawing lines, and the view that law must reflect the political relationships of the various groups that compose society. Holmes could have thought that how judges placed the poles of legal development and drew the line of constitutional authority depended on political realities. It is, after all, very difficult to fit Holmes's ideas into pre-*Lochner* and post-*Lochner* periods. The case that Kellogg primarily uses to exemplify Holmes's earlier common-law approach, *Hudson Water Company v. McCarter*, 209 u.S. 349 (1908), in fact came well after *Lochner*. Moreover, Holmes's 1873 article on the Gas Stokers' strike suggests that he had a clear understanding of how battling socioeconomic groups influenced legal development well before *Lochner* (see Holmes, "The Gas Stokers' Strike," *American Law Review* 7 (April 1873), in *The Mind and Faith of Justice Holmes*, ed. Max Lerner (Boston: Little, Brown, 1943), 48–51. And his realization that political power as directly related to legal development does not mean that he entirely denied judges a policy-making role. Though he practiced judicial restraint, he did occasionally exercise the power of judicial review. As the text will make clear, my understanding is that Holmes would invalidate a statute if it conflicted with the will of the sovereign American people. Kellogg, in my opinion, is not sufficiently sensitive to Holmes's understanding of the judge as a special representative of the American people and, for that reason, fails to see how the two models of constitutional adjudication (that he defines and discusses) are in fact complimentary facets of a deeper underlying theory of American constitutionalism.

64. *Lochner v. New York,* 198 U.S. 45, 76 (1904).

65. 260 U.S. 393 (1922).

66. Id. at 416.

67. 207 U.S. 79 (1907).

68. *Interstate Consul. R. Co. v. Massachusetts,* 207 U.S. 79, 87 (1907).

69. *Noble State Bank v. Haskell,* 219 U.S. 104, 112 (1910).

70. *Missouri, Kansas, & Texas Ry. v. May,* 194 U.S. 267, 269 (1904). See also letters from Holmes to F. Pollock, 28 May 1914 and 26 October 1919, in *Holmes-Pollock letters,* ed. Mark D. Howe, 2 vols. (Cambridge: Harvard University Press, 1942), 1:216, 2:28.

71. *Paddell v. New York,* 211 U.S. 446, 448 (1908).

72. Yosal Rogat, "Mr. Justice Holmes: A Dissenting Opinion," *Stanford Law Review* 15 (March 1963): 280–87.

73. 219 U.S. 219 (1911).

74. *Kuhn v. Fairmont Coal Company,* 215 U.S. 349, 372 (1909).

75. *Prentis v. Atlantic Coast Line Company,* 211 U.S. 210, 226 (1908).

76. *Springer v. Philippine Islands,* 277 U.S. 189, 210 (1927).

77. Letter from Holmes to Dr. Wu, 26 August 1926, in *Justice Oliver Wendell Holmes: His Book Notices and Uncollected Letters and Papers,* ed. Harry C. Shriver (New York: Central Book Company, 1936), 188.

78. See Rabban, "The Emergence of Modern First Amendment Doctrine," especially 1257–83, and idem, "The First Amendment in Its Forgotten Years," especially 533–36, 579–86. Rabban agrees with the view, discussed in the previous section, that Holmes's opinion in *Patterson v. Colorado* supported Blackstone's limitation of freedom of speech to a protection from prior restraints. Rabban, however, implies that Holmes gave up this reactionary view before *Schenck,* perhaps when he wrote his dissent in *Toledo Newspaper Co. v. United States,* but never abandoned the bad-tendency doctrine, if he ever did, until *Abrams.* Holmes's deeper commitment was therefore to the bad-tendency doctrine (see Rabban, "The Emergence of Modern First Amendment Doctrine," 1260, 1266).

79. See Fred D. Ragan, "Holmes, Chafee, and Free Speech," especially 29–36.

80. Ibid., 1267. Another branch of Rabban's argument that Holmes was an adherent of the bad-tendency doctrine is an analysis of his free-speech opinions. I have criticized this side of Rabban's reasoning in chap. 3.

81. Yosal Rogat, "The Judge as Spectator," 221–26. See also Yosal Rogat and James M. O'Fallon, "Mr. Justice Holmes: A Dissenting Opinion—The Free Speech Cases," *Stanford Law Review* 36 (1984): 1361–68.

82. Ibid., 224.

83. Ibid., 225.

84. Ibid.

85. Rabban, "The Emergence of Modern First Amendment Doctrine," 1269–70.

86. Ibid., 1276.

87. *Southern Pacific Co. v. Jensen* 224 U.S. 205, 222 (1917). For further cites, see Pohlman, *Justice Oliver Wendell Holmes and Utilitarian Jurisprudence* (Cambridge: Harvard University Press, 1984), 194 n. 58.

88. Holmes, review of "Law and Command," by F. Pollock, *American Law Review* 6 (1872), in *Harvard Law Review* 44 (March 1931): 788–89.

89. *Heard v. Sturgis*, 146 Mass. 545, 549 (1888).

90. *Holmes-Laski Letters*, 1:115.

91. Holmes, "Gas Stokers' Strike," in *The Mind and Faith of Justice Holmes*, 51. Holmes's criticism of Spencer was the following: "It has always seemed to us a singular anomaly that believers in the theory of evolution and in the natural development of institutions by successive adaptations to the environment, should be found laying down a theory of government intended to establish its limits once for all by a logical deduction from axioms" (50).

92. Certainly Holmes had no idea that the Supreme Court was sovereign. After he received letters critical of his denial of two stays in the Sacco and Vanzetti case, Holmes ironically told Laski that they assumed "that I had the power of Austin's sovereign over the matter" (*Holmes-Laski Letters*, 2:974).

93. *Opinions of the Justices to the House of Representatives*, 160 Mass. 586, 594 (1894).

94. Id. at 594–95.

95. *Nation* 13 (1871): 38. See generally Mark D. Howe, *Justice Oliver Wendell Holmes: The Proving Years* (Cambridge: Harvard University Press 1963), 38–42.

96. Holmes, review of *Treatise on Constitutional Limitations*, by Thomas Cooley, *American Law Review* 6 (October 1871), in *Holmes: His Book Notices*, 98.

97. See James F. Stephen, *Liberty, Equality, Fraternity*, ed. R. J. White (Cambridge: Cambridge University Press, 1867), 165–66: "the question between the North and South [cannot be decided] by lawyers' metaphysics about the true meaning of sovereignty or by conveyancing subtleties about the meaning of the Constitution. . . . You might as well try to infer the fortunes of a battle from the shape of the firearms."

98. And when the will of the North waned, Reconstruction ended and the tragic era of Jim Crow began.

99. Letter from Holmes to Harold Laski, 29 January 1926, in *Holmes-Laski Letters*, 2:822.

100. See Rabban, "The Emergence of Modern First Amendment Doctrine," 1261, 1276. See also Gunther, "Learned Hand and the Origins of Modern First Amendment Doctrine: Some Fragments of History," *Stanford Law Review* 27 (February 1975): 737.
101. What is puzzling is that Rabban recognizes that Holmes required proximity to harm in attempts and that he measured the proximity by the nearness, the greatness, and the probability of harm, plus the apprehension felt by the community (see his "The Emergence of Modern First Amendment Doctrine," 1272–73). Hence, it is not at all clear how Rabban could conclude that Holmes's standard was indistinguishable from the bad tendency test, since the latter did not require any proximity to harm (see ibid., 1294–95).
102. Rogat, "The Judge as Spectator," 216.
103. See Zechariah Chafee, Jr., "Freedom of Speech in War Time," *Harvard Law Review* 32 (1919): 967. Chafee, citing *Peaslee v. Massachusetts,* 177 Mass. 267 (1901), correctly argued that Holmes's theory of speech required proximity to harm since it was derived from his doctrine of attempts.
104. See Rogat, "The Judge as Spectator," 215–16; Rabban, "The Emergence of Modern First Amendment Doctrine," 1276; Bogen, "Holmes and Free Speech," 157, 160, 168–69, 186.
105. Holmes, *The Common Law,* 61 and, generally, 54–61.
106. Ibid., 56.
107. Rabban argues that Holmes "judged the intent requirement of the Espionage Act by the tendency of words rather than through an effort to uncover the defendants' actual states of mind" (see his "Emergence of Modern First Amendment Doctrine," 1276). Yosal Rogat also implied that no matter what Holmes said about actual intent, his emphasis on external standards excluded the agent's actual intent from any consideration (see his "The Judge as Spectator," 215–16 n. 13). Gunther is puzzled how intent could play any role in Holmes's theory (see his "Learned Hand," 737, 743). David Bogen believes that unlawful intent was one of several factors used to measure the proximity of harm in cases of attempts. Upon his interpretation, Holmes would at some point favor liability, even if the speaker's intent was innocent. Liability would become appropriate, regardless of intent, as the likelihood, imminence, and seriousness of harm increased and as the apprehensions of the community were raised (see his "The Free Speech Metamorphosis of Mr. Justice Holmes," 157, 186).
108. Freund argued that "to be permitted to agitate at your own peril, subject to a jury's guessing at motive, tendency and possible effect, makes the right of free speech a precarious gift" (see his "The *Debs* Case and Freedom of Speech," *The New Republic,* 3 May 1919, in the *University of Chicago Law Review* 40 [Winter 1973]: 240). Learned Hand and many later commentators have shared this concern. See the letter from Learned Hand to Holmes, March 1919, and Letter from Hand to Zechariah Chafee, 8

January 1920. Both letters are appended to Gunther, "Learned Hand,"
759 and 766, documents 4 and 11 respectively. See also Gunther, "Learned
Hand," 740; Ragan, "Holmes, Chafee, and Free Speech," 39–40; Rabban,
"The Emergence of Modern First Amendment Doctrine," 1229–35, 1280–
83.

109. *Nash v. United States*, 229 U.S. 373, 377 (1912).
110. The Letter, dated 12 May 1919, was addressed to Herbert Croly, editor of
The New Republic, but Holmes sent it to H. Laski instead (see *Holmes-Laski Letters,* 1:203).
111. Holmes, *The Common Law,* 96.
112. Ibid.
113. Ibid., 100–101.
114. Holmes, "Law in Science and Science in Law," *Harvard Law Review* 12
(1899), in Holmes, *Collected Legal Papers* (New York: Peter Smith, 1952),
238.
115. Ibid., 99.
116. 233 U.S. 655, 688 (1911). Cases cited by Holmes include *Egan v. Hart*
165 U.S. 188, 189 (1896); *Almonester v. Kenton,* 9 How 1, 7 (1850);
Dower v. Ritchards, 151 U.S. 658, 663 (1893); *Gardner v. Bonesteel,* 180
U.S. 362, 365, 370 (1901); *Thayer v. Spratt,* 189 U.S. 346, 353 (1902);
German Sav. & L. Soc. v. Dormitzer, 192 U.S. 125, 129 (1903); *Adams v.
Church,* 193 U.S. 510, 513 (1904).
117. 192 U.S. 125–28 (1903). Holmes cited Justice Blatchford's opinion in
Horner v. United States, 143 U.S. 570 (1891) to support his interpretation
of the Court's jurisdiction under the act of 1891.
118. *Cedar Rapids Gas Light Co. v. Cedar Rapids,* 223 U.S. 655, 668–69
(1911).
119. *Direction Der Disconto-Gesellschaft v. United States,* 267 U.S. 22, 29
(1930).
120. *Louisville Gas & E. Co. v. Coleman,* 277 U.S. 32, 41 (1927), Holmes
dissenting. Also see *Interstate Consol. Street R. Co. v. Massachusetts,* 207
U.S. 79, 88 (1907); "It is not enough that a statute goes to the verge of
constitutional power. In case of real doubt a law must be sustained."
Noble State Bank v. Haskall, 219 U.S. 104, 110 (1910): "We have few
scientifically certain criteria of legislation, and as it often is difficult to
mark the line where what is called the police power of the states is limited
by the Constitution of the United States, judges should be slow to read
into the latter *a nolumus mutare* as against the law-making power." See
also *Dominion Hotel v. Arizona,* 249 U.S. 265, 268 (1918).
121. *Missouri, Kansas, and Texas Railway Co. of Texas v. May,* 194 U.S. 267,
270 (1904).
122. *Bain Peanut Co. v. Pinson,* 282 U.S. 499, 501 (1930). Also see *Noble State
Bank v. Haskell,* 219 U.S. 104, 110 (1910): "we must be cautious about
pressing the broad words of the 14th Amendment to a drily logical extreme."

123. *Truax v. Corrigan,* 257 U.S. 312, 342 (1921), Holmes dissenting. Also see *Louisville & N.R. Co. v. Barber Asphalt Paving Co.,* 197 U.S. 430, 434 (1904).

124. *Tyson Brothers v. Banton,* 273 U.S. 418, 445 (1918).

125. *Hudson County Water Co. v. McCarter,* 209 U.S. 349, 355 (1907). Also see Holmes's review of Thomas Cooley, *A Treatise on the Constitutional Limitations,* in *Holmes: His Book Notices,* 100: "We suppose this phrase [the police power] was invented to cover certain acts of the legislature which are seen to be unconstitutional, but which are believed to be necessary." Also see a letter from Holmes to Dr. Wu, 4 November 1923, in *Holmes: His Book Notices,* 168: Holmes outlined two senses of the term police power, one being "a conciliatory phrase-to cover those cases where the legislature is held justified in contravening the literal meanings of constitutional protections."

126. *Noble State Bank v. Haskell,* 219 U.S. 104, 111 (1910).

127. Letter from Holmes to F. Pollock, 23 April 1910, in *Holmes-Pollock Letters,* 1:163.

128. Remark of Holmes to Chief Justice Hughes, cited by Merlo J. Pusey, *Charles Evans Hughes,* 2 vols. (New York: MacMillan, 1951), 1:287.

129. *Truax v. Corrigan,* 257 U.S. 312, 343 (1921), Holmes dissenting.

130. *Blinn v. Nelson,* 222 U.S. 1, 7 (1911).

131. *Forbes Pioneer Boatline v. Bd. of Commissioners,* 258 U.S. 338, 340 (1921). See also *Bain Peanut Company v. Pinson,* 282 U.S. 499, 501 (1930); *Missouri, Kansas, & Texas Railway Co. of Texas v. May,* 194 U.S. 267, 270 (1904).

132. Holmes, *"Learning and Science,"* a speech delivered to the Harvard Law School Association, 25 June 1895, in *Collected Legal Papers,* 139.

133. Holmes did support judicial review even though he thought that the country would survive if the Supreme Court lost its power to declare federal law unconstitutional. See Holmes, "Law and the Court," a speech given at a dinner of the Harvard Law School Association, 15 February 1913, in *Collected Legal Papers,* 295–96.

134. *Missouri, Kansas, & Texas Ry. v. May,* 194 U.S. 349, 355–56 (1904).

135. *Otis v. Parker,* 187 U.S. 606, 608–9 (1903).

136. See Duguit, "The Law and the State," *Harvard Law Review* 31 (November 1917): 1–185.

137. Letter from Holmes to H. Laski, 4 March 1920, in *Holmes-Laski Letters,* 1:248.

138. *The Common Law,* 120.

139. Holmes, "Law in Science and Science in Law," an address delivered before the New York Bar Association, 17 January 1899, in *Harvard Law Review* 12 (1899), in *Collected Legal Papers,* 239.

140. 216 U.S. 358 (1909).

141. Id. at 366.

142. Holmes, "Law and the Court," in *Collected Legal Papers*, 295.
143. The cases were *Ottinger v. Consolidated Gas Co.*, 272 U.S. 576 (1926), and *Ottinger v. Brooklyn Union Co.*, 272 U.S. 579 (1926).
144. Letter from Holmes to H. Laski 23 October 1926, in *Holmes-Laski Letters*, 2:887–88.
145. Holmes, review of *A Treatise on the Constitutional Limitations*, by Thomas Cooley, in *Holmes: His Book Notices*, 98–99.
146. Holmes, "Law and the Court," a speech delivered to the Harvard Law School Association of New York, 15 February 1913, in *Collected Legal Papers*, 292.
147. Ibid., 294–95.
148. Letter from Holmes to Charles Owen, 5 February 1912, cited by Mark DeWolfe Howe, *Justice Oliver Wendell Holmes: The Proving Years*, 175.
149. Holmes, "Law and the Court," 295.
150. Letter from Holmes to F. Pollock, 19 September 1919, in *Holmes-Pollock Letters*, 2:25. See also letters from Holmes to Laski, 15 September 1916 and 13 May 1919, in *Holmes-Laski Letters*, 1:21 and 203 respectively.
151. Holmes, "Path of the Law," 181.
152. Letter from Holmes to H. Laski, 13 May 1926, in *Holmes-Laski Letters*, 2:837.
153. Holmes, "Montesquieu," an introduction to a reprint of *Esprit des lois* (1910), in *Collected Legal Papers*, 258.
154. See the letter that Holmes wrote to Herbert Croly but sent to Laski instead, 12 May 1919, in *Holmes-Laski Letters*, 1:203: "Moreover, I think the *clauses under consideration* not only were constitutional but were proper enough while the war was on." Note that Holmes confined his endorsement to the provisions of the Espionage Act that were the basis of the attempt and conspiracy convictions in the early 1919 cases. He probably had real constitutional doubts about the 1918 amendments to the Espionage Act.

Afterword

JUSTICE HOLMES HAD a coherent and a moderately protective doctrine of free speech. He was not speech's greatest defender, but he was hardly hostile to it or insensitive to its value. His doctrine reflected his legal positivism and his basic understanding of American constitutionalism, but his theory of legal liability provided the basic framework of his approach. The key factor was therefore whether the speech was harmful in itself, constituted an attempt, or was part of a conspiracy. In the first instance, a speaker was punishable if the speaker knew facts that should have warned of the harmful character of his or her speech; in the second, if the speaker intended a harm that was proximate to his or her speech; and in the third, if the speaker was acting in concert with others to obtain an illegal result. Other jurists of Holmes's generation treated speech much more harshly, especially if the legislature had prohibited the specific type of speech uttered or published. Holmes, however, understood judges to have a representative function independent of the legislature. They were to represent the long-term interests and values of the sovereign American people. Therefore, when federal and state officials began to impose liability on speech that failed to satisfy Holmes's theory of liability, he refused to go along. He did not think that the American people really wanted to punish speech that was not liable according to his general theory of liability. Speech was not to be treated more harshly than any other form of action.

Of course, the above picture of Holmes is no more than an interpretation. One might object that the coherence and moderation discovered in this book exist more in the eyes of the beholder than in Holmes's thought and writings. But in the history of ideas, the more interesting questions are not susceptible of direct proof. We come up against the limits of our knowledge very quickly, and to go beyond them is necessarily to enter a very gray world—a world, if the truth be told, of conjecture, intuition, and guess.

In the case of Holmes's legal thought, the problem is compounded. As Brandeis put it, Holmes did not "sufficiently consider the need of others to understand."[1] He "liked to say that he wrote for the one man who did understand," but Francis Biddle added that "sometimes Holmes missed him."[2] Putting the puzzle of his ideas together is simply not an easy task. It is not the case that certain pieces are lost or not yet found. All that is significant is on the table. The problem is putting the pieces together in a coherent manner when they seem to change shape and color depending on where they are placed in the larger picture.

Beyond the difficulties inherent in the subject matter itself, there is the additional problem that the issues that bear on any interpretation of Holmes's legal philosophy—free speech, skepticism, legal positivism, social Darwinism—are controversial even today. All too readily the intellectual commitments of today's observer can influence his or her understanding and evaluation of Holmes. The result is that the commentary is plagued by anachronism.[3] He is still too close to us; there is not enough historical distance between him and us to treat him dispassionately; his opinions must either be extolled or condemned because they still play a role in the continuing battle of ideas. The job of expounding his legal thought is therefore not an easy one. Holmes's writings are difficult, and the issues that demand attention are hot to handle.

No one's view of Holmes can climb above the status of an interpretation. That is all that is possible. Yet, it is still true that not all interpretations are equal. In this book, I have argued that differences between the free-speech cases that came before him explain why he decided them as he did. There may, no doubt, have been some incremental changes in his theory. In chapter 4, I discussed how he was willing late in life to use free speech to prevent the government from denying mail service or citizenship, something that he was unwilling to do in analogous cases earlier in his judicial career. And it is very possible that his late realization that the framers' intended, by free speech, to do something more than prevent prior restraints may well have induced him to adopt this more protective attitude toward speech. But even so, my thesis is that Holmes's *basic* approach to free speech remained stable throughout his life.

The now-orthodox interpretation argues that all the espionage cases were essentially similar, implying that at some point in 1918–1919 Holmes underwent some kind of intellectual and emotional metamorphosis in favor of free speech. There is disagreement concerning the nature and the timing of this transformation, but many think that the early Holmes was hostile, insensitive, or indifferent to free speech, that sometime during 1918–1919 he was reborn, and that his pro-speech dissent in *Abrams* was the result.

Certainly these two opposing interpretations of Holmes can not be equally valid. But which is preferable? I would like to point out a few things that help to explain my position. It is simply hard to believe that Holmes would have underwent an intellectual metamorphosis at the age of seventy-seven.[4] And even if such an argument, resting heavily on stereotypical assumptions, should have little weight, there are a few special facts about Holmes that make it even less likely that he underwent such a conversion. Since he derived his epistemology from the British utilitarians,[5] he accepted associationist psychology. According to it, what a person believed and valued was determined by their particular experiences, especially their early ones. Ideas were rooted in one's personality, and intellectual transformations were therefore thought to be particularly painful. One "can not be wrenched from the rocky crevices into which one has grown for many years without feeling that one is attacked in one's life."[6] Accordingly, if Holmes did undergo some kind of intellectual and emotional transformation in 1918–19, he would have considered it a "painfully wrenching" experience. One can not but think that he would have clearly expressed this personal anguish in some form that would have been preserved. But to my knowledge, there is no *explicit* evidence that Holmes's ideas and life were at any time "torn up from the roots." The entire argument that he did undergo some such experience rests on inference, not *direct* evidence.

Also, on many different issues and occasions Holmes gave every indication that he was a man of conviction, unwilling to change his mind, perhaps to the point of dogmatism.[7] For example, Sir Frederick Pollock, one of the very few people whose knowledge of the common law Holmes considered equal to his own, repeatedly tried to convince him that his theory of contract—a theory that reduced contracts to torts and denied that there was any duty to fulfill one's contract—was wrong. But Pollock had no luck, and in the end the two great men had to agree to disagree.[8] If so, would an opinionated, if not dogmatic, judge in his late seventies, who believed that intellectual transformations involved "wrenching up the roots of one's identity," have undergone a metamorphosis in his commitment to free speech? No doubt it is conceivable, but Holmes's epistemology and documented intellectual intransigence cast a large shadow over any such interpretation.[9] Accordingly, even if all the various pictures of Holmes that exist in the commentary are interpretations, they are not all equal.[10]

Of course the validity of my interpretation has no bearing on the validity of Holmes's legal philosophy. Whether I am right about Holmes is a question that should be kept strictly separate from the issue of whether he was right. It is a mistake to confuse history with a substantive consideration of the issues themselves. To avoid any misunderstandings, however, a few things can be said. Clearly, time has passed by much of Holmes's approach to free speech. One reason why this has happened is that his theory of legal liability is no longer thought to be an accurate reflection of law, especially criminal law. It strikes our generation, at least some of us at certain times, as unjust to punish a person merely because he or she knew facts that would have warned an average person of the dangerous character of his or her act, especially if the person did not have the capacities necessary to foresee the harm. The idea that a speaker could be punished for harmful speech irrespective of intent or of personal ability is therefore one that is difficult for us to swallow. This is most obviously the case with libel. It is well known that today a newspaper must act, at least in regard to public officials and figures, with malice or with reckless disregard of the truth before any liability is incurred. In contrast, Holmes would punish a newspaper that falsely published material to the detriment of some individual, even if it acted reasonably and in good faith. It is fairly clear that libel is not now thought to be so harmful as to justify this kind of harsh treatment.

It is less clear that there are no forms of speech activity that should not be treated according to Holmes's external standard of liability. The issue is whether there is some type of speech that is so harmful that a person who engages in it is punishable irrespective of foresight or intent. Libel no longer qualifies, but perhaps there are other forms of speech that would. Holmes's old example of falsely shouting "fire" in a theater seems to be a case in point. Would it be unconstitutional for a state to punish the shouter if that person only meant it as a joke and never foresaw the resulting panic? Would the person's limited capacity of foresight make any difference? Or what about contempt of court? Here again the actor knows facts that would have warned an average person of the danger of his or her speech, and it seems arguable that liability would be appropriate even if the agent neither intended or foresaw the harm. In both cases, the speech is seriously harmful in itself. The state has a serious interest in preventing the resulting harms whether the actor intended or foresaw them or not. An additional problem is that if the external standard is not used, actors with bad intent could possibly escape liability by feigning good faith, ignorance, or incapacity. To discourage these kinds of seriously harmful speech, the community might insist on punishment, especially if the harms became at all prevalent.

Whether Holmes's external standard should be applied in a specific instance or not, however, is not the main point. The underlying insight that does have value even today is that speech is multifaceted. Some of it is good, some indifferent, and some is positively bad. There is therefore not one set of criteria that can answer all the questions about liability for speech. If conspiracy is set aside, Holmes divided speech into harmful speech, which was subject to liability according to the external standard, and illegal advocacy, which required an unlawful intent and a proximity to the harm. Perhaps his theoretical framework was not as complicated as we would like it to be, and perhaps we would not agree with the types of speech that he placed in either category. Nevertheless, he saw that speech had to be broken down into more manageable portions with different criteria of liability applicable to each. This insight was a real step forward. It avoided the fiction that no speech was punishable and the myth that all types of speech were protected to an equal degree.

Holmes's treatment of illegal advocacy also has some merit. His focus on the intent of the speaker and the proximity of the speech to an actual harm seems to coincide with common sense. If the intent was unlawful and if a serious harm that raised the apprehension of the community was imminent, Holmes imposed liability on the speaker regardless of the words used. A speaker did not have to incite illegality literally before incurring liability. This point of view is valuable because there is some indication that constitutional law has drifted away from Holmes's criteria. Ever since the Supreme Court decided *Brandenburg v. Ohio*,[11] there has been the growing impression that only literal incitement is outside of the Constitution. But it seems fairly clear that the rule of literal incitement would be very difficult to live with in a real crisis. If illegal advocacy was becoming generally efficacious, if serious illegal acts were becoming widespread, it would be impossible to let off the hook the agitator who veiled his or her unlawful intent with language just short of literal incitement. The community would not stand for it. And since a constitution can not transcend the popular will that gives it power and force, a constitutional right of free speech has to be understood accordingly.

It was Holmes's opinion that the strong and enduring feelings of the community were always important to determine the limits of both harmful speech and illegal advocacy. Indeed, his entire theory of constitutional adjudication rested on his understanding that the judge's job was to adapt "slowly but not too slowly" the Constitution to the beliefs, wishes, and values of the community. At the very least, it seems that this suggestion is a fair description of what has happened in the long run. During the New Deal, the Commerce Clause was interpreted expansively, well beyond what the framers intended, because public opinion would have it no other way. The incorporation of the Bill of Rights against the states, the application of equal protection against the federal government, the movement toward racial and sexual equality, and the creation of the right of privacy have been developments of constitutional law whose legitimacy depends on popular will. Having grown up with the country, the Constitution was a living or organic entity, not a dusty eighteenth-century document. Holmes was one of the first to formulate this understanding of the American Constitution that has played such a prominent role in the twentieth century. He deserves recognition on this basis alone.

No longer, of course, is the idea of a living Constitution linked to a theory of popular sovereignty as it was in Holmes's mind. Today, it functions more as a license for judicial activism against public opinion. When someone says that the Constitution is living, more than likely that person means that judges have the ultimate authority to decide constitutional questions in accordance with their own personal values. I am sure that Holmes would regret this development. In his view, the idea of a living Constitution was wedded to a doctrine of judicial deference to the legislature and submission to the American people. The contemporary fear, one with which I sympathize, is that this type of approach does not provide enough protection for individual rights. It encourages a judge to help the community achieve its wishes, whether its goal is heaven or hell. Individual rights now thought to be sacred might well be trampled on.

It is pointless to deny that Holmes's Constitutionalism does have this fatalistic character. In his view, political power will have its way, and the judge's job was eventually to bow to the inevitable. Those who believe in natural law might think that a judge should never serve the ends of injustice. But who is to say what natural law requires? Certainly there is no reason to think that the Supreme Court will be right and the American people wrong. Recruited from the practicing bar, judges have no qualifications to be platonic Guardians, even if an objective morality exists. The same is true for those who believe that there is no standard beyond the judgment of history. The Court in the past has made some very serious errors. And it will not be for some time before the place of *Roe v. Wade* in history is clear, whether it exemplifies the Supreme Court at its best or worst. Evolving public opinion will largely determine what happens in regard to this issue, and this is true whether abortion is understood in terms of natural law or conventional morality. Is *Roe* more like *Dred Scott* or *Brown v. Board of Education?* The jury is still out. But it is hard to avoid the conclusion that in our democratic society and culture the jury is the American public.

Holmes, of course, had little faith in the wisdom of the masses. He was perfectly willing to concede that judicial deference to democratic will would end in disaster. But he knew that in the American constitutional order, there was no other choice. That was the way it was. In contrast, many contemporary theorists leave the impression that there are all kinds of alternatives.[12] This optimism may be refreshing, but it might rest on a delusion. Holmes's brand of American constitutionalism can serve as an effective, if somewhat bitter, antidote. Above and beyond providing us with the idea of a living Constitution, it forms a perspective from which to evaluate whether contemporary theories of constitutional adjudication are utopian in character or not.

Notes

1. Alexander Bickel, ed., *The Unpublished Opinions of Mr. Justice Brandeis* (Chicago: University of Chicago Press, 1957), 226–27.

2. Francis Biddle, *Justice Holmes, Natural Law, and the Supreme Court*, (New York: Macmillan 1961), 37–38.
3. See G. Edward White's discussion of how Holmes's reputation has shifted according to the intellectual outlook of successive generations ("The Rise and Fall of Mr. Justice Holmes," *University of Chicago Law Review* 39 [1971]: 51–77).
4. See letter from Holmes to Lewis Einstein, 30 December 1903, in *The Holmes-Einstein Letters* (London: St. Martin's Press, 1964), 8–9: "[A]t my age a man has his final formula made up, and my cosmos goes into a pretty small package. It is not likely to change its contents very much, or to let in either Hegel or the Catholic Church."
5. H. L. Pohlman, *Justice Oliver Wendell Holmes and Utilitarian Jurisprudence* (Cambridge: Harvard University Press, 1984), chap. 4.
6. Ibid.
7. See Yosal Rogat, "The Judge as Spectator," *University of Chicago Law Review* 31 (Winter 1964): 214, 253–55; Also see Francis Biddle, *Mr. Justice Holmes* (New York: Scribner, 1942), 85: "Holmes . . . has found his dominant conceptions before he was forty and never thereafter saw any reason to change them."
8. See the letters exchanged between Holmes and Pollock that are reprinted in *Holmes-Pollock Letters*, ed. Mark D. Howe, 2 vols. (Cambridge: Harvard University Press, 1942), 1:3, 21, 79–80, 119–20, 177, 2:55, 200, 201–2, 233–35. The letters cited begin with the first letter of the correspondence in 1874, and the last letter to mention this issue is one that Pollock sent Holmes in 1928.
9. The interpretation that Holmes underwent a metamorphosis is only credible if it can be established who induced him to a more pro-speech position. Learned Hand or Justice Brandeis have served as good candidates for this role. Even if Hand was much younger than Holmes, all three were federal judges, and there was a fair amount of communication among them, whether by correspondence or by personal contact. There is, however, the persistent view that Zechariah Chafee, Jr., was the person responsible for Holmes's new commitment to free speech. But in 1918 Chafee was a relatively unknown law professor at Harvard Law School specializing in commercial law and equity. He was separated from Holmes in age, stature, and reputation, and he had only the slightest contact with him. Indeed, one commentator who argues that Chafee had significant influence on Holmes places a great deal of weight on a meeting at which they had tea together. Of course such evidence unintentionally reveals the problematical quality of the entire argument. See Fred D. Ragan, "Justice Oliver Wendell Holmes, Jr., Zechariah Chafee, Jr., and the Clear and Present Danger Test for Free Speech: The First year, 1919," *Journal of American History* 58 (June-March 1971–72): 43.
10. It is also difficult to fit Holmes's decisions into opposing chronological periods. For example, David Rabban believes that Holmes restricted free

speech to protection from prior restraints before *Toledo Newspaper Company v. United States,* which was decided in 1918. He supposedly adopted a truly speech-protective standard in this case, but then reverted back to the bad-tendency doctrine in the 1919 espionage cases. If so, then Holmes took two steps beyond Blackstone in *Toledo Newspaper Company,* retreated to the bad-tendency doctrine in *Schenck, Frohwerk,* and *Debs,* and returned to a speech-protective standard in his dissent in *Abrams v. United States.* If the "metamorphosis-thesis" has to become this complicated to explain Holmes's decisions, at some point it loses credibility. In my judgment that point is not only reached but clearly surpassed when Rabban implies that Holmes, in his 1920 concurrence in *Gilbert v. Minnesota,* reverted back to some variant of the bad-tendency doctrine (see Rabban, "The Emergence of Modern First Amendment Doctrine," *University of Chicago Law Review* 50 [Fall 1983]: 1266 n. 366, 1317–19).

11. 395 U.S. 444 (1969).
12. See, for example, Laurence H. Tribe, *Constitutional Choices* (Cambridge: Harvard University Press, 1985); Ronald Dworkin, *A Matter of Principle* (Cambridge: Harvard University Press, 1985); Sotirios Barber, *On What the Constitution Means* (Baltimore: John Hopkins University Press, 1984); Judith A. Baer, *Equality under the Constitution* (Ithaca, N.Y.: Cornell University Press, 1984); Michael J. Perry, *The Constitution, the Courts, and Human Rights* (New Haven: Yale University Press, 1982); Bernard H. Siegen, *Economic Liberties and the Constitution* (Chicago: University of Chicago Press, 1981); John Hart Ely, *Democracy and Distrust* (Cambridge: Harvard University Press, 1980); Raoul Berger, *Government by the Judiciary* (Cambridge: Harvard University Press, 1977).

Index

American Socialist party, 60, 65, 68, 70, 106; left wing, 82
Amidon, Judge, 159, 170, 216
Atiyah, Patrick, 22–24
Austin, John, 22

Bad-tendency test: Holmes's purported conversion from, 96 n.144, 255–57; Holmes's purported relationship to, 66–67, 77, 89 n.48, 90 n.59, 91 n.79, 92 n.84, 93 n.114, 122, 222–23, 227; supporters of, 180–84
Bentham, Jeremy, 22
Biddle, Francis, 255
Blackstone, William, 165, 202, 206, 207, 210
Bogen, David S., 94 n.122, 201, 207, 241 n.4, 244 n.42, 250 n.107
Brandeis, Louis, 69–70, 98, 100, 101, 104, 105, 106, 107, 110, 115, 120, 121, 164, 181, 255, 261 n.9; on clear and present danger in conspiracy, 108–9; applied clear and present danger doctrine to false statements, 152–53; commitment to Holmes's approach, 149–52, 159–62; distinctive justification for free speech, 163–64; war theory of free speech, 153–58; role of jury in deciding truth of statements, 116–17; on Supreme Court's rules of jurisdiction, 111–12
Butler, Justice, 110

Chafee, Zechariah, Jr., 93 n.114, 138, 139, 140, 147, 148, 149, 150, 151, 159, 163, 201, 202, 210, 211, 227, 261 n.9; his deductive approach, 166–68, 193 n.174,

216; critique of traditional definitions of free speech, 164–66, 193 n.181, 194 n.182; policy versus limit of free speech, 168–69, 170–73, 194 nn.187, 189, 195 nn.191, 193; preference for Holmes's constitutional test of free speech, 173–76
Clarke, Justice, 182
Clayton, Judge, 78–79, 80
Communist Labor party, 106, 126 nn.36, 44
Constitutional adjudication, 1–2, 9, 14–15; conservative character of constitutional law, 236–38; Holmes's common-law approach, 217–20, 247 n.63; Holmes as formalist, 214–17, 246 n.59; accuracy of Holmes's theory, 259; judges' active role, 220–22; jury's role, 229–31; relevance of founders' intent, 213–14
Contempts, 201, 206, 207; distinguished by Holmes from reasonable comment, 210; harmful acts, 56, 58; malice not required, 57–58; truth not a defense, 56–57, 202–3, 205
Cooley, Thomas, 179, 208–9, 211, 242 n.25
Corwin, Edward S., 89 n.50, 90 n.59, 183–84, 214
Cover, Robert, 192 n.152

Darwinism, 237, 255
Duguit, Leon, 233
Duty: Holmes's theory of, 12–14, 18 n.45

Frankfurter, Felix, 150, 154
Freund, Ernst, 180, 228; direct provoca-

About the Author

H. L. POHLMAN is an associate professor of political science at Dickinson College. He is the author of *Justice Oliver Wendell Holmes and Utilitarian Jurisprudence* and the editor of *Political Theory and the American Judiciary.*